HISTORY AND BELONGING

Representations of the Past in Contemporary European Politics

Edited by Stefan Berger and Caner Tekin

berghahn
NEW YORK · OXFORD
www.berghahnbooks.com

First published in 2018 by
Berghahn Books
www.berghahnbooks.com

Library of Congress Cataloging-in-Publication Data
Names: Berger, Stefan, editor. | Tekin, Caner, editor.
Title: History and belonging : representations of the past in contemporary
European politics / Edited by Stefan Berger and Caner Tekin.
Description: First edition. | New York : Berghahn, 2018. | Series: Making
Sense of History: Studies in Historical Cultures ; volume 33 | Includes
bibliographical references and index.
Identifiers: LCCN 2017056917 (print) | LCCN 2018021143 (ebook) | ISBN
9781785338816 (ebook) | ISBN 9781785338809 (hardback : alk. paper)
Subjects: LCSH: Europe--Politics and government--20th
century--Historiography. | Political culture--Europe. | Collective
memory--Europe.
Classification: LCC D443 (ebook) | LCC D443 .H57 2018 (print) | DDC
940.5072--dc23
LC record available at https://lccn.loc.gov/2017056917

British Library Cataloguing in Publication Data
A catalogue record for this book is available from the British Library

ISBN 978-1-78533-880-9 hardback
ISBN 978-1-78533-881-6 ebook

Contents

Towards a 'Europeanized' European History?

CANER TEKIN AND STEFAN BERGER

In 1988, the prominent British historian A.J.P. Taylor wrote about the topic of European history: 'It must take place in or derive from the area we call Europe. But as I am not sure what exactly that area is meant to be, I am pretty well in a haze about the rest'.[1] The European project has been trying to blow away the haze since the 1970s, beginning to mobilize culture in order to further European integration.[2] An important part of this cultural reinvention of Europe was history. Until the 1970s the European Economic Community had relied heavily on its economic success and attractiveness, but then came the realization that something else, apart from the economy, was needed to guarantee the success of European idea. Today, this 'something else' includes the House of European History, a museum that opened in 2017 right next to the European Parliament in Brussels. In it, a narrative of European integration history meets some of the traditional national narratives; but whether this merger, inside and outside of the museum, is successful or not will contribute to determining whether the citizens of Europe have a less hazy idea about Europe than A.J.P. Taylor had almost thirty years ago.

The aim of this volume is to give an introduction to the representations of European history, in particular the history of European integration after 1945, in both European and national contexts. The European Union's history politics forms an important part of these representations, which have remained, to this day, extraordinarily contested. We can subdivide the

---

Notes for this section begin on page 13.

EU's presentation of history into two groups: expressions on history made within the EU's institutions, and the history narrative that the EU strives to systematize. The first group includes celebrations of historical events that the EU deems critical to European memory, such as the European Parliament's resolutions on the Remembrance of the Holocaust, anti-Semitism and Racism (2005), on the Armenian Genocide (1989), and on the Armenian Genocide's centenary (2015). The speeches given by diplomats and politicians representing the European Union's stance on specific historical events can also be considered in this category.

The second group consists of more systematic attempts to create a discourse on history underpinned by a political strategy. The EU initiated its cultural and identity policies in the 1970s in order to strengthen its legitimacy in the face of economic crises.[3] The EU's Declaration on European Identity, signed by (West) European foreign ministers in 1973, called for the first time for the foundation and advancement of a common conception of European identity by means of activities that would further European unification and analyse Europe's 'common heritage'. Since then the EU's institutions, in particular the European Commission and European Parliament, strived to contribute to the public awareness of European culture and identity within the framework of a common cultural policy.[4] The EU's history politics should be considered in this context. The recent projects presenting European memory and history serve the same aims, creating an awareness of identity and legitimizing the EU's institutions.[5] Thus, for example, the European Commission's former president Romano Prodi initiated the group of intellectuals called 'The Spiritual and Cultural Dimension of Europe', who upheld notions of multiculturalism in the European Union against the powerful arguments about an alleged 'Clash of Civilizations'.[6]

In another example, the European Commission and European Parliament worked together in 2013–14 in a project entitled 'New Narrative for Europe', to overcome the recurring discussions on the EU's political legitimacy following its financial crisis in 2008.[7] In 2013, the European Commission and European Parliament also started 'Active European Remembrance' as a joint endowment to sponsor projects stressing the memory of the totalitarian past of Europe.[8] The fourth example is the already mentioned House of European History, the idea for which was introduced by the European Parliament in 2008 with a similar political rationale of creating identity. Hans-Gert Pöttering, the then president of the European Parliament, stated that the House of European History 'will bring Europe's history alive for everyone, but especially young people, and will thereby help promote an awareness of European identity'.[9]

What recent publications on the EU's history politics can agree upon is that the objective of legitimizing the EU brings a tendency to write

European history as a cumulative, linear process leading up to a positively accentuated European Union. In this way, the attempts by the EU to shape a European integration narrative become part and parcel of the ongoing process of European integration. As Stråth and Leggewie write separately, the EU-sponsored European integration history evokes an ethical position against wars and in favour of democracy and welfare.[10] Gerard Delanty argues in the same direction that today coping with the contemporary problems of the European Union entails bringing into focus European history as a transnational history.[11] A number of scholars, however, have recently voiced their scepticism about such functionalization of the past. Oriane Calligaro, Wolfram Kaiser, Fabrica Larat and Tuuli Lähdesmäki have recently reminded us that the single narrative of European integration is part of a streamlined and streamlining objective of legitimizing European institutions at the grass-roots level.[12] The EU's history projects are described as initiatives of top-down cultural engineering.[13]

In a similar vein, the House of European History (HEH) is criticized as a legitimatory project making the case for European integration. So, for example, Kaiser questioned its teleological perspective, rooted in the idealism of Pöttering and finding expression in the museum's first Conceptual Basis (2008).[14] Huistra, Molema and Wirt have argued that the HEH, through its conceptualization of European history, has an inbuilt automatism that moves history in the direction of democracy and diversity.[15] The narrative presents the two world wars as temporary breaks with an otherwise continuous history of European values that were born in previous centuries and have come into their own with the foundation and development of EU institutions.

Partly as a result of such criticisms, the House of European History changed its narrative scope and reduced the tone of its teleological argument about European integration.[16] Yet, following Wolfram Kaiser, it remains a problem that the museum's exhibition does not cover a longer-term historical perspective on European integration, and focuses attention on the developments emanating after the Second World War.[17] As Veronika Settele adds, it remains deeply problematic that some important aspects of European integration underpinning the value of diversity, including colonial relations of European nation states or immigration into Europe, are sidelined in the HEH's exhibition.[18] Another major critique focuses on the tendency of the museum to present European integration as a success story. To Ben Wellings and Ben Power this is a typical attempt to vindicate the European Union.[19] The official EU representations of the past rely to some extent on positive perceptions of the European past, including its ancient heritage, its Christian culture, its Enlightenment tradition and, not least, the process of European integration after the Second World War.[20] At the same, however, official EU statements on the past also present a darker picture of Europe – a picture dominated by wars, civil wars, violence and genocide. The EU can then be presented as an inheritor of the good traditions of Europe and, at the same time, as an instrument with which to overcome the darker aspects of the past.

Yet this officially preferred version of European history has been difficult to align with national conceptions of Europe that are still characterized by wide contestation over the precise relationship between the national and the European and over the contribution of diverse nation states to a wider European space.[21] Different nationalized conceptualizations of Europe, which dominate European historical consciousness today, rely on very different narrative framings of key events, including the history of the two world wars in the twentieth century.[22] As the following chapters in our volume also demonstrate, the memory landscape of the Second World War has an important impact on the way in which various nation states in Europe position themselves vis-à-vis democratic politics and Europeanization.[23] Recent publications on the memory of those wars therefore call for analyses of rituals, landscapes, symbolic representations and other elements of war memories to understand better the importance of national interests in framing national identity and to arrive at an understanding both of the commonalities and the differences of war remembrances across Europe.[24]

The Holocaust has become an integral part of that war memory, and today forms the core of a European remembrance culture that assumes commonality but often hides substantial differences. In fact, the assumed European foundational narrative of the Holocaust has a very different place in diverse national collective memory. On the one hand, the European Union has invested heavily in putting the Holocaust at the centre of its historical self-understanding and in influencing national understandings of the Holocaust in diverse European nation states. In their article, Buttner and Delius take the remembrance of the Holocaust as an example of the universalization of a single-memory culture in the Western world.[25] Aline Sierp, in her book on the changes in Holocaust commemorations in Germany and Italy, discusses the connection between national politics, European politics and remembrance at length. She shows how the European Union's initiatives are emphasizing the singularity of the Holocaust and how they make the Holocaust the principal event to remember in European history.[26] The Council of Europe is producing a range of programmes on Holocaust remembrance, intending to further its understanding as an important anchor of European identity creation.[27] On the other hand, this remembrance of the Holocaust is still centrally linked to the particular agendas of national history politics. Even if European nation states are all, to a certain extent, presenting the Holocaust as illiberal 'other' to their self-presentation today, its weight in national memory politics differs substantially.[28] Especially in Eastern Europe, it is ranked far below the memory of the Communist past.[29]

With regard to British Holocaust memory, Sharon Macdonald concurs with this view as she looks into the Holocaust memorial ceremonies in Britain, which were first organized in 2001. She states: 'Depicting the nation itself as cosmopolitan, as open to different cultures and traditions was, then, a central ambition of the new Holocaust commemoration'.[30] Indeed, as Chantal Mouffe and, in her wake, Anna Bull and Hans Lauge Hansen have argued, such forms of cosmopolitan politics and memory have become dominant in European politics and memory cultures. However, cosmopolitan politics and memory, they contend, may well be the problem rather than the solution to European politics and memory cultures, as they depoliticize politics and memory, and make contention over politics and memory a near impossibility. Hence, they call for agonistic forms of politics and memory, which would allow renewed political debate that does not fall back into the antagonistic forms of politics and memory that were often at the heart of earlier military conflicts in Europe.[31]

A uniform cosmopolitan understanding of history and memory as sometimes championed by the European Union is likely to be challenged by national contexts, and recent publications already explore the disagreements expressed by Central and East European countries on two occasions. First, the principal importance given to the Holocaust's representation is intrinsic to Western Europe, whereas in the East it is the memory of the crimes committed in the Communist era that take centre stage.[32] True, from the European enlargement in 2004, the Holocaust is not the only event memorialized within the European Union as new members often call for the remembrance of Stalinist and other Communist crimes in the East. As Marek Kucia discusses, the new members of the European Parliament from Central and East European countries have included these crimes in the European Parliament's resolutions.[33] However, the West European understanding of European memory primarily resting on the Holocaust memory is still visible in many official proclamations emanating from the EU, and also in the narration of the House of European History. According to Kaiser, the HEH does cover the memory of Stalinist and Communist crimes but it still takes the Holocaust as the single most important criminal event in human history.[34]

Ultimately the memorial landscapes of Central and Eastern Europe cannot be expected to be the same as those of Western Europe. In Eastern Europe, as many scholars, such as Berger and Leersen, point out, nationalisms and national representations of history were revitalized in the 1990s, when the Cold War and the Soviet Union's ideological influence came to an end.[35] Consequently, and as Fabrice Larat's work also reminds us, the EU's new members from Central and Eastern Europe today have particular relationships with their national pasts and with the concept of European inte-gration.[36] This particularity focuses on a foreign-imposed Communist past that excluded East-Central and Eastern Europe from the post-war 'success story' of the European Union. Therefore, one of the main challenges for European historical consciousness today remains how to bring together the very different post-war memorial landscapes of Western and Eastern Europe, divided for so long by the Cold War.

This is not, of course, to deny the very important differences between the memorial cultures within Eastern, Central and Western Europe. Thus, the revival of nationalism has by no means been restricted to Eastern Europe. Nationalist movements and nationalist memory politics have been growing in many West European nation states, including France, and a range of small nation nationalisms, for example in Scotland and Catalonia, have been threatening the existence of long-established multinational states, such as the United Kingdom and Spain.[37] At the same time, nationalist memory politics in East-Central and Eastern Europe show important specificities that should not be lost amidst blanket charges of a nationalist memory politics in those regions of Europe. Thus, for example, the Polish memory landscape as a major site of both the Holocaust and Soviet war crimes is quite different from the memory landscape of Hungary, where the trauma of the Trianon treaty still looms large over national memory.[38]

The chapters of the present volume attend to these interlinked debates on the pitfalls of the EU's history politics, representations of history in European and national contexts, and memory politics in Central and Eastern Europe. They also reflect on the relevance of specific concepts regarding interconnected histories and memories in Europe. The first is 'transnational memory': how national memory landscapes impact on each other, and how, in a dialogic exchange, memory landscapes often transcend the boundaries of the nation state. Transnational memory has emerged as a relatively recent concept in memory studies, and is particularly employed by constructivist approaches taking national identities as invented.[39] There are two main-stream viewpoints connecting transnational memory to either supranational (global/European) or national contexts. A number of scholars have been arguing that, in the case of the Holocaust, memory receives global recogni-tion and takes precedence over national memory.[40] Civil dialogue, including the presentations and exhibitions discussed through international mass media, museums, and academia, plays a decisive role in the emergence of a globalized Holocaust memory.[41] The second viewpoint maintains that nation states are still the primary agents of memory politics throughout Europe that continue to determine the direction of transnational memories.[42] Disagreements on the definition and scope of transnational memories do exist in many instances, and many of them stem from national politics. The representation of the

Holocaust is an example. The media have contributed to a global awareness of the Holocaust, but the authenticity and purpose of these contributions cannot always be the same.[43] Thus, the media in different nation states have juxtaposed the memory of the Holocaust and the memory of Stalinist crimes to differing degrees, making a problematic aspect of transnational memory in contemporary Europe.[44] Another example is the memory politics in most post-Yugoslav states, which link the negative remembrance of Yugoslavia, in their separate ways, to the positive remembrance of their national identities.[45] The contributions to this volume deal with all of these issues, and together provide further commentary on the importance of transnational memory in the representation of Yugoslav history between Balkan nations, the Soviet (Stalinist) history between West and East European countries, and the remembrance of the Holocaust between Europe and Israel.

Conceptualizations of 'self' and 'other' also feature strongly in the present volume. Lionel Gossman, Gregory Sterling and Jörn Rüsen have all separately pointed to the importance of such binaries in historical meaning-making.[46] National memory, through its constructions of evils, heroes and victims, plays a major role in re-enforcing these binaries, as it strengthens an in-group identity vis-à-vis its 'others'.[47] What the EU's official history politics primarily takes as its 'other' are the periods in the previous century marked by authoritarianism, totalitarianism and violence, in which many of the EU's member states and candidates for accession were entangled. Yet, arguably the most contested 'other' today is Turkey. Political debates on Turkey's accession to the EU already reveal contestations between political camps over Turkish history in relation to European history.[48]

The book gathers ten chapters, all dealing with either the European Union's attempts to promote a 'shared' narrative of European history or national contestations over such unifying narrative frames. In the opening chapter, Daniel Rosenberg reviews the debates over the House of European History (HEH). Rosenberg first introduces the main approaches taken towards an understanding of European civilization and subsequently critiques those approaches for not being pluralist enough. He then reviews a range of museums dedicated to European history, and compares them with the HEH. After reflecting on its scope and aims, he contends that the coverage of the HEH is in harmony with the general purpose of the primary supranational EU institutions, namely to produce a streamlined pan-European discourse of a uniform European civilization. To Rosenberg, the HEH is not designed to show an accumulation of diverse European histories that might at certain points converge but also diverge; on the contrary, it is designed as an attempt to give a narrative frame to the pan-European idea.

The second chapter reviews the role of European institutions in the historiography of European integration. Oriane Calligaro argues that the

European Commission has attempted to promote a particular take on
European history in academia. To achieve this objective, the Commission
first supported the project of European integration history at the European
University Institute during the 1970s. As this project 'failed' in 1980, the
Commission initiated the Liaison Committee – a network of scholars
working on the subject of European integration – and continued to endorse
it until the mid-1990s. According to Calligaro, the Commission was partially successful in these attempts. From the 1980s the Liaison Committee
did well in bringing together a network of scholars writing on European
integration and streamlining a standard terminology, which fed into popular
concepts like 'identity', 'memory' and 'integration'. In the end, however,
the European Commission did not succeed in creating a singular dominant
'Europeanized' form of history writing.

The first two chapters beg the question of why the EU was relatively
unsuccessful in forging a dominant European historical narrative, when
the nineteenth-century nation states of Europe were so successful in doing
so.[49] Part of the answer lies in the rather half-hearted and almost ashamed
attempts by the EU institutions to drive a determined history politics from
above. Much of this may well have to do with the recognition that the
construction of such narratives streamlines and excludes contention over the
very narratives that are at the heart of any democratic politics. As democrats,
EU politicians subscribe to the necessity for such contention and pluralist
perspectives, which makes it far more difficult to arrive at a European master
narrative of history. Furthermore, there is also far greater respect for the
autonomy of the historical sciences among European politicians than was
the case amongst the politically powerful in nineteenth-century nation states.
The latter had a much more functionalist approach to historical writing. And
as it always takes two to tango, the professional historians in contemporary
Europe are also far less willing to become the prophets of Europe in the way
that their nineteenth- and early twentieth-century predecessors were the
prophets of their nations.[50]

Because historiographical nationalism is today perceived as having contributed to some of the major disasters of modern history, including civil
war, world war and genocide, it has been tainted and is not likely to be
revived at European level without contention. This is precisely what we
have witnessed in the debates over the European House of History, referred
to above. But a European master narrative is struggling to emerge, and not
just because of unwilling politicians and historians; in effect, the content
of that master narrative is also difficult to construct. Just as some national
histories were easier to construct than others, a homogenizing and unifying
European history is difficult to write. After all, what disunited Europeans in
the past is so much more visible and obvious than what united them. All of

the potentially unifying narratives have their flaws. For example, classical Greece as birthplace of democracy included parts of the Mediterranean that are now firmly outside of Europe, and it excluded large parts of Northern Europe that are now an integral part of the EU. It is also questionable to what extent imperial Rome should serve as a model for the contemporary EU. Christianity contains some history of bloody separation and division that cost the lives of millions, as did its equally bloody struggles against alleged 'infidels'. Humanism and the Enlightenment contained a dialectic that could and did turn its enlightening intentions into their mirror opposites.[51] The Holocaust and hyper-nationalism producing two world wars marked the high point of the crisis of European civilization against which the European Union is often defined; but can a European master narrative be built on negative foundational myths alone. Even if we answer this question in the affirmative, the wars as well as the Holocaust concerned and touched European nations to very different degrees. And finally, the success story of the EU itself arguably lacks all the heroism and gripping storylines that national histories were made of in the nineteenth century. Thus the difficulties of coming up with a convincing European master narrative have to be added to the hesitancy of its main agents to explain why all those attempts to frame such a narrative have not been entirely convincing or successful.

After discussing in the first two chapters the relatively limited success of the EU to promote a streamlined version of European history, Claudia Schneider asks in the third chapter to what extent EU members actually uphold a supranational representation of European history and culture? She addresses this question through her analysis of national images presented at the European Union National Institutes for Culture (EUNIC), the network of national cultural institutes of the EU member states. One of the network's aims is to encourage 'cultural dialogue and exchange' at the European level. Despite that, the principal objective of each individual EU member of EUNIC is to put forward national self-images. The question as to what extent these are shared (or not) by other EU member states is all too rarely addressed. Thus, member states of EUNIC voluntarily come together to exhibit to each other their national cultural heritages, whilst arguments on common or shared European memory remain rather superficial. The emphasis on being European, as Schneider concludes, is in fact no more than a side effect of EUNIC.

The fourth chapter then turns its attention from cultural initiatives to school curricula and textbooks. Falk Pingel discusses changing conceptions of European integration in national school curricula and textbooks from the 1990s onwards. He reviews teaching materials and additionally makes use of Eurobarometer surveys. Although national textbooks in Europe move within a shared memory space, 'nation' remains the core point of reference not only

for curricula experts and textbook authors but also in pupils' concepts of
collective identities. The stronger national identities of European schoolchil-
dren may thus well contribute to a growing Euroscepticism, especially when
the latter is pushed by important populist forces across many nation states in
Europe. For these reasons, Pingel argues that a common history education
about Europe and the European Union is becoming more and more central
for the European project today. And yet, we seem to be far away from any
such developments becoming a reality, despite the good intentions of some
politicians, history educators and historians who have been pushing for the
development of joint schoolbooks. The Franco–German schoolbook, the
first volume of which (on the post-1945 period) was launched in 2006,[52] has
been followed by a Polish–German one, launched in 2016,[53] and the model
has been received well in many places. However, there is currently little
evidence that the Franco–German schoolbook is actually being used widely
in either France or Germany. The Polish–German initiative is as yet too new
to be able to judge its future success.

If there has been a long-standing tension between national and
European narratives, this tension has been particularly marked in the case
of Britain, more specifically England. In the fifth chapter, Ben Wellings
and Chris Gifford explore the uses of history in contemporary discussions
of Euroscepticism in England, which they grouped into 'soft' and 'hard'
versions. Together these groups construe England as the birthplace of
representative democracy and an empire of free trade. The main difference
between the two is that the hard version of Euroscepticism completely
rejects the idea of coexistence between European and British histories,
whereas the soft one confirms intersections during certain times in history.
According to Wellings and Gifford, political camps with hard and soft
versions of Euroscepticism conflicted each other harshly during the Brexit
debates. The authors analyse the arguments put forward by both camps on
a range of historical themes, including 'representative democracy', 'Empire'
and the 'Second World War'.

The sixth, seventh and eighth chapters explore the meaning of the
Second World War in memory politics of diverse other European nation
states. The sixth chapter, written by Jelena Dureinovic, addresses the
memory of Yugoslavia in various post-Yugoslavian states. The remembrance of the Second World War was the primary source of legitimacy
of the state in socialist Yugoslavia. Socialist leaders constructed a narrative
framing the war as the triumph of antifascism. As a form of resistance to the
Yugoslav state, independence movements in the 1980s put forward alternative, nationalist narratives celebrating anticommunist movements going back
to the Second World War. This legitimation of quasi-fascist movements in
the struggle against Communist Yugoslavia and its version of Yugoslavism

was exacerbated during the secessionist wars in 1992. And it remained an important part of history politics in many of the post-Yugoslav states. The Second World War was now interpreted very differently, as it symbolized the defeat of nations by communism. Antifascism was delegitimized as the ideology of Serbian nationalism allegedly oppressing other nationalities in the Balkans. In this narrative framing, nationalist Croatian warlords, often in alliance with German and Italian fascism, could be reinterpreted as national heroes. In the early 1990s, Serbian and Croatian narratives about the Second World War were often constructed against each other, yet, according to Dureinovic, they also showed a number of interesting parallels in their framing of stories of resistance, collaboration and victimhood. Overall, as Ulf Brunnbauer has shown, the important role of history in contributing mentally and culturally to the dissolution of Yugoslavia would have been unthinkable without the move towards more nationalist historiographies and a more nation-centred history politics in the individual federal states making up Yugoslavia throughout the 1980s.[54]

The rewriting of national pasts in pre- and post-Communist Yugoslavia finds intriguing parallels across much of post-Communist Eastern Europe. In the seventh chapter, Claudia Weber discusses contemporary East European memory cultures surrounding the histories of Stalinism. The agents of memory politics in Eastern Europe are acutely aware of the West European preoccupations with Holocaust memory, and are often arguing that the memory of Stalinist and Communist crimes, which had been a taboo topic under Communism in Eastern Europe, deserves a stronger hearing and emphasis in a post-Cold War European memory space. Giving examples from European and national politics prioritizing the memory of the Holocaust, Weber therefore rightly cautions us against making a hierarchy of humanitarian crimes.

European memory today undoubtedly finds one of its strongest anchors in the Holocaust, but to what extent is this memory a shared one? In the eighth chapter, Judith Müller reviews Lizzie Doron's literary work, *On the Brink of Something Beautiful*, and questions the existence of a uniform contemporary European discourse connecting Holocaust memories with Europeanness. Hesi, Doron's fictional character, is a young scholar who meets witnesses of the Holocaust in Poland and France, observing disagreements between the narratives with which he was raised in Israel and the ones he finds in Europe. The memory of the Holocaust, Hesi has to conclude, is not a uniform one: victims' perspectives can vary, and today's media and literature can represent it very differently. The chapter concludes that the Holocaust should certainly play a key role in Europe's commemoration of its past, but a more pluralistic way of representing identity and history in relation to the Holocaust also needs to be found.

If there is no uniformity in relation to European Holocaust memory, there is also no uniformity of European images of and dealings with Turkey, a long-time candidate for EU accession and arguably one of the key 'others' of Europe. The ninth and tenth chapters are reserved for analyses of contemporary memory debates surrounding Turkey. Paul Levin begins his chapter with the evolution of the Turkish image in Europe in the longue durée. He shows how Europe's historical identity was partially forged in relation to the Islamic image of the Ottoman Empire. Levin argues that Turkey's religious exclusion from Europe continues today, and he finds much evidence of this in the European Union's membership negotiations with Turkey, which have been ongoing since 2005. He concedes that Turkey's inability to democratize has also played a decisive role in the continuing failure of the negotiations, but he can also demonstrate how European political elites have been characterizing Turkey using its historically 'non-European' traits, especially its Islamic character. These characterizations have, according to Levin, contributed to Turkey's 'othering', and sometimes Turkey-sceptical political camps even explained the democratic problems of the candidate with its religious history. Once again, we encounter in Levin's chapter the importance of historical arguments for excluding one country, Turkey, from belonging to an association of other countries, the EU. History has become a weapon with which to question the compatibility of Turkey with the Europeanness.

In the final chapter, Caner Tekin explores the specific examples from Turkish history that European political camps discussed in the European Parliament during the 2000s, particularly from the beginning of the membership negotiations in 2005 onwards. He argues that these prominent historical images of Turkey find very little reflection in the accession criteria that are based on a range of political and economic conditions that Turkey, like any other accession country, has to meet. Yet especially among European conservatives a distinct historical discourse on Turkey, problematizing in particular its belonging to the Islamic world, in fact augments the accession criteria and has led to the continued exclusion of Turkey from Europe. As these conservatives tend to define Europe (again with reference to history) as 'Christian Europe', an Islamic Turkey, by definition, does not belong. Tekin exemplifies such exclusionary practices with a collection of parliamentary statements on the historical image of Turkey.

Overall the chapters in this volume shed light on the complex and multifaceted relationships between vernacular national memorial landscapes and attempts to arrive at European memorial landscapes. Europe has for a long time been part and parcel of national memories and vice versa, and European memory reappropriates in manifold ways national memories. The mismatches and internal contradictions of the national memory landscapes in

Europe make the emergence of a European landscape so difficult. Ultimately history may well be what divides rather than what unites Europe, which might explain the futility of building Europe on history.

Stefan Berger is professor of history at the Ruhr University Bochum, where he is the director of the Institute of Social Movements and the chairman of the History of the Ruhr Foundation. He was appointed honorary professor at Cardiff University in 2017. He has published numerous books and articles on historiography and comparative labour history, and his most recent book publications include *Industrial Heritage and Regional Identities* (edited with Christian Wicke and Jana Golombek, 2018), *The Transnational Activist: Transformations and Comparisons from the Anglo-World since the Nineteenth Century* (edited with Sean Scalmer, 2018), and *Popularizing National Pasts: 1800 to the Present* (edited with Chris Lorenz, 2017).

Caner Tekin is a member of the Centre for Mediterranean Studies at the Ruhr University Bochum, where he has recently received his doctoral degree. He worked previously at the Georg-Eckert Institute for International Textbook Research in Brunswick, Germany as a postdoctoral fellow. He is also a review editor working for H-Nationalism, the online scholarly forum on nationalism studies. His research interests revolve around the linkages between nationalisms, representations of the past, and migration.

Notes

1. A.J.P. Taylor et al., 'What is European History?' in J. Gardiner (ed.), *What is History Today?* (Houndmills and London: Macmillan Press, 1988), 143.

2. C. Shore, '"In Uno Plures" (?) EU Cultural Policy and the Governance of Europe', *Cultural Analysis* 5 (2006), 12–13.

3. C. Shore, *Building Europe: The Cultural Politics of European Integration* (London: Psychology Press, 2000).

4. Commission of the European Communities, 'A People's Europe'. Communication from the Commission to the European Parliament, Com(88) 331 Final, Brussels, 7 July 1988, 11.

5. O. Calligaro, 'Legitimation through Remembrance? The Changing Regimes of Historicity of European Integration', *Journal of Contemporary European Studies* 23(3) (2005), 330–43; W. Kaiser, 'Clash of Cultures: Two Milieus in the European Union's "A New Narrative for Europe" Project', *Journal of Contemporary European Studies* 23(3) (2015), 364–77.

6. See K. Biedenkopf, B. Geremek and K. Michalski, The Spiritual and Cultural Dimension of Europe: Concluding Remarks (Vienna, Austria: Institute for Human. Sciences / Brussels: European Commission, 2004), which were in stark contrast to S. Huntington, *The Clash of Civilisations and the Remaking of World Order* (New York: Simon and Schuster, 1996).

7. European Commission, 'General Report on the Activities of the European Union 2013' (Luxembourg: Publication Office of the European Union, 2014), 15.

8. European Commission, 'Europe for Citizens Programme 2007–2013, Programme Guide 2013', 49–52, http://eacea.ec.europa.eu/citizenship/programme/documents/2013/guide_2013_en_final%20.pdf [last accessed 2 February 2017].

9. 'EP Bureau Decides to Set Up a "House of European History"', Press Release, Directorate for the Media, 20081216IPR44855.

10. B. Stråth, 'Methodological and Substantive Remarks on Myth, Memory and History in the Construction of a European Community', *German Law Journal* 6(2) (2005), 264; C. Leggewie, 'Seven Circles of European Memory', *Cultural Memories* 4 (2011), 123–43.

11. G. Delanty, 'Entangled Memories: How to Study Europe's Cultural Heritage', *European Legacy* 22(2) (2017), 129–45.

12. Calligaro, 'Legitimation through Remembrance?' 340–41; W. Kaiser, 'Unreliable Narrators: Witness Accounts and the Institutionalization of European History', *Eurozine*, 24 November 2011; F. Larat, 'Present-ing the Past: Political Narratives on European History and the Justification of EU Integration', *German Law Journal* 6(2) (2005), 27–90; T. Lähdesmäki, 'Narrativity and Intertextuality in the Making of a Shared European Memory', *Journal of Contemporary European Studies* 25(1) (2017), 57–72.

13. Kaiser, 'Clash of Cultures', 364–77.

14. W. Kaiser, 'Limits of Cultural Engineering: Actors and Narratives in the European Parliament's House of European History Project', *JCMS: Journal of Common Market Studies*, 3 October 2016, 2.

15. P. Huistra, M. Molema and D. Wirt, 'Political Values in a European Museum', *Journal of Contemporary European Research* 10(1) (2014), 124–36.

16. Kaiser, 'Limits of Cultural Engineering', 2.

17. ibid., 13.

18. V. Settele, 'Including Exclusion in European Memory? Politics of Remembrance at the House of European History', *Journal of Contemporary European Studies* 23(3) (2015), 405–16.

19. B. Wellings and B. Power, 'Euro-myth: Nationalism, War and the Legitimacy of the European Union', *National Identities* 18 (2015), 157–77.

20. S. Berger, 'History and Forms of Collective Identity in Europe: Why Europe Cannot and Should Not be Built on History', in L. Rorato and A. Saunders (eds), *The Essence and the Margin: National Identities and Collective Memories in Contemporary European Culture* (Amsterdam: Rodopi, 2009), 21–36.

21. S. Woolf, 'Europe and its Historians', *Contemporary European History* 12(3) (2003), 324–25.

22. J.H. Gillis, *Commemorations: The Politics of National Identity* (Princeton, NJ: Princeton University Press, 1994); S. Berger and C. Lorenz (eds), *The Contested Nation: Ethnicity, Class and Gender in National Identities* (Basingstoke: Palgrave Macmillan, 2008); S. Sumartojo and B. Wellings (eds), *Nation, Memory, and Great War Commemoration: Mobilizing the Past in Europe, Australia, and New Zealand* (Bern: Peter Lang, 2014); A. Sierp, *History, Memory, and Trans-European Identity: Unifying Divisions* (London: Routledge, 2014).

23. See the contributions in R.N. Lebow, W. Kansteiner and C. Fogu (eds), *The Politics of Memory in Postwar Europe* (Durham, NC: Duke University Press, 2006).

24. E.T. Woods and R. Tsang, 'Ritual and Performance in the Study of Nations and Nationalism', in R. Tsang and E.T. Woods (eds), *The Cultural Politics of Nationalism and Nation-Building, Ritual and Performance in the Forging of Nations* (London and New York: Routledge, 2014), 1–18; T. O'Keeffe, 'Landscape and Memory: Historiography, Theory, Methodology', in N. Moore and Y. Whelan (eds), *Heritage, Memory and the Politics of Identity: New Perspectives on the Cultural Landscape* (Aldershot: Ashgate, 2007), 3–18; D. Zuev and F. Vircchow, 'Performing National Identity: The Many Logics of Producing National Belongings in Public Rituals

and Events', *Nations and Nationalism* 20(2) (2014), 191–99; S. Sumartojo, 'Commemorative Atmospheres: Memorial Sites, Collective Events and the Experience of National Identity', *Transactions* 41(4) (2016), 541–53; S. Sumartojo 'On Atmosphere and Darkness at Australia's Anzac Day Dawn Service', *Visual Communication* 14(3) (2015), 267–88. See also the Horizon 2020 project 'Unsettling Remembering and Social Cohesion in Transnational Europe', www.unrest.eu [last accessed 9 February 2017], which is seeking to explore the directions in which war memories have been developing over the last decades.

25. S. Buttner and A. Delius, 'World Culture in European Memory Politics? New European Memory Agents between Epistemic Framing and Political Agenda Setting', *Journal of Contemporary European Studies* 23(3) (2015), 394.

26. A. Sierp, *History, Memory, and Trans-European Identity: Unifying Divisions* (London: Routledge, 2014).

27. E. Kuebler, 'Holocaust Remembrance in the Council of Europe: Deplorable Victims and Evil Ideologies without Perpetrators', *Jewish Political Studies Review* 23(12) (2012).

28. For insights into the political instrumentalization of memory, see M. Pakier and B. Stråth, 'Introduction: A European Memory?' in M. Pakier and B. Stråth (eds), *A European Memory? Contested Histories and Politics of Remembrance* (New York: Berghahn Books, 2010), 7–11.

29. On the impact of Holocaust memory in Eastern Europe, see M. Kucia, 'The Europeanization of Holocaust Memory and Eastern Europe', *East European Politics and Societies and Cultures* 30(1) (2016), 97–119; E. Droit, 'Le Goulag contre le Shoah', *Vingtième Siècle* 94 (2007), 101–20.

30. S. Macdonald, *Memorylands: Heritage and Identity in Europe Today* (Abingdon and New York: Routledge, 2013), 205.

31. C. Mouffe, 'An Agonistic Approach to the Future of Europe', *New Literary History* 43(4) (2012), 629–40. Also see A. Bull and H.L. Hansen, 'On Agonistic Memory', *Memory Studies* 9(4) (2016), 390–404.

32. Buttner and Delius, 'World Culture in European Memory Politics?', 394.

33. Kucia, 'The Europeanization of Holocaust Memory and Eastern Europe', 106–7.

34. Kaiser, 'Limits of Cultural Engineering', 11–12.

35. S. Berger, 'Narrating the Nation: Historiography and Other Genres', in S. Berger, L. Eriksonas and A. Mycock (eds), *Narrating the Nation: Representations in History, Media and the Arts* (New York: Berghahn Books, 2008), 3–4; J. Leerssen, *National Thought in Europe: A Cultural History* (Amsterdam: Amsterdam University Press, 2007), 242–43.

36. Larat, 'Present-ing the Past', 273–90.

37. On the memory politics of the Front National in France, see C. Flood, 'The Politics of Counter-memory on the French Extreme Right', *Journal of European Studies* 35(2) (2005), 221–36; and G. Goodliffe, 'From Political Fringe to Political Mainstream: The Front National and the French Municipal Elections of 2014', *French Politics, Culture and Society* 35 (2017), 126–47. On the memory politics of Scotland and Catalonia, compare I. Robertson and T. Hall, 'Memory, Identity and the Memorialisation of Conflict in the Scottish Highlands', in N. Moore and Y. Whelan (eds), *Heritage, Memory and the Politics of Identity: New Perspectives on the Cultural Landscape* (Aldershot: Ashgate, 2007), 19–36; R. Mann and S. Fenton, *Nation, Class and Resentment: The Politics of National Identity in England, Scotland and Wales* (Basingstoke: Palgrave MacMillan, 2017); D.A. Messenger, 'Contemporary Memory Politics in Catalonia: Europeanizing and Mobilizing the History of the Spanish Civil War', in C. Kraenzle and M. Mayr (eds), *The Changing Place of Europe in Global Memory Cultures: Usable Pasts and Futures* (Basingstoke: Palgrave MacMillan, 2017), 49–62.

38. On Poland, see P. Madajczyk, 'Experience and Memory: The Second World War in Poland', in J. Echternkamp and S. Martens (eds), *Experience and Memory: The Second World War in Europe* (New York: Berghahn Books, 2010), 70–85; on Hungary, compare K. Gerner,

'Open Wounds? Trianon, the Holocaust and the Hungarian Trauma', in C. Mithander, J. Sundholm and M. Holmgren Troy (eds), *Collective Traumas: Memories of War and Conflict in Twentieth-Century Europe* (Brussels: Peter Lang, 2007), 79–110.

39. S. Berger and B. Niven, 'Introduction', in S. Berger and B. Niven (eds), *Writing the History of Memory* (London and New York: Bloomsbury Academic, 2014), 16; A. Assmann, 'Transnational Memories', *European Review* 22 (4) (2014), 546–47; A. Sierp and J. Wüstenberg, 'Linking the Local and the Transnational: Rethinking Memory Politics in Europe', *Journal of Contemporary European Studies* 23(3) (2015), 322.

40. D. Levy and N. Sznaider, *Erinnerung im globalen Zeitalter: der Holocaust* (Frankfurt: Suhrkamp, 2001). A similar and newer approach prioritizes the role of Europeanization in the existence of transnational memory. See C. de Cesari and A. Rigney (eds), *Transnational Memory: Circulation, Articulation, Scales* (Berlin: De Gruyter, 2014); and Sierp and Wüstenberg, 'Linking the Local and the Transnational'.

41. See E. Lehrer, 'Can There Be a Conciliatory Heritage?', *International Journal of Heritage Studies* 16(4–5) (2014), 269–88. D. Levy and N. Sznaider, 'Memory Unbound: The Holocaust and the Formation of Cosmopolitan Memory', *European Journal of Social Theory* 5(1) (2002), 87–106.

42. S. Berger and B. Niven, 'Writing the History of National Memory', in S. Berger and B. Niven (eds), *Writing the History of Memory* (London and New York: Bloomsbury Academic, 2014), 150. K.K. Patel, 'In Search of a Second Historicization: National Socialism in a Transnational Perspective', in K.H. Jarausch and T. Lindenberger (eds), *Conflicted Memories: Europeanizing Contemporary Histories* (New York: Berghahn Books, 2007), 99.

43. A. Assmann, 'The Holocaust – A Global Memory? Extensions and Limits of a New Memory Community', in A. Assmann and S. Conrad (eds), *Memory in a Global Age: Discourses, Practices and Trajectories* (Houndmills: Palgrave Macmillan, 2010), 113–14.

44. Assmann, 'Transnational Memories', 552.

45. G. Kirn, 'Transnationalism in Reverse: From Yugoslav to Post-Yugoslav Memorial Sites', in C. de Cesari and A. Rigney (eds), *Transnational Memory: Circulation, Articulation, Scales* (Berlin: De Gruyter, 2014), 328.

46. L. Gossman, 'History as Decipherment: Romantic Historiography and the Discovery of the Other', *New Literary History* 18(1) (Autumn 1986), 23–57; G.E. Sterling, *Historiography and Self-Definition: Josephos, Luke-Acts and Apologetic Historiography* (Leiden: Brill, 1992); J. Rüsen, 'Historical Thinking as Intercultural Discourse', in J. Rüsen (ed.), *Western Historical Thinking: An Intercultural Debate* (New York: Berghahn Books, 2002), 1–14.

47. D.S.A. Bell, 'Mythscapes: Memory, Mythology, and National Identity', *British Journal of Sociology* 54(1) (2003), 69–70; C. de Cesari and A. Rigney, 'Beyond Methodological Nationalism', in C. de Cesari and A. Rigney (eds), *Transnational Memory: Circulation, Articulation, Scales* (Berlin: De Gruyter, 2014), 9. Also see, P. Nora and D.L. Kritzman (eds), *Realms of Memory* (New York: Columbia University Press, 1996).

48. C. Tekin, 'Discussing Turkey in "European Terms"? Conceptualisations of Turkey and the European Union between European Political Camps during the Accession Talks in the 2000s'. Unpublished PhD thesis (Bochum: Ruhr Universität Bochum, 2016).

49. As documented in the eight-volume book series *Writing the Nation*, edited by S. Berger, C. Conrad and G. Marchal (Basingstoke: Palgrave MacMillan, 2007–2015).

50. S. Berger and C. Conrad, *The Past as History: National Identity and Historical Consciousness in Modern Europe* (Basingstoke: Palgrave MacMillan, 2015).

51. M. Horkheimer and T.W. Adorno, *Dialects of Enlightenment: Philosophical Fragments* (Stanford, CA: Stanford University Press, 2002).

52. C. Defrance and U. Pfeil, 'German–French School Textbook: Some Considerations about its Origins and the First Two Volumes'. Conference paper, 2008, https://www.bpb.de/system/files/pdf/IK3TE4.pdf [last accessed 11 February 2017].

53. Ministry of Foreign Affairs of the Republic of Poland, 'Foreign Ministers Present Polish–German History Textbook', 23 June 2016. http://www.msz.gov.pl/en/news/foreign_ministers_present_polish_german_history_textbook_;jsessionid=60E6BFE46A014C43DD9 D48F8C915E045.cmsap5p [last accessed 11 February 2017].

54. U. Brunnbauer (ed.), *(Re)writing History: Historiography in Southeast Europe after Socialism* (Münster: Lit-Verlag, 2004).

Bibliography

Archival Sources

Commission of the European Communities. 'A People's Europe'. Communication from the Commission to the European Parliament, Com(88) 331 Final, Brussels, 7 July 1988, 11.

European Commission. 'General Report on the Activities of the European Union 2013'. Luxembourg: Publication Office of the European Union, 2014.

European Commission. 'Europe for Citizens Programme 2007–2013. Programme Guide, 2013'. http://eacea.ec.europa.eu/citizenship/programme/documents/2013/guide_2013 _en_final%20.pdf [last accessed 2 February 2017].

European Parliament. 'Declaration of the European Parliament on the Proclamation of 23 August as European Day of Remembrance for Victims of Stalinism and Nazism', 23 September 2008, Brussels, P6_TA(2008)0439.

European Parliament. 'EP Bureau Decides to Set Up a "House of European History"'. Press Release, 20081216IPR44855. http://www.europarl.europa.eu/sides/getDoc.do?language=en&type=IM-PRESS&reference=20081216IPR44855 [last accessed 2 February 2017].

Horizon 2020 Project. 'Unsettling Remembering and Social Cohesion in Transnational Europe'. www.unrest.eu [last accessed 9 February 2017].

House of European History, Brussels. https://historia-europa.ep.eu/en [last accessed 7 November 2017].

Ministry of Foreign Affairs of the Republic of Poland. 'Foreign Ministers Present Polish–German History Textbook', 23 June 2016. http://www.msz.gov.pl/en/news/foreign_ministers_present_polish_german_history_textbook_;jsessionid=60E6BFE46A014C43 DD9D48F8C915E045.cmsap5p [last accessed 11 February 2017]

United Nations Outreach Programme. 'About the Holocaust and the United Nations Outreach Programme'. http://www.un.org/en/holocaustremembrance/ [last accessed 11 February 2017].

Secondary Sources

Assmann, A. 'The Holocaust – A Global Memory? Extensions and Limits of a New Memory Community', in A. Assmann and S. Conrad (eds), *Memory in a Global Age: Discourses, Practices and Trajectories* (Houndmills: Palgrave Macmillan, 2010), 97–118.

———. 'Transnational Memories'. *European Review* 22(4) (2014), 546–56.

Bell, D.S.A. 'Mythscapes: Memory, Mythology, and National Identity'. *British Journal of Sociology* 54(1) (2003), 63–81.

Berger, S. 'Narrating the Nation: Historiography and Other Genres', in S. Berger, L. Eriksonas and A. Mycock (eds), *Narrating the Nation: Representations in History, Media and the Arts* (New York: Berghahn Books, 2008), 1–16.

———. 'History and Forms of Collective Identity in Europe: Why Europe Cannot and Should Not be Built on History', in L. Rorato and A. Saunders (eds), *The Essence and* the Margin: National Identities and Collective Memories in Contemporary European Culture (Amsterdam: Rodopi, 2009), 21–36.

Berger, S., and C. Conrad. *The Past as History: National Identity and Historical Consciousness in Modern Europe*. Basingstoke: Palgrave MacMillan, 2015.

Berger, S., C. Conrad and G. Marchal. *Writing the Nation*. 8 volumes. Basingstoke: Palgrave MacMillan, 2007–2015.

Berger, S., and C. Lorenz (eds). *The Contested Nation: Ethnicity, Class and Gender in National Identities*. Basingstoke: Palgrave Macmillan, 2008.

Berger S., and B. Niven. 'Introduction', in S. Berger and B. Niven (eds), *Writing the History of Memory* (London and New York: Bloomsbury Academic, 2014), 1–24.

———. 'Writing the History of National Memory', in S. Berger and B. Niven (eds), *Writing the History of Memory* (London and New York: Bloomsbury Academic, 2014), 135–56.

Biedenkopf K., B. Geremek and K. Michalski. *The Spiritual and Cultural Dimension of Europe: Concluding Remarks*. Vienna, Austria: Institute for Human. Sciences / Brussels: European Commission, 2004.

Brunnbauer, U. (ed.). *(Re)writing History: Historiography in Southeast Europe after Socialism*. Münster: Lit-Verlag, 2004.

Bull, A., and H.L. Hansen. 'On Agonistic Memory'. *Memory Studies* 9(4) (2016), 390–404.

Buttner, S., and A. Delius. 'World Culture in European Memory Politics? New European Memory Agents between Epistemic Framing and Political Agenda Setting'. *Journal of Contemporary European Studies* 23(3) (2015), 391–404.

Calligaro, O. 'Legitimation through Remembrance? The Changing Regimes of Historicity of European Integration'. *Journal of Contemporary European Studies* 23(3) (2005), 330–43.

Cesari, C. de, and A. Rigney (eds). *Transnational Memory: Circulation, Articulation, Scales*. Berlin: De Gruyter, 2014.

———. 'Beyond Methodological Nationalism', in C. de Cesari and A. Rigney (eds), *Transnational Memory: Circulation, Articulation, Scales* (Berlin: De Gruyter, 2014), 1–25.

Defrance, C., and U. Pfeil. 'German–French School Textbook: Some Considerations about its Origins and the First Two Volumes'. Conference paper, 2008, https://www.bpb.de/system/files/pdf/IK3TE4.pdf [last accessed 11 February 2017].

Delanty, G. 'Entangled Memories: How to Study Europe's Cultural Heritage'. *European Legacy* 22(2) (2017), 129–45.

Droit, E. 'Le Goulag contre le Shoah'. *Vingtième Siècle* 94 (2007), 101–20.

Flood, C. 'The Politics of Counter-memory on the French Extreme Right'. *Journal of European Studies* 35(2) (2005), 221–36.

Gerner, K. 'Open Wounds? Trianon, the Holocaust and the Hungarian Trauma', in C. Mithander, J. Sundholm and M. Holmgren Troy (eds), *Collective Traumas: Memories of War and Conflict in Twentieth-Century Europe* (Brussels: Peter Lang, 2007), 79–110.

Gillis, J.H. *Commemorations: The Politics of National Identity*. Princeton, NJ: Princeton University Press, 1994.

Goodliffe, G. 'From Political Fringe to Political Mainstream: The Front National and the French Municipal Elections of 2014'. *French Politics, Culture and Society* 35 (2017), 126–47.

Gossman, L. 'History as Decipherment: Romantic Historiography and the Discovery of the Other'. *New Literary History* 18(1) (Autumn 1986), 23–57.

Horkheimer, M., and T.W. Adorno. *Dialects of Enlightenment: Philosophical Fragments*. Stanford, CA: Stanford University Press, 2002.

Huistra, P., M. Molema and D. Wirt. 'Political Values in a European Museum'. *Journal of Contemporary European Research* 10(1) (2014), 124–36.

Huntington, S. *The Clash of Civilisations and the Remaking of World Order*. New York: Simon and Schuster, 1996.

Kaiser, W. 'Unreliable Narrators: Witness Accounts and the Institutionalization of European History'. *Eurozine*, 24 November 2011.

———. 'Clash of Cultures: Two Milieus in the European Union's "A New Narrative for Europe" Project'. *Journal of Contemporary European Studies* 23(3) (2015), 364–77.

———. 'Limits of Cultural Engineering: Actors and Narratives in the European Parliament's House of European History Project'. *JCMS: Journal of Common Market Studies*, 3 October 2016, 1–17..

Kirn, G. 'Transnationalism in Reverse: From Yugoslav to Post-Yugoslav Memorial Sites', in C. de Cesari and A. Rigney (eds), *Transnational Memory: Circulation, Articulation, Scales* (Berlin: De Gruyter, 2014), 313–38.

Kucia, M. 'The Europeanization of Holocaust Memory and Eastern Europe'. *East European Politics and Societies and Cultures* 30(1) (2016), 97–119.

Kuebler, E. 'Holocaust Remembrance in the Council of Europe: Deplorable Victims and Evil Ideologies without Perpetrators'. *Jewish Political Studies Review* 23(12) (2012).

Lähdesmäki, T. 'Narrativity and Intertextuality in the Making of a Shared European Memory'. *Journal of Contemporary European Studies* 25(1) (2017), 57–72..

Larat, F. 'Present-ing the Past: Political Narratives on European History and the Justification of EU Integration'. *German Law Journal* 6(2) (2005), 273–90.

Lebow, R.N., W. Kansteiner and C. Fogu (eds). *The Politics of Memory in Postwar Europe*. Durham, NC: Duke University Press, 2006.

Leerssen, J. *National Thought in Europe: A Cultural History*. Amsterdam: Amsterdam University Press, 2007.

Leggewie, C. 'Seven Circles of European Memory'. *Cultural Memories* 4 (2011), 123–43.

Lehrer, E. 'Can There Be a Conciliatory Heritage?' *International Journal of Heritage Studies* 16(4–5) (2014), 269–88.

Levy, D., and N. Sznaider. *Erinnerung im globalen Zeitalter: der Holocaust*. Frankfurt: Suhrkamp, 2001.

———. 'Memory Unbound: The Holocaust and the Formation of Cosmopolitan Memory'. *European Journal of Social Theory* 5(1) (2002), 87–106.

Macdonald, S. *Memorylands: Heritage and Identity in Europe Today*. Abingdon and New York: Routledge, 2013.

Madajczyk, P. 'Experience and Memory: The Second World War in Poland', in J. Echternkamp and S. Martens (eds), *Experience and Memory: The Second World War in Europe* (New York: Berghahn Books, 2010), 70–85.

Mann, R., and S. Fenton. *Nation, Class and Resentment: The Politics of National Identity in England, Scotland and Wales*. Basingstoke: Palgrave MacMillan, 2017.

Messenger, D.A. 'Contemporary Memory Politics in Catalonia: Europeanizing and Mobilizing the History of the Spanish Civil War', in C. Kraenzle and M. Mayr (eds), *The Changing Place of Europe in Global Memory Cultures: Usable Pasts and Futures* (Basingstoke: Palgrave MacMillan, 2017), 49–62.

Mithander, C., J. Sundholm and M. Holmgren Troy (eds), *Collective Traumas: Memories of War and Conflict in Twentieth-Century Europe* (Brussels: Peter Lang, 2007), 79–110.

Mouffe, C. 'An Agonistic Approach to the Future of Europe'. *New Literary History* 43(4) (2012), 629–40.

Nora, P., and D.L. Kritzman (eds). *Realms of Memory*. New York: Columbia University Press, 1996.

O'Keeffe, T. 'Landscape and Memory: Historiography, Theory, Methodology', in N. Moore and Y. Whelan (eds), *Heritage, Memory and the Politics of Identity: New Perspectives on the Cultural Landscape* (Aldershot: Ashgate, 2007), 3–18.

Pakier, M., and B. Stråth. 'Introduction: A European Memory?' in M. Pakier and B. Stråth (eds), *A European Memory? Contested Histories and Politics of Remembrance* (New York: Berghahn Books, 2010), 1–20.

Patel, K.K. 'In Search of a Second Historicization: National Socialism in a Transnational Perspective', in K.H. Jarausch and T. Lindenberger (eds), *Conflicted Memories: Europeanizing Contemporary Histories* (New York: Berghahn Books, 2007), 96–116.

Robertson, I., and T. Hall. 'Memory, Identity and the Memorialisation of Conflict in the Scottish Highlands', in N. Moore and Y. Whelan (eds), *Heritage, Memory and the Politics of Identity: New Perspectives on the Cultural Landscape* (Aldershot: Ashgate, 2007), 19–36.

Rüsen, J. 'Historical Thinking as Intercultural Discourse', in J. Rüsen (ed.), *Western Historical Thinking: An Intercultural Debate* (New York: Berghahn Books, 2002), 1–14.

Settele, V. 'Including Exclusion in European Memory? Politics of Remembrance at the House of European History'. *Journal of Contemporary European Studies* 23(3) (2015), 405–16.

Shore, C. *Building Europe: The Cultural Politics of European Integration*. London: Psychology Press, 2000.

————. '"In Uno Plures"(?) EU Cultural Policy and the Governance of Europe'. *Cultural Analysis* 5 (2006), 7–26.

Sierp, A. *History, Memory, and Trans-European Identity: Unifying Divisions*. London: Routledge, 2014.

Sierp, A., and J. Wüstenberg. 'Linking the Local and the Transnational: Rethinking Memory Politics in Europe'. *Journal of Contemporary European Studies* 23(3) (2015), 321–29.

Sterling, G.E. *Historiography and Self-Definition: Josephos, Luke-Acts and Apologetic Historiography* (Leiden: Brill, 1992).

Stråth, B. 'Methodological and Substantive Remarks on Myth, Memory and History in the Construction of a European Community'. *German Law Journal* 6(2) (2005), 255–71.

Sumartojo, S. 'On Atmosphere and Darkness at Australia's Anzac Day Dawn Service'. *Visual Communication* 14(3) (2015), 267–88.

————. 'Commemorative Atmospheres: Memorial Sites, Collective Events and the Experience of National Identity'. *Transactions* 41(4) (2016), 541–53.

Sumartojo, S., and B. Wellings (eds). *Nation, Memory, and Great War Commemoration: Mobilizing the Past in Europe, Australia, and New Zealand*. Bern: Peter Lang, 2014.

Taylor, A.J.P., et al. 'What is European History?' in J. Gardiner (ed.), *What is History Today?* (Houndmills and London: Macmillan Press, 1988), 143–54.

Tekin, C. 'Discussing Turkey in "European Terms"? Conceptualisations of Turkey and the European Union between European Political Camps during the Accession Talks in the 2000s'. Unpublished PhD thesis. Bochum: Ruhr Universität Bochum, 2016.

Wellings, B., and B. Power. 'Euro-myth: Nationalism, War and the Legitimacy of the European Union'. *National Identities* 18 (2015), 157–77.

Woods, E.T., and R. Tsang. 'Ritual and Performance in the Study of Nations and Nationalism', in R. Tsang and E.T. Woods (eds), *The Cultural Politics of Nationalism and Nation-Building, Ritual and Performance in the Forging of Nations* (London and New York: Routledge, 2014), 1–18.

Woolf, S. 'Europe and its Historians'. *Contemporary European History* 12(3) (2003), 323–37.

Zuev, D., and F. Virchow. 'Performing National Identity: The Many Logics of Producing National Belongings in Public Rituals and Events'. *Nations and Nationalism* 20(2) (2014), 191–99.

CHAPTER 1

Exhibiting Post-national Identity

The House of European History

DANIEL ROSENBERG

Introduction

The question about the nature of exhibiting European identity through the medium of museums has been increasingly discussed since the turn of the third millennium. The emergence of a distinctly European museum culture, in the context of memory as well as more general historiography, has encouraged the appearance of important scholarly works that address the identity dimension of European exhibits and collections. Among these works, scholars have noticeably raised the issue of the unique aspect of European identity and the difficulty in framing it in a traditional visual narrative, with respect to the discrepancy between the political-administrative nature of the European Union and European culture as a whole.

The inauguration of the House of European History (HEH) project puts the spotlight on this question. Discussed, deliberated and debated on a myriad of platforms, the HEH is turning out to be one of the most controversial museum projects in recent history. Dedicated entirely to the documentation, dissemination and celebration of Europe as an ideal, the very idea of a museum institution is related to the problem of the overall abstractness and indeterminacy of the European project. This issue is largely

Notes for this section begin on page 33.

amplified by the politicized nature of the HEH, which has led some of its critics to see it as merely a 'paean to Brussels'.

The present chapter will examine the HEH in the context of the discussion about the roots and nature of European identity. The first section will discuss the idea of European identity as a coherent political constellation, which appears in relevant theories and schools of thought. These theories, which stress the unique position of Europe as a pluralistic political unit, can be seen as encompassing an explanatory principle for exhibiting and concretizing European identity. The second section will elaborate on the representation of European identity and history, through the examination of several existing museums. It will discuss the various ways in which these museums demonstrate a pluralistic notion of European identity. The third section will explore the House of European History, with an emphasis on the underlying narrative involved in its founding documents.

Contours of European Identity

The question of European heritage has become more crucial in recent years. Ever since the talk about a political, rather than merely institutional and economic unification of Europe gained speed, the question of a political identity has similarly gained prominence. One of the more common theoretical ways of approaching European integration has been to regard it as an agglomeration of different nation states, whether it is a centralized or a 'federative' structure, a liberal or a regulative one. According to this approach, integration is viewed as a process through which different peoples come together as part of their respective nation states. To give one example, Anthony Smith, in his influential 1992 article, presents a clear case for a coherent, quasi-national European identity – an identity that stems from history and from heritage. This is a very assertive form of identity which takes the form of cultural content, and constitutes a 'reiterated reference to a community of common public culture which reveals the continuing influence of ethnicity and its common myths, symbols and memories'.[1] Smith's idea of a European identity can thus largely be seen as a cultural identity: for him, although the European identity certainly offers something post-national, its essence is conceived along rather traditional ethnic-nationalist lines.

In recent decades, a different approach has emerged, emphasizing the unique character of the European Union's unification process and the manner in which the EU has introduced a qualitatively new political structure. It emphasizes Europe's political identity as relying on an institutional arrangement rather than on a shared cultural tradition. This school, associated with numerous thinkers and scholars,[2] marks Europe as a 'post-sovereign' or 'post-national' entity, and tends to reject the notion of political sovereignty as applied to the European configuration. Instead, those scholars opt for a European political identity rooted in civic commitment to a set of European political institutions, itself not replacing but rather supplementing the existing national identities. Those institutions may be associated with a number of constitutionally defined activities, including political participation and decision making, along with educational, cultural and other programmes.

As an outgrowth of these notions, I would like to suggest a different type of understanding of the European political entity – that of Europe as heritage. This approach to European identity lacks the theoretical elaboration of the two mentioned above, and largely implies a longer foundation period transcending the periods dominated by the ethnic-national and the post-sovereignist paradigms. An important formulation of this approach can be found in François Guizot's discussion on the notion of European civilization, which, despite being written in the early nineteenth century, is not outdated. Guizot, a French historian and intellectual, described the political form of Europe as constantly happening and shifting its shape according to various principles:

> All the principles of social organization are found existing together within it; powers temporal, powers spiritual, the theocratic, monarchic, aristocratic, and democratic elements, all classes of society, all the social situations, are jumbled together, and visible within it; as well as infinite gradations of liberty, of wealth, and of influence. These various powers, too, are found here in a state of continual struggle among themselves, without any one having sufficient force to master the others, and take sole possession of society.[3]

This pluralism, according to Guizot, consists of a perpetual process in which certain tribes, peoples and social and religious movements all left imprints on the idea of Europe, by means of integrating some of their ideas into the founding institutions of European civilization.

I argue that this idea lies at the centre of the contemporary understanding of European identity with an emphasis on the political structures, which are indispensable in the process of European integration. Most importantly, this idea gives a political character to the components of European identity, namely national identities, including national institutions and, naturally, European institutions. In this way, Guizot's European identity addresses the concerns of continuity and evolution (staples of the 'ethnic' school), as well as those of participation and rulership (commonly discussed in the frame of the 'post-sovereign' school).

Precedents in European Musealization

As we have seen, this European idea is somewhat ambivalent in relation to
the idea of a coherent 'national' European identity. As such, it is not a fixed
identity composed of a collection of relics that need to be salvaged from the
depths of history. It involves a testament to the living process of historical
and cultural evolution that eventually gave birth to the European ideal.
This section will discuss three of the main institutions that have become
virtually synonymous with the process of the musealization of European
identity. These three museums represent different forms of acceptance of the
same issue, namely the notion of European plurality. As has been discussed
by other scholars, all three museums point to the same trend, in which
homogeneity is substituted for diversity of cultures, languages, religions
and so on.[4] As will be seen, this diversity serves a post-national identity
but does not entirely imply a uniform, 'positive' identity. It rather exists by
merely accumulating different elements, without necessarily presenting a
new, unique persona. In other words, the leading philosophies behind these
museums, although they are novel with respect to their content and purpose,
remain well within the 'classical' national paradigm.

European History from Below: The Musée de l'Europe

An early attempt at a museal institution that would address European identity
was the Musée de l'Europe in Brussels, the plans for which were drafted in
2001, and it has been operating on and off since 2006, mostly on the basis
of temporary exhibitions. The Musée's enterprise is largely different from
the HEH; it is smaller in scale, mostly financed by private donors and the
Belgian state, and it functions as a more conventional museum, and as such
is a member of the Network of European Museum Organizations (NEMO).
The Musée's association with the European establishment was largely developed a posteriori, after the concept for the museum had already been put in
place by regional bodies and civil society organizations;[5] thus in a way it is
largely opposed to the HEH.

   However, in some ways, the Musée can be seen as prefiguring some
of the themes of the HEH, namely its broader political-cultural objective of revealing or, perhaps, establishing a single European identity, and
the objective of forming, in the words of the directors, 'a cultural link
between Europe and the citizen'.[6] This project is to be accomplished not
only by artistic means but also in educational terms, as one intention is to dis-
seminate the 'spirit of Europe'. This idea is expressed in some of the specific

initiatives of the institution, such as the intention to publish a textbook on European history, as well as its close involvement with the Network of European Museums (not to be confused with NEMO), an international group of museums working collaboratively in the framework of European civilization.[7]

This educative purpose is also prominent in the curative choices of the museum's collection, which aspire to serve, according to Christine Cadot, as a 'civic ritual'[8] in the style of older and more traditional national museums. The museum's plan presents European history, as some commentators critically indicate, as a 'teleological tale' – a narrative in which the humanistic tradition of Europe culminates in the integrative process of the post-war era. The Musée has been criticized for failing to specify exactly what would be the nature of this integration; it presents and lauds Europe, but does not supply it with any concrete identity or meaning.[9] One exhibition, entitled 'C'est Notre Histoire' (It's Our History) was established in 2007 in the Musée de l'Europe, and was peculiarly juxtaposed with one additional segment: '1945: Europe, année 0' (1945: Europe Year Zero).[10]

This exhibition presents a kind of history 'from below' by focusing on stories of individuals and exhibiting their immediate social environments as proclaimed by '27 ordinary citizens from the 27 countries of the European Union. Each of them has an exciting story to tell'.[11] Almost all of the stories represent the same kind of triumphalism that characterizes the general line of the Musée on the European Union at large, a triumphalism that acts (according to some commentators) as a substitute for authentic social negotiation between the various member states.[12]

The exhibition is joined by another one entitled 'Le Chambre des cartes', or Chamber of Maps. This part of the permanent exhibition takes a longer-term approach to European unification, as it traces it back much further than 1945. The narrative presented in this part indicates, by the use of historical maps, the three major periods of unification (ancient-classical, early modern, and that beginning in 1989), separated by two major fractures (the Middle Ages and modern totalitarianism). This very wide and abstract segment of the exhibition can be seen as an attempt to complement the more concrete and short-term narrative displayed in the first chamber; their juxtaposition, it seems, would allow a more panoramic perspective of European integration, encompassing both popular and elitist points of view.

The triumphalism that is stressed in the content of the exhibition is exacerbated by another issue, that of uniformity. The similarity between the different installations that comprise this 'uniform' narrative tends to erase the diversity that exists on the cultural, social and political levels in favour of a somewhat superficial and redundant materiality. Its attempt to incorporate a more segmented view of the development of European unity, formed by the periodization in the second chamber, remains a somewhat secondary effort with respect to its ultimate result, that of the post-1945 European edifice.

Two characteristics of the Musée de l'Europe raised criticism – referring to the project as a 'failure', they said: first, the museum had laid excessive emphasis on historical teleology, which is not backed by a similar insistence on the demonstration of the pluralism of Europe; and second, the museum had chosen to frame the European story only as a narrative of elites and abstract individuals.[13] These criticisms did not arise from the museum's inability to present European culture in a way that transcends national boundaries (something the Musée does quite effectively), but rather from its inability to address a notion of Europe that encompasses its different layers – social, cultural and institutional – through a historical perspective. As will be seen in the following section, this is largely the point of departure of ethnographic museums, which accomplish this particular aspect yet miss others.

Tracing the Genealogy of Europe: The 'Musée des Civilisations de l'Europe et de la Méditerranée' and the 'Museum Europäischer Kulturen'

Another project that should be discussed in this context is the Musée des Civilisations de l'Europe et de la Méditerranée (MuCEM), which was initiated in Marseille in 2000 on the basis of the collection hosted in the Parisian Musée des Arts et Traditions Populaires, and which was officially inaugurated in 2013 as the hallmark event of Marseille European Capital of Culture 2013. MuCEM has received far less attention than the Musée de l'Europe, and has apparently little in common with its museological concept, yet in many ways its project corresponds and even responds to the one displayed in the institution in Brussels.

In its scope, the MuCEM project is more ambitious than that of the Musée de l'Europe, as it presents European civilization not as a historically enclosed unit, but as part and parcel of the wider civilization of the Mediterranean basin. Thus, the permanent exhibitions also refer to Europe in terms of a coherent unit whose cumulative growth is documented and presented via a collection of material objects. The different sections are organized in such a way as to give the viewer a concept of certain spheres of life in ancient and premodern societies and their development until now; one of the exhibitions, for example, that touches on the origins of agriculture, begins with the Neolithic period and ends with capitalist industrialization.

In a certain way, this form of presentation is more committed to the idea of Europe as a pluralist entity, namely by showing the diverse and qualitatively different elements that brought it together from ancient technology,

Eastern religions, and early urbanity. This narrative is not only largely different from the commonplace narrative of Greece, Rome and Christianity but also represents the dialectical and mutual influence that gave birth to European civilization; the museum's announcement lists Latin, Muslim, Christian, Middle Eastern, Jewish, Greek and Slavic cultures as participating in the process of creating the emergence of European civilization.[14]

In the ethnographical context, this tendency means the reframing of European history in a more heavily teleological and even slightly anachronistic context. The tracing of European identity to premodern and pre-industrial times, without necessarily accounting for evolutionary processes, can be seen as an attempt to reconstruct a European 'ethnicity', an attempt that faces the usual issues, especially when confronted with the plethora of material-culture practices of the entire Mediterranean. While being a very pertinent strategy for a European-focused ethnographic exhibition, it also runs the risk of effacing any unique formal aspects of Europe as a civilization as well as a political project.[15]

The museological concept reflects a material perspective of social development, usually associated with the *longue durée* school, which integrates particular national history into the more extensive frame of material history – in other words, the narratives about the 'Europeanization' of already existing ethnographic collections across the continent. This idea is best demonstrated in the case of the former Museum für Volkskunde in Berlin, which has undergone significant changes in the direction of Europeanization. The museum changed its name to the Museum Europäischer Kulturen (MEK) in 1999 accordingly, and later merged with several other ethnographic museums as part of the Dahlem Museum Complex (Museumszentrum Berlin-Dahlem).

This relabelling represents for some not only a semantic move, but also 'an act of redefining and reorganizing objects'.[16] Similar to the case of MuCEM, the MEK suggests an anthropological and ethnographic approach to the study of European civilization, but unlike the institution in Marseille, the latter adopts a decidedly more modernist dynamic. The narrative presented in both institutions generally revolves around the emergence of general European culture in the modern age, and particularly in the last few decades of the twentieth century. But the narrative traced by the Berlin museum specifically bonds the past and present and creates an intercultural dialogue, by exhibiting, for example, traditional garb from different corners of the continent, as well as contemporary forms of material culture in an 'inter-national' context, such as among immigrants and expatriates. According to the museum's mission statement: 'We focus on particular themes and thus expand the collection, depending on the project, to include new regional, social and/or temporal realms in agreement with our partner museums throughout Europe. Because cultural interactions commonly reach across geographic and national boundaries and determine cultural expression in European regions even today, cooperation is a cornerstone of our work'.[17]

The museal strategy adopted by both the museums can be defined as 'quantitative' integration, in which the various aspects of European culture – different ethnicities, nationalities and languages – are juxtaposed in order to emphasize the diversity of European identity. European unification is seen in this context as a forum for the contact of different cultures, which in itself is a neutral platform devoid of any inherent identity of its own. While the two museums share what some commentators have identified as a critical approach towards the 'essentialist representation of European history',[18] it is still not entirely clear whether a truly distinct object of representation arises from the juxtaposition of a number of national cultures.

The focus on modern history allows the MEK to cover many specific topics, from the First World War to the current issue of migration to Europe. In a similar way to the treatment offered by the collection at MEK, the exhibitions mentioned above tend to emphasize a sort of 'identity in diversity' through the promotion of common motifs and themes in objects from different cultures and settings. Yet they reach the overarching identity from different approaches. It may be argued that while the Musée de l'Europe tends to significantly underplay nationality and ethnicity at both the contemporary and the historical level, the other, ethnographic museums tend to overplay them, assuming a position that views European civilization as essentially an accumulation of differences.

The House of European History in Brussels, on the other hand, rather opts for a different idea of representation, which can be defined as 'qualitative' integration. Instead of a simple amassment of different cultures, this form of representation emphasizes the unique institutional and historical nature of the unification as a political programme.

Diversity and its Stakes: The House of European History

The House of European History has been one of the central cultural initiatives undertaken by the European Parliament. The project has been exceptional not only regarding its scale and budget (€31 million as of early 2016), but also with regard to its underlying thought. The concept of the museum was advanced by a committee of experts, almost exclusively art historians, led by Professor Hans Walter Hütter, who previously served as head of the House of the History of the Federal Republic of Germany (located in Bonn).[19] The process of drafting the HEH's 'conceptual basis' can be defined as largely centralized and discreet, unlike the initiation of the Musée de l'Europe, which, significantly, was open to the public.

The HEH project has been an object of controversy since the day of its inception, as reflected in the criticism raised by commentators, especially from Britain, not only with regard to the scale of the project but also to its goals. While some criticism has been directed towards certain parts of its historical narrative, a more general line of criticism has been aimed at the very attempt to find a common and uniform historical narrative for the European continent; the think tank Civitas went so far as to call that aspiration a 'disingenuous paradox'.[20]

This critique largely stems from the so-called 'sovereignist' type of Euro-scepticism, which essentially views national sovereignty and democracy as viable institutions only within the framework of the nation state. In response to this critique, it can be argued that the project's plan refers indirectly to those issues. By embedding the concept of the post-national European identity in the larger project of European pluralism, it essentially bypasses the national question and proposes a different form of representation.

This mission statement was put in very direct terms in the inaugural address of the HEH in 2007, given by the European Parliament president Hans-Gert Pöttering:

> European history is nearly always presented as a national history, represented in national museums. I would like to provide a place of memory and of the future in which the idea of Europe can flourish and develop further. I would like to propose the construction of a 'House of European History'. This should be no boring, dull museum, but instead a place in which our memory of European history and the work of European unification can be cultivated in common, which is however also open to the future development of Europe's identity by all present and future citizens of the European Union.[21]

Indeed, questions regarding the politicization involved in its founding have been characteristic of the discussion revolving around the HEH. As indicated by Taja Vovk van Gaal and Christine Dupont, two members of the Academic Project Team, the understanding of the HEH as a political initiative has been intrinsic to the rationale of the project, much more than the other initiatives discussed above. This understanding is also linked to the idea that humanities (including social sciences) and politics intersect in the representation of European identity and history, and that European intellectuals and political elites have a large role to play here.[22]

Because the HEH has opened relatively recently, it is not yet possible to assess fully the success of the project. However, the HEH has already been defined in the 'Conceptual Basis for a House of European History' issued in October 2008, as well as in the project overview published in 2012. Both of these documents offer clear guidelines regarding the general setting and the curative style of the project. As they made clear, the usage of 'house' in the title instead of 'museum', which arose largely for technical reasons (to avoid confusion with the Musée de l'Europe, as well as various legal ramifications), serves also as a leading idea for the visual style of the exhibition: the space itself is designed not in the classical manner of museums, but as a 'house', with the objects scattered throughout its rooms and hallways, on tabletops and bookshelves.[23] This setting, seemingly inspired by the immersive style of the Haus der Geschichte in Bonn, seems to imply a non-linear presentation of European history – one in which different historical periods do not replace each other as much as are 'amassed' on top of each other.

The very first glance at the HEH's mission statement, entitled 'Conceptual Basis', makes clear that it is not narrating/displaying the history of Europe, the continent, but rather that of the 'European union' ('u' in lowercase); it is the history of the formation of a common identity among groups and cultures that compose European civilization, and particularly its formation within the elites or the more intellectually refined classes. The idea of European unification is conceptualized primarily as that of a movement – a movement of people, of armies, of commodities and of ideas. Europe has not grown up in a linear manner through a vindication of the progress of reason and liberty, as much as through the accumulation of institutions and ideas, and their transformation and conveyance across borders and centuries.[24]

As a result, there is not a unique, distinguishable element that can be identified as the progenitor of the notion of European unification, due to its fluidity and its abstract nature. Migration then becomes a key to concretizing European integration. In one of the document's paragraphs we encounter the 'phenomenon of migration and of colonies', both of which represent two aspects of the same principle, that of contact and communication and of the carrying of ideas and people over geographic and cultural borders.[25] Those processes do not indicate progress by virtue of their original content, because of the identity of the immigrants, but due to the fact of migration itself. What is encountered in the HEH's Conceptual Basis is the institutional form taking the place of national symbols and ethoses as the agents of identity. This is the case especially regarding the description of migration, which receives much more central attention than is paid to the European and Europeanized exhibitions. By way of an example, the Berlin MEK 'demoted' migration in Europe to merely an additional aspect of European integration.

In its 'Conceptual Basis', the HEH also depicts the spread and transformation of religious ideas as another factor strengthening Europe's transition. Yet, religion represents here not the vindication of spiritual ideas as much as a principle for institutional and cultural unification and stabilization. Any religious apologia is opposed, and, for the most part, counterbalanced by the 'hermetic' aspect of European civilization addressed in the previous paragraphs. Religion is rather associated with unification (in the case of bringing Latin to the fore as a common language), with preservation (in the case of cathedrals and other architectonic wonders), and with ordering societies according to metaphysical principles.[26]

As these cases clearly exemplify, the House of European History is not dedicated to exhibiting any particular national narrative. In fact, national narratives were conspicuously absent from the plan.[27] This choice raised some controversy. For example, the plan was criticized by Polish commentators for failing to include central parts of its own national narratives such as the Battle of Vienna in 1683 and the 1944 Warsaw Uprising.[28] This omission does not arise from a preference for certain national cultures over others, nor from a strategy of erasure of national identities, but, as we have seen, from the different perspectives of the development of Europe as a civilization. As such, nationalism, in general, receives very meagre treatment in the Conceptual Basis, as the entire period between the Napoleonic Wars and the Great War is characterized by developments in the fields of education, technology, economy, culture and the media, and even by the growth of museums. The emergence of nationalism, marked by events such as the revolutions in 1848, is narrated in parallel with 'the rise of internationalism and cosmopolitanism'. It is also credited with being an opposite and a countervailing force, through the term 'national emancipation', which is posited together with 'liberal emancipation' – two of the major tendencies of the nineteenth century.[29] None of these principles truly encompasses the essence of European identity as such, as partially shown in the triumphalist story introduced by initiatives such as the Musée de l'Europe. The HEH tries not to read the European past through the retrospective prism of a single value, but rather as a pluralist, institutional constellation.

The treatment of the developments in the continent throughout the twentieth century understandably forms the bulk of the institution's programme. The outline of the Conceptual Basis places particular emphasis on the Second World War, which includes a detailed treatment of strategic and political developments; the war is rarely presented in terms of an ideological or a larger philosophical conflict, but rather as a military struggle, more or less. It is only after the Second World War that the relationship between Europe (at least its western part) and democracy is emphasized, in contradistinction to the Soviet rule of Eastern Europe. Thus, democracy is presented not as the final form of European civilization, but, more accurately, as a new and somewhat contingent addition to the European edifice.

The HEH traces democracy in the modern institutions of Europe: they are portrayed as one result of a necessary rebuttal of the Soviet centralization, and are juxtaposed to another symbol of international cooperation – that of

NATO. The process of European integration from the 1980s is depicted to
be a more intensive one that corresponded with democracy and the progress
of liberal values. Further, it was the 'renaissance of the nation state' in the
period after the Maastricht Treaty (1992) that led to what the HEH's document defines as 'parliamentarisation in the European Union'.[30]

The narrative drawn in the Conceptual Basis is thus different in several
respects from those drawn by the other museums dedicated specifically to
European heritage. Primarily, and most importantly perhaps, it shuns a story
of Europe that is read as a *Drang nach Brussel*, a retroactive vindication of one
type of social and democratic order, in favour of a story that is more genuine
as well as more educationally honest – as a tale marked by contingency and
volatility. Furthermore, it avoids almost all evocations of particular national
histories to favour an integrated story of Europe as a civilization, in a way that
suggests a more cohesive narrative and averts possible claims of imbalance.[31]

Following this exegesis, we can estimate the way in which the HEH
interprets the pluralist thesis regarding European identity. The most significant characteristic of the narrative of HEH is that it is careful not to reduce
the history of Europe to a story of the linear movement of human rights
and deliberative democracy, or alternatively to the coalescence of different
ethnic cultures and origins. The attempt to evade those two somewhat
superficial visions, which I believe do not do justice to the unique position
of Europe as a political idea, is very well-established in the museal practice
envisioned by the HEH progenitors.

This conscious attempt, however, also introduces some issues of its
own; namely, how can this narrative be concretized and brought forward
as a museal theme? While the project definition seems convincing, there
remains a problem of concretization, not only because of the nature of the
project, but also because its narrative is perhaps too theoretical and thematic.
By avoiding national and other traditional narratives, the museum also runs
the risk of remaining devoid of any concrete symbols or icons. Surely, these
concerns stem in part from the attempt to exhibit not a historical object but
an ongoing project in constant formation and negotiation.

Conclusion

As this paper has suggested, one of the most important tendencies in the
formation of a museum strategy is the emphasis on the notion of European
identity as heritage. The practice of seeing Europe as heritage transcends the
more typical path of interpreting European identity along the lines of nation
states. Rather than attempting to score a proper balance between nationality
and integration, the heritage model depicts integration as a common as well

as a pluralist phenomenon, situated in continuity with the political history of the continent. The goal of the HEH is thus to offer a perspective on European history which considers it at once as a unified and heterogeneous historical unit, whose diversity is reflected in the way it retains the traces of different cultural, institutional and intellectual developments which took place on the continent and in relation to it.

As discussed here, this ambitious and novel approach is not without its particular limitations and challenges. The HEH in particular leads a programme that is at once intentional in its vindication of the integration project, and prudent in its attention to the elaborate and multifaceted histori- cal nature of this integration. Unlike other exhibition projects, the HEH is not a kind of teleological or 'providential' interpretation of the process of integration. In opposition to the other museums reviewed here, the HEH does not introduce a pre-conceived solution or a finalized story, but a more open-ended narrative. The most significant element in the exegesis put forward by the HEH initiators is the episodic and non-causal nature of the formation of European identity. Thus, in more than one way, the project proposes a political programme that is more compatible with contemporary challenges facing the continent. European integration is thus seen at once as an almost determinist process due to the unified nature of Europe, as well as a complex process due to the diverse and multifaceted nature of Europe.

Daniel Rosenberg is a late-stage doctoral candidate in the Department of Political Science at the Hebrew University of Jerusalem. His doctoral thesis is entitled 'The Elite Idea in French Liberalism, from Napoleon to De Gaulle'. Rosenberg's academic interests include the history of political thought in Europe, and in particular in France; he has written and published on figures such as Joseph de Maistre, Bertrand de Jouvenel and Paul Valéry.

Notes

1. A. Smith, 'National Identity and the Idea of European Unity', in *International Affairs* (Royal Institute of International Affairs, 1944 –) 68(1((January 1992), 62.

2. See, for example: N. MacCormick, 'Liberalism, Nationalism and the Post-sovereign State', *Political Studies* 44(3) (1996); O. Waever, 'Identity, Integration and Security: Solving the Sovereignty Puzzle in EU Studies', *Journal of International Affairs* 48(2) (1995), 553–567. Most famously, this approach is commonly associated with the notion of 'constitutional patriotism', which has been originated in the writings of Jürgen Habermas and developed further by J.W. Müller – cf. J. Habermas, 'The European Nation State: On the Past and Future of Sovereignty and Citizenship', in J. Habermas et al. (eds), *The Inclusion of the Other: Studies in Political Theory* (Cambridge, MA: MIT Press, 1988), 106–127; J.W. Müller, *Constitutional Patriotism: An Introduction, International Journal of Constitutional Law* 6(1) (2008), 67–71.

3. F. Guizot, *General History of Civilization in Europe* (New York: D. Appleton and Company, 1896), 30–31. See also the helpful discussion in G. Delanty, 'The European Heritage from a Critical Cosmopolitan Perspective', LSE 'Europe in Question' Discussion Paper Series, February 2010, http://www.lse.ac.uk/europeanInstitute/LEQS%20Discussion%20Paper%20Series/LEQSPaper19b.pdf.

4. B. Rogan, 'The Emerging Museums of Europe', *Ethnologia Europaea* 33(1), 53–54.

5. V. Charléty, 'L'invention du Musée de l'Europe: Contribution à l'analyse des politiques symboliques européenne', *Regards sociologiques*, 27(2) (2004), 149–166, here p. 153.

6. Musée de l'Europe – Rapport d'activité 2014, 14.

7. Ibid., 158–59.

8. C. Cadot, 'Can Museums Help Build a European Memory? The Example of the "Musée de l'Europe" in Brussels in the Light of "New World" Museums' Experience', *International Journal of Politics, Culture, and Society* 23(2/3), Arts and Politics: A French–American Perspective (September 2010), 129.

9. W. Kaiser et al., *Europa ausstellen: Das Museum als Praxisfeld der Europäisierung* (Vienna: Böhlau, 2014), 34.

10. http://www.expo-europe.be/content/view/45/78/lang.fr/, pp. 29–35 (the installation is reproduced on p. 30).

11. 'Ces 27 personnes sont des citoyens ordinaires des 27pays de l'Union Européenne. Elles ont chacune une histoire passionnante à raconter'. Quoted in Kaiser et al., *Europa ausstellen*, 22.

12. Ibid., 23–26.

13. A similar point regarding the overly teleological narrative which discards national identity is raised in Cadot, 'Can Museums Help', 135.

14. Taken from the introductory text on the MuCEM website: http://www.mucem.org/en/mucem/museum-europe-and-mediterranean.

15. The emphasis on the inclusion of non-European cultures and their integration into a pan-European identity has been criticized by one journalist as 'a melange of everything and nothing, a case of mixing all the colours and ending up with mud, of serving vague political ideals at the expense of curatorial direction' (R. Moore, 'Museum of the Civilisations of Europe and the Mediterranean (MuCEM) – Review', *Guardian*, 9 June 2013).

16. C. Snekkers et al., 'Exhibiting Europe: The Development of European Narratives in Museums, Collections and Exhibitions', Research Group Exhibiting Europe, Faculty of Humanities, Norges teknisknaturvitenskapelige Universitet Trondheim, 2011.

17. Mission Statement Museum Europäischer Kulturen Staatliche Museen zu Berlin, 1–2. Retrieved from http://www.smb.museum/fileadmin/website/Museen_und_Sammlungen/Museum_Europaeischer_Kulturen/Leitbild_des_MEK_en_2014_NEU.pdf (last accessed 11 July 2016).

18. Kaiser et al., *Europa ausstellen*, 78.

19. in an informative exposition on the decision-making process leading up the drafting of the HEH programme, Wolfram Kaiser points out that the almost strictly professional nature of the committee was also selected as to fend off possible concerns about political-partisan bias (W. Kaiser, 'Limits of Cultural Engineering: Actors and Narratives in the European Parliament's House of European History Project', *Journal of Common Market Studies*, 2016, 8–9).

20. B. Waterfield, 'Anger at Plans for "Official" European history', *Guardian*, 2 January 2009; 'Rewriting History', Civitas, 7 April 2011 (www.civitas.org.uk/2011/04/07/rewriting-history/).

21. Quoted in Kaiser et al., *Europa ausstellen*, 44. The original address (in the German language) can be found at http://hieronymi.de/PDF%20Dokumente/Programmrede.13.2.2007.DE.pdf.

22. T.V. van Gaal and C. Dupont, 'The House of European History', in Bodil Axelsson et al. (eds), *Entering the Minefields: The Creation of New History Museums in Europe*. Conference Proceedings from EuNaMus, European National Museums: Identity Politics, the Uses of the Past, and the European Citizen. Brussels, 25 January 2012, 47.

23. Sketches in 'Building a House of European History: A Project of the European Parliament', 2012. Retrieved from http://www.europarl.europa.eu/visiting/ressource/static/files/en_building-a-house-of-european-history.pdf (last accessed 11 July 2016).

24. The 'Conceptual Basis' has been analysed in similar terms in Huistra et al., 'Political Values in a European Museum', *Journal of Contemporary European Research* 10(1) (2014), 124–36.

25. Committee of Experts, 'Conceptual Basis for a House of European History' (Brussels: European Parliament, 2007), 11.

26. Ibid., 12.

27. The document's attention to avoiding any Western regional bias is noticeable in several sections; for example, the discussion on the Renaissance omits any mention of Italy, France or England, while Lutheran conversion is described as taking place 'on the shores of the Baltic Sea', and the English Reformation is absent (Committee of Experts, 13).

28. Kaiser et al., *Europa ausstellen*, 124.

29. Committee of Experts, 14.

30. Ibid., 24.

31. Kaiser indicates that the narrative presented by the HEH represents a compromise between different political interests, including West and Central/East European members of the EU. This compromise is reflected in the focus on the post-1945 period in the HEH narrative, as well as the de-emphasis of certain religious and cultural motifs (Kaiser, 'Limits of Cultural Engineering', 12–13).

Bibliography

Archival Sources

Building a House of European History: A Project of the European Parliament, 2012. http://www.europarl.europa.eu/visiting/ressource/static/files/en_building-a-house-of-european-history.pdf (last accessed 11 July 2016).

Mission Statement Museum Europäischer Kulturen Staatliche Museen zu Berlin, 1–2. http://www.smb.museum/fileadmin/website/Museen_und_Sammlungen/Museum_Europaeischer_Kulturen/Leitbild_des_MEK_en_2014_NEU.pdf (last accessed 11 July 2016).

Secondary Sources

Cadot, C. 'Can Museums Help Build a European Memory? The Example of the "Musée de l'Europe" in Brussels in the Light of "New World" Museums' Experience'. *International Journal of Politics, Culture, and Society* 23(2/3), Arts and Politics: A French–American Perspective (September 2010), 127–36.

Charléty, V. 'L'invention du Musée de l'Europe: Contribution à l'analyse des politiques symboliques européenne', *Regards sociologiques*, 27(2) (2004), 149–166.

Civitas. 'Rewriting History', 7 April 2011 (www.civitas.org.uk/2011/04/07/rewriting-history/).

Committee of Experts. 'Conceptual Basis for a House of European History'. Brussels: European Parliament, 2007.

Delanty, G. 'The European Heritage from a Critical Cosmopolitan Perspective'. LSE 'Europe in Question' Discussion Paper Series, February 2010. http://www.lse.ac.uk/europeanInstitute/LEQS%20Discussion%20Paper%20Series/LEQSPaper19b.pdf.

Gaal, T.V. van, and C. Dupont. 'The House of European History', in Bodil Axelsson et al. (eds), *Entering the Minefields: The Creation of New History Museums in Europe*. Conference Proceedings from EuNaMus, European National Museums: Identity Politics, the Uses of the Past, and the European Citizen. Brussels, 25 January 2012, 43–53.

Guizot, F. *General History of Civilization in Europe*. New York: D. Appleton and Company, 1896.

Habermas, J. 'The European Nation State: On the Past and Future of Sovereignty and Citizenship', in J. Habermas et al. (eds), *The Inclusion of the Other: Studies in Political Theory* (Cambridge, MA: MIT Press, 1988), 106–127.

Huistra, P., et al. 'Political Values in a European Museum'. *Journal of Contemporary European Research* 10(1) (2014), 124–36.

Kaiser, W. 'Limits of Cultural Engineering: Actors and Narratives in the European Parliament's House of European History Project'. *Journal of Common Market Studies* 55(3) (2016), 1–17.

Kaiser, W., et al. *Europa ausstellen: Das Museum als Praxisfeld der Europäisierung*. Vienna: Böhlau, 2014.

MacCormick, N. 'Liberalism, Nationalism and the Post-sovereign State'. *Political Studies* 44(3) (1996), 553–567.

Moore, R. 'Museum of the Civilisations of Europe and the Mediterranean (MuCEM) – Review', *Guardian*, 9 June 2013.

Müller, J.W. 'Constitutional Patriotism: An Introduction'. *International Journal of Constitutional Law* 6(1) (2008), 67–71.

Musée de l'Europe – Rapport d'activité. 2014.

Rogan, B. 'The Emerging Museums of Europe'. *Ethnologia Europaea* 33(1), 51–60.

Smith, A. 'National Identity and the Idea of European Unity'. *International Affairs* (Royal Institute of International Affairs, 1944–) 68(1) (January 1992), 55–76.

Snekkers, C., et al. 'Exhibiting Europe: The Development of European Narratives in Museums, Collections and Exhibitions'. Research Group Exhibiting Europe, Faculty of Humanities, Norges teknisknaturvitenskapelige Universitet Trondheim, 2011.

Waever, O. 'Identity, Integration and Security: Solving the Sovereignty Puzzle in EU Studies'. *Journal of International Affairs* 48(2) (1995), 389–431.

Waterfield, B. 'Anger at Plans for "Official" European History', *Guardian*, 2 January 2009.

CHAPTER 2

The European Union and the Historiography of European Integration

Dangerous Liaisons?

ORIANE CALLIGARO

Introduction

In 1965, the creator and historical director of the Press and Information Service of the European Communities (EC), Jacques-René Rabier, described in a public lecture the legitimizing effect that academic knowledge can have on the European political project: 'University lends the phenomenon [European integration] a sort of legitimacy of a great significance by making it the object of research, teaching and examination'.[1] His service, which would become the European Commission's Directorate-General for Information (DG X) in 1967, had early on identified the university milieu as one of its priority targets.[2] An objective was hence to promote research and teaching on European integration in all relevant human sciences. The concept of 'European studies' appeared first in law and economics during the 1960s, when the impact of European integration on the legal and economic systems of the European countries became obvious. The emergence of concurrent political conceptions of the European project also aroused the interest of political scientists, eager to develop integration theories by the yardstick of the European case. Compared to these disciplines, which closely mirror their immediate social and political contexts, history has to some extent more latitude in terms of the choice of the themes on which it focuses. Moreover, the temporal distance required for historical research accounts for the later development of the history of European integration, which occurred for the most part during the 1980s.

Because the historical discipline posed particular challenges, the European Commission developed specific actions in this field which are worthwhile analysing. In line with critical sociologists of European integration who argued that knowledge producers (scientists, experts, lawyers, economists, etc.) played a key part in shaping the European Union (EU),[3] this chapter focuses on the relationships between the EU institutions and the historians of European integration. Some scholars have studied the research networks that contributed to the emergence of the history of European integration as a discipline.[4] Others have described the EU action in the academic field,[5] with some focusing on the initiatives taken by the EU institutions to have their own history written.[6] This literature has revealed the existence of different types of EU support schemes for historiographical enterprises. The proximity between certain networks of historians and the EU inevitably raises suspicion. The historian Antonio Varsori, himself a protagonist of these networks, articulated this issue bluntly: 'Is the historiography of European integration a political creation by Eurocrats in Brussels?'[7] This provocative question invites us to explore, over the long term, from the 1970s until the 2000s, the exact nature and evolution of the partnerships that associated historians to the EU institutions, to assess their impact on historiographical research, to analyse the changing EU's expectations towards historiography, and to make sense of the historians' disparate interests in this institutional support.

Based on archival sources from the European University Institute (EUI), the European Commission and pivotal actors (DG X officials and historians), and on interviews with key protagonists, this chapter first explores the commission's initial project in the mid-1970s to create a durable centre of research on the history of European integration at the EUI, a project that failed as early as 1980. As a consequence of this failure, the commission helped in the creation of a transnational network, the Liaison Committee of Historians by the European Commission – an atypical group launched in 1982 and which played a crucial role in the development of the history of European integration. After studying the exchanges between the Liaison Committee and the European institutions, and showing the porosity between the institutional and academic agendas in some cases, the chapter eventually describes the conflicts that put an end to their collaboration.

The interactions between the historians and their institutional partners cannot be merely described as a top-down influence of the European institutions. The historians' involvement often followed logics internal to their profession. However, proximity to the institutions had concrete effects on their research agenda and methodology. The difficulties and resistances that the EU encountered in its relationships with the historians illustrate the fundamental problems posed by an institutional intervention in the politically and culturally sensitive field of history. For those historians concerned, these problems largely pertained to their scientific independence and the validity of a teleological approach to European history.

A First Attempt: The History of European Integration at the EUI

The European University Institute offered the first frame in which the European Commission tried to promote a historiographical project very directly. The EUI, created by an international agreement in 1972, was an atypical postgraduate research and teaching centre closely related to the EC and dedicated to the human and social sciences. A declared objective of the institute was to go beyond a national approach to social sciences and create a 'European frame of mind and dimension'.[8] Transnational collaboration between scholars of different national origins was hence central. This transnationalization of research was also a fundamental principle in the historiographical projects supported by the European Commission from the mid-1970s onwards. Indeed, the European Commission had no competence to interfere in the content of the research, but it could however try to influence the conditions in which it was conducted. Jacqueline Lastenouse, who worked on the academic milieu during her entire career at the commission, from 1962 until 2001, insists that the Information Service has seen the creation of international networks as one of its central tasks in this domain.[9] The EUI was ideally suited to the creation of such networks. Even before the institute was officially opened in 1976, the European Commission launched a historiographical project based at the EUI History and Civilization Department.

The origin of this project lies in a contract signed in March 1975 between the EUI and the Secretary-General of European Commission, Émile Noël. Proposed by the latter, it concerned the setting up of a 'Projet d'histoire de la Communauté européenne'.[10] The EUI asked Pascal Fontaine, history professor at Sciences Po Paris, to produce a note concerning the preparation and the realization of this project.[11] Fontaine was at the time, and had been since 1971, Jean Monnet's private assistant. His father, François Fontaine, was head of the commission's Press and Information Office in Paris, and one of the promoters of Jean Monnet's memoirs. The Fontaines were among the key actors in the creation of a '*récit des origines de la construction européenne*'.[12] Pascal Fontaine's involvement shows how this project of history of the

European Communities at the EUI was part of a larger design aiming at the production and promotion of a European master narrative.

As he was asked to give feedback on Fontaine's proposal, Peter Ludlow, a young English historian who was then associate professor at the EUI, expressed his concerns about the risk of a too federalist and teleological approach:

> We say that we want to write a history of the European Community? But what *is* the latter? [*original emphasis*] Western Europe is a community in process of formation, without a single centre and without a clearly defined future. There may one day be a single political entity, but there are at the present, as there have been in the past, many different forms of association and cooperation, and as historians of European integration we must allow for the variegated and partial character of what we are trying to describe. We have to base our work on a concept of Europe which is neither a collection of nation states, nor, still less, a new nation: a conceptual framework which allows free rein to the many different elements, official and unofficial governments and multinational companies, market forces and cultural and ideological enthusiasms, pro-Europeans and 'antis', which have moulded the politics of our community.[13]

In September 1977, the research programme 'History of European Integration' was launched under the lead of Walter Lipgens, chair of Contemporary European History at the EUI.[14] Lipgens, in his 1977 monograph on the origins of European integration, adopted a clear federalist stance: the European nations being too weak to remain in control of their destiny, unity was the only way to preserve Europe and its culture.[15] In a letter to his collaborators in the 'History of European Integration' programme, Lipgens affirmed the political dimension of the initiative. The EUI department had 'the *duty* to promote multinational cooperation', which was 'indispensable to the study of the common history of Europe', a history that corresponded to an institutional need: 'For the European Community, it is also important to acquire a proper and historical consciousness resting on scientific bases'.[16] The European Community *needed* a history, and the EUI History Department would produce it. The 'History of European Integration' project had a very ambitious agenda, including the publication of a series on the archival sources of European integration and of four monographs presenting its main phases. Only a part of this agenda was actually achieved. The first monograph, published in 1982, was a translated and expanded version of Lipgens' 1977 monograph, originally published in German.[17] The book, now considered as a pioneer work for European integration history, was hence made accessible to a larger audience, which increased the visibility of this emerging field of research.[18]

More generally, the 'History of European Integration' project allowed Lipgens to lay the foundations for a transnational cooperation through conferences and publications, which brought together historians of international relations who had never worked together before. Thanks to these meetings, the historians could also formulate demands regarding the archives of the EC, which adopted in 1978 the thirty-year rule for the opening of its archives, and created a dedicated service.[19] Although this dynamic of cooperation started at the EUI, its History Department did not turn into a permanent, attractive research centre on European integration, as the commission had originally wished. This failure is mainly due to the complex relations that bound the project 'History of European Integration', Walter Lipgens, the EUI and the European Commission. In September 1979, Lipgens' contract at the EUI ended. He expressed the desire to pursue the project at his home university in Saarbrücken and asked for a transfer of the European Commission's subsidies devoted to the project.[20] The European Commission refused, arguing that the project was legally attached to the EUI and could not be carried out in another research institution.[21] However, no professor at the EUI took on the project. Peter Ludlow had remained very sceptical towards its Europeanist stance, and completely ceased to collaborate in 1980.[22] As a result, the project stopped at the EUI and was partly continued in Saarbrücken, supported by private sponsors.[23] Since the partnership the European Commission had envisaged with EUI historians did not survive after Lipgens' departure, the commission had to find new interlocutors in the academic community to help to promote the history of European integration.

A Privileged Partner for the European Institutions: The 'Liaison Committee of Historians by the European Commission'

The creation of the Liaison Committee of Historians and the long process of opening the archives of the European Communities are closely inter-twined. To organize the access to and the exploitation of these archives, the European Commission needed to engage with the historians likely to use this material. Since the link with the EUI historians was weakened, new forms of collaboration had to be invented.[24] To this end, in 1982 the commission's DG X organized an international conference of professors of contemporary history under the chairmanship of Gaston Thorn, president of the European Commission.[25] Academics, many of whom had participated in the 1977 conference at the EUI, and EC officials gathered for three days to discuss the issue of the archives and the writing of European integration history. Thorn gave an inaugural speech in which he shared his conviction that historians could help in bringing the European project 'out from behind closed doors' and closer to the citizens.[26] He denied, however, any intention on the part of the EC to use history as an instrument of propaganda:

The purpose is most certainly not to campaign for European unification under the cloak of scientific research. It would be just as bad to deliberately 'refocus' studies in line with a European political Grand Design in order to make Europeans, as to continue treating the facts from each country's particular standpoint only in order to preserve patriotism, as has been done regularly in the last century and is too often still done today.[27]

At the same time, he called for a necessary 'cultural extraterritoriality of science'.[28] While criticizing the nationalist use of history, he nonetheless invited historians to write history in a way that could be beneficial for the transnational nature of European integration.

Paradoxically, Thorn's denial of any attempt to promote a 'European Grand Design' was contradicted by Walter Lipgens' subsequent intervention, in which he proposed a militant approach to history. The former EUI professor explained to his pairs that the contemplation of the past and of the present was bound 'to arouse in any historian the fundamental feeling that the road to European Union [was] a historical necessity'.[29]

It is up to the historian to show that none of the European nation states is in a position to fulfil the most basic tasks of central government on its own – namely, the security and the welfare of their people. It is up to the historian to show that this can only be done by continental unions like the USA and the USSR, and such as the 'United States of Europe' could be.[30]

Lipgens hence reaffirmed his idea of the historians' duty to European unification. In his eyes, this duty was not performed at the expense of objectivity. Since Europe's unity was a fact and not a project, historians did not need to distort reality but to say 'purely and simply what happened'.[31] Consequently, writing the history of Europe consisted both in demonstrating 'the century-old unity of European culture' and showing the necessity of a United States of Europe.[32] Like Thorn, Lipgens underlined the negative role played by the academics who harmed the unity of European spirit in the name of national culture.[33] However, the political mission that Lipgens attributed to the 'European' historian was ironically very similar to the one of the 'nation-builder' historian whom he criticized.

It is in this highly politicized context that the most important network of historians of European integration was created. Following a proposal from René Girault, professor at the Sorbonne, the participants unanimously approved the launching of the 'Groupe de Liaison des professeurs d'histoire contemporaine près la Commission européenne', eventually created in 1983. It gathered historians from Germany, France, Belgium, Luxembourg, the Netherlands, Italy, Ireland and the United Kingdom. Walter Lipgens himself was on the committee. Considering Lipgens' militant discourse and the commission's explicit call for an approach to history favourable to European unification, the question of the motivations and views on

European integration of the members of the Liaison Committee shall be posed. Antoine Marès, scientific secretary of the committee from 1982 to 1987, explains that Lipgens' position aroused suspicion and even irritation in the group.[34] Michel Dumoulin, professor at Louvain-la-Neuve in Belgium, confirms that although a significant number of the participants were pro-European, Lipgens' 'rabid federalism' was not shared by all the historians, who sometimes had a very different vision of European integration.[35] Dumoulin explains that René Girault, the first chairman and an influential figure on the Liaison Committee, was not, unlike Lipgens, convinced that European unification was a historical necessity. This divergence is well reflected in a debate that took place shortly after the creation of the group. Girault criticized the denomination of 'historian of European integration' proposed by Lipgens because it took up uncritically an expression used by the EC institutions, and spoke rather of 'European construction'.[36] Therefore, the involvement of a person like Girault on the Liaison Committee was not an act of European activism but a pragmatic decision. Girault was convinced of the necessity of creating networks of historians, and saw the action of the commission as an opportunity to launch transnational projects.[37] Moreover, for historians of international relations like those who joined the Liaison Committee, to specialize on European integration was also a way to renew their research and gain legitimacy in a historical discipline that was increasingly dominated by social and cultural history.[38]

The creation of the Liaison Committee of Historians is hence the result of a conjunction of interests: on the one hand, the commission's interest in the legitimizing effect of historical research on European integration, and on the other hand, the historians' interest in a new and promising topic, which could help them to obtain recognition in their discipline while benefiting from EC financial support. The conditions of birth of the Liaison Committee and its funding by the European Commission raise the question of the actual institutional interference in its activities. The missions originally assigned to the committee remained relatively vague. One of them was 'to initiate or encourage meetings between historians' in the field of European integration. This mission constituted the most regular and probably the most consensual activity of the group. Since 1984 the Liaison Committee has organized an international conference more or less every two years.[39] Another main task was to collaborate with the European institutions for the creation of archives of the European Communities, which the committee fulfilled as well.[40] However, since the institutions were eager to keep a narrow control over their archives, the negotiations with the historians were sometimes contentious.[41] Although Jacqueline Lastenouse from the DG X took part in the committee's meetings for more than a decade, the commission was never involved in the production of historical knowledge.[42] However, it repeatedly tried to influence the conditions of production of this knowledge, either through the creation of multinational networks – which was the main objective of the Liaison Committee – or through an influence on the production of and access to archives.

Institutional Influences on the Historians' Agenda: Divergence and Porosity between the Political and Academic Spheres

The creation of oral archives on European integration offers a good example of such an attempt. At the 1982 conference, the DG X had invited the historians to include in their work the testimonies of actors of European integration, this 'living source'.[43] Although the Liaison Committee had originally very limited interest in such practice, at the request of DG X it charged Antoine Marès with the drafting of a document on the possibility of creating a fund of oral archives.[44] In his report submitted in 1984, Marès recommended an 'elitist' approach for the constitution of oral archives with the testimonies of actors who played an important role in European integration.[45]

However, this elitist approach was not in keeping with the political agenda of the EC at the time. In the period that followed the creation of the Liaison Committee, the European institutions showed an increasing interest in a European historiography capable of raising the public's interest. The European Council's Solemn Declaration on European Union of June 1983 recommended an improvement in 'the level of knowledge about other Member States of the Community and of information on Europe's history and culture' in order to promote the citizens' 'European awareness'.[46] In June 1985, the EC launched its People's Europe campaign, which was meant to bring the citizens closer to the European project.[47] In this context, in December 1985, the EC ministers of culture discussed the importance of historiography:

> A People's Europe without History is not conceivable: our historians are writing it, with the help of our archivists. . . . However, if we intend to constitute a 'historical fund of the Community', we should take care to involve the citizens themselves. The Council and the Ministers of Culture invited the Commission to take steps in this sense.[48]

The expression 'our historians', which probably refers to the Liaison Committee, is striking. The method proposed by the ministers was called 'Lived history of European integration' and consisted of the collection, especially through tape recording, of the memories of the man in the street concerning the beginnings of the integration process.[49] The European Commission asked the Liaison Committee about the feasibility of such a project. The historians judged the idea preposterous for the simple reason that the 'man on the street' probably had very few, if any, memories of these events, and concluded that this grass-roots approach could not succeed.[50] The committee proposed to concentrate on high-ranked personalities: 'The issue is to save the European memory of the decision-takers and of the important witnesses. With the support of the European Commission, this task could be carried out by the Liaison Committee of Historians'.[51] In 1987, the committee formed a group to work on this oral-sources project, but its agenda was not followed. It was mainly because of a lack of time and of means, but also because the historians' interest in this type of archives was weak.[52]

This attempt by the European Commission to put on the agenda of the Liaison Committee a project that was in keeping with its own political objectives first failed. In 1996, Émile Noël, former secretary-general of the European Commission and since 1987 president of the EUI, proposed to organize a conference gathering historians and witnesses for the fortieth anniversary of the Treaty of Rome in 1997.[53] Subsequently, the DG X proposed to the Liaison Committee to collect interviews on this occasion.[54] The 'Project of Oral History of the Jean Monnet Chairs in History' was launched. At the time, almost all members of the Liaison Committee were the recipients of a Jean Monnet Chair – an EU-funded chair specialized on European integration. Administrative notes and letters inviting the professors to realize interviews at the 1997 conference give evidence of the fact that the project was initiated and organized by the European Commission.[55] However, ulterior commission documents presented this project as emanating from the professors. A 2000 note reads: 'In 1997, in the wake of the conference on the "40 years of the Treaties of Rome", a large project of oral history has been launched by Jean Monnet professors in History of European integration'.[56] This presentation of the facts shows that in a sensitive domain like historical research, the institutional interference is sometimes better obscured: it can cast doubts on the independence of academic actors and reveal the commission's foray into a domain for which it was not competent. To be sure, the project of oral history conducted by the Jean Monnet professors did provide the historians with new sources, but many of them remained sceptical about their scientific quality.[57] It is therefore remarkable that this approach proposed by the commission, and for which the historians showed very little enthusiasm, eventually integrated their agenda.

Besides these direct attempts by the European Commission at influencing the historians' methods, convergence between the institutional and academic approaches could also follow more subtle paths, through a reorientation of the scholars' research agenda. In the late 1980s, René Girault proposed to go beyond a strictly diplomatic and institutional approach to European integration and integrate the cultural dimension of this process. He conceived the project 'European identity and consciousness in the twentieth century', which introduced elements usually absent from the history of international relations.[58] As this letter addressed by Girault to his colleagues shows, the project was originally imagined in the framework of the Liaison Committee:

> The central objective of the Liaison Committee since its creation has been to contribute to the scientific research on the history of the Communities. This objective found its motivation in the need felt by the Communities to popular-ize a recent past which is positive but too often ignored. This objective is still relevant. We take as a premise that a new step towards European integration will be made possible by the awareness of our cultural convergences. In order to smooth down political opposition, the peoples have to understand what unites them today: in our eyes, it is a common cultural history, a unique civilization.[59]

With the expression 'popularize', Girault recognized that the Liaison Committee took part in an information action, as originally conceived by the European Commission. In the description of his project, he insisted on informational and political objectives rather than on scientific ones. This indicates a significant change in his attitude towards European integration. While he was sceptical of Lipgens' militant stance in 1982, the presentation of this later project adopted a comparably teleological approach to European history. Like Lipgens, Girault claimed that the historical analysis of different expressions of European unity in the past could inspire the Europeans of the present in their attempts to integrate Europe:

> We, Western Europeans, despite our distinct national histories, have been participating for a long time in a common civilization. Does this not constitute the deep source of the transformations achieved in the last thirty or forty years? When the founding fathers joined to attempt to create Europe, did not they share common methods of thinking, ideals . . . as much as incidental interests? To put it in a nutshell, what has been the cultural environment of a Jean Monnet and why could he find around him people of his generation willing to follow him, beyond his personal qualities?[60]

The project was eventually launched in 1989 at the University Paris I Pantheon-Sorbonne and conducted with the support of DG X.[61] Although not officially an initiative of the Liaison Committee, many of its members participated in its realization.[62] According to Antonio Varsori, the project was to some extent disappointing since it failed to define common characteristics of European identity.[63] This confirms that a normative impetus characterized this project, whose scientific agenda reflected a vision of Europe that could not be demonstrated empirically. The follow-up project was hence entitled 'European identities' to better correspond to empirical and historical facts.[64] W. Loth remarks that most of the members of the group remained sceptical about the concept of European identity and that, in collective projects, it was usually dealt with by external contributors.[65] Nonetheless, in the following years, members of the Liaison Committee proposed seminars on these topics –

for example, 'The Issue of European Identity: Historical and Philosophical Analysis' (Michel Dumoulin, University of Louvain-la-Neuve) and 'The Experience of European Unity in the 20th Century: European Awareness and New Identities' (Gérard Bossuat, University of Cergy-Pontoise).[66] Concepts like European identity and European consciousness or awareness, which were high on the EC institutions agenda, were hence integrated into the committee's scientific activities. This does not mean that the historians were uncritically following an injunction coming from the institutions, but it shows that the proximity between the committee and its object of research resulted in a porosity between the political and scientific agendas.

Resistances and Conflicts: The End of a Privileged Partnership

This atypical collaboration eventually evolved into irreconcilable divergences. In 1998, an official note from the commissioner for education and culture to the president of the commission exposed the motives justifying the end of the commission's support to the Liaison Committee. It explained that the committee functioned 'as a closed community, constituted of a dozen professors co-opted ad personam', which was not in contact anymore with the active university milieu, neglecting hence one of its main missions: to strengthen a network of specialists of the European integration history.[67] The network called for by the commission had eventually been achieved through the Jean Monnet Chairs programme.[68] In a context of increasing budgetary control after the scandal of the Santer Commission in 1999, the commission considered it useless 'to maintain two parallel networks' and intended, 'for the sake of efficiency, transparency and coherence, to rationalize its relationship with the historians in the framework of the Jean Monnet Action'.[69] Moreover, the *Journal of European Integration History*, created in 1995 by the Liaison Committee at the request of the commission, and funded by the DG X, had a too limited number of subscribers. As a result, in 1999 the commission stopped its permanent subvention to the Liaison Committee and to its journal,[70] and to this day the committee has continued its activities without the commission's support. To be sure, many members of the Liaison Committee were assigned the positions of Jean Monnet Chair, but history has been weakly represented in the Jean Monnet Action, and only about 10 per cent of the projects were co-financed by the commission in the 2000s.[71] Since the mid-1990s, the European Commission's interest in the history of European integration has markedly decreased.[72]

However, the commission did mobilize the historians for the writing of its own history as an institution. Two books on the history and memories of the European Commission, partly based on the oral history database constituted since 1997 at the commission's request, were published in 2007 and 2014. Members of the Liaison Committee coordinated these projects, selected after a call from the commission, and many contributors were also members of the group.[73] As Michel Dumoulin, coordinator of the first volume, explains, the process of writing this history did not come without tensions and eventually resulted in a 'negotiated interpretation' between the commission, the witnesses and the historians.[74] Through its cooperation with the Liaison Committee and its project of oral archives, the European Commission succeeded in getting a certain number of historians working on topics it considered relevant – the most striking example being its own history, partly based on actors' testimonies.

Conclusion

The EU's sponsorship of academic research and of history writing in particular may give rise to criticism regarding the independence and objectivity of the knowledge produced in this framework. Without pretending to assess the scientific quality of the EU-sponsored historiographical projects, this chapter has investigated the nature and effects of various partnerships between EU institutions and historians of European integration. It appears that such partnerships have existed since the 1970s, first in the framework of the EC action in the university milieu, which itself was part of an information policy designed to increase popular support for the emerging European institutions. The historians were chosen as privileged interlocutors because of their capacity to create narratives of and spread knowledge on European integration. The collaboration with the historians could function either because they shared the Europeanist agenda of the institutions, like in the case of Lipgens, or because it was a means to develop international cooperation and to gain more legitimacy in their discipline, like in the case of Girault. In both cases – militant or pragmatic – porosity between the scientific and institutional agendas can be observed. The Liaison Committee of Historians was created in a period in which the EC intended to enhance the 'human' dimension of European integration. The members of the committee, mostly historians of international relations, soon integrated into their research concepts new to their historiographical practice but which were then extensively used in the EC official discourse – European consciousness, identity, awareness, etc. While guaranteeing EC subsidies, this allowed for a diversification of their research in a context of competition within the discipline. This conjunction of interests made a partnership with the EC beneficial. However, certain attempts of the commission, regarding, for instance, the oral sources and the focus on a 'popular' memory, faced the historians' resistance. The ending of the collaboration between the DG X and the Liaison Committee eventually revealed the incompatibility of two agendas. The European Commission, for whom the Liaison Committee was part of an information policy, was more interested in teaching and vulgarization activities than in research, which in contrast remained at the centre of the historians' agenda. These diverging logics led to the dissolution of their atypical partnership. It remains true, however, that the European Commission did contribute, through its convening and financial power, to the emergence of transnational collaborations, which, in turn, allowed for the establishment of a new discipline – the history of European integration.

Oriane Calligaro is a research fellow and lecturer at the Institute for European Studies, Université libre de Bruxelles, and a visiting professor at the College of Europe (Bruges). She holds a PhD from the European University Institute in Florence, and worked as a research assistant for the Robert Schuman Centre for Advanced Studies. She was also a Humboldt Foundation Research Fellow and a lecturer in european studies at the Maastricht University. She authored the monograph *Negotiating Europe: The EU Promotion of Europeanness since the 1950s* (Palgrave Macmillan, 2013).

Notes

1. J.-R. Rabier, 'L'information des Européens et l'intégration de l'Europe'. Lessons on 17 and 18 February 1965, Complementary course 10, Université libre de Bruxelles, Institut d'Etudes Européennes, 15.

2. A. Reinfeldt, 'Promoting a Knowledge of Europe: The Youth and European Integration', History of European Integration Research Society third conference (Geneva: Graduate Institute of International Studies, 16–17 March 2007), 65.

3. A. Vauchez, 'The Force of a Weak Field: Law and Lawyers in the Government of the European Union', *International Political Sociology* 20(2) (2007), 128–44; A. Favell and V. Guiraudon, 'The Sociology of the European Union: An Agenda', *European Union Politics* 10(4) (2009), 550–76; S. Mudge and A. Vauchez, 'Building Europe on a Weak Field: Law, Economics, and Scholarly Avatars in Transnational Politics', *American Journal of Sociology* 118(2) (2012), 449–92; O. Calligaro, *Negotiating Europe: The EU Promotion of Europeanness since the 1950s* (New York: Palgrave Macmillan, 2013); R. Adler-Nissen and K. Kropp, 'A Sociology of Knowledge Approach to European Integration: Four Analytical Principles', *Journal of European Integration* 37(2) (2015), 155–73.

4. A. Varsori, 'From Normative Impetus to Professionalization: Origins and Operation of Research Networks', in W. Kaiser and A. Varsori (eds), *European Union History Themes and Debates* (Basingstoke: Palgrave Macmillan, 2010), 6–25; M. Le Boulay, 'Investir l'arène européenne de la recherche: Le Groupe de Liaison des historiens auprès de la Commission européenne', *Politix* 89 (2010), 103–24; W. Loth, 'La contribution du Groupe de Liaison à l'histoire des institutions européennes', in M. Mangenot and S. Schirmann (eds), *Les institutions*

européennes font leur histoire: Regards croisés soixante ans après le traité de Paris (Brussels: Peter Lang, 2012), 47–58.

5. E. Torquati, 'L'azione Jean Monnet, unicum nelle iniziative della Commissione Europea per l'Università', in A. Varsori (ed.), *Sfide del mercato e identità europea* (Milan: Franco Angeli, 2012), 111–43; Calligaro, *Negotiating Europe*, 15–35.

6. M. Mangenot and S. Schirmann (eds), *Les institutions européennes font leur histoire: Regards croisés soixante ans après le traité de Paris* (Brussels: Peter Lang, 2012).

7. Varsori, 'From Normative Impetus', 7.

8. French Ministry of Foreign Affairs, quoted in J.-M. Palayret, *A University for Europe: Prehistory of the European University in Florence (1948–1976)* (Rome: Presidency of the Council of Ministers, Department of Information and Publishing, 1996), 121.

9. Interview with J. Lastenouse, Brussels, 3 September 2008.

10. Historical Archives of the European Union (HAEU): Fund Walter Lipgens WL-96, 1946–1980. Memorandum addressed by Peter Ludlow to Walter Lipgens, March 1979.

11. HAEU: Fund EUI-10, 1974–1981. Research project 'History of European Co-operation and Integration', 'Etude sur les origines du Marché commun et de la Communauté Européenne' by P. Fontaine (03/1976).

12. A. Cohen, 'Le "père de l'Europe": La construction sociale d'un récit des origines', *Actes de la recherche en sciences sociales* 166–167 (2007), 20.

13. HAEU: Fund EUI-10, 1974–1981. Letter from Peter Ludlow to Pascal Fontaine, 6 March 1976.

14. HAEU: Fund EUI-10, 1974–1981. Note de dossier, Historique du projet de recherche de l'Institut Universitaire Européen de Florence sur l'histoire de la coopération et de l'intégration européenne, DG X, 4 January 1980.

15. W. Lipgens, *Die Anfänge der europäischen Einigungspolitik 1945–50, Erster Band: 1945–1947* (Stuttgart: Klett, 1977).

16. HAEU: Fund Walter Lipgens, WL-179 03/1977-09/1977. Invitation letter to the symposium 'Problèmes méthodologiques et pratiques d'une histoire de l'intégration européenne depuis la deuxième guerre mondiale' 29/09/1977–01/10/1977, European University Institute, 10 March 1977.

17. W. Lipgens, *A History of European Integration, 1945–1947: The Formation of the European Unity Movement* (Oxford: Clarendon Press, 1982).

18. On the impact of this book on the discipline, see e.g. N.P. Ludlow, 'Widening, Deepening and Opening Out: Towards a Fourth Decade of European Integration History', in W. Loth (ed.), *Experiencing Europe: 50 Years of European Construction 1957–2007* (Baden-Baden: Nomos, 2009), 33–44.

19. C. Audland, 'The Historical Archives of the European Union: Their Opening to the Public, Management and Accessibility', *Journal of the Society of Archivists* 8(2) (2007), 177–192.

20. HAEU: Fund EUI-10, 1974–1981. Letter from Walter Lipgens to Christopher Auland, 31 October 1979. 'Note de dossier: Historique du projet de recherche de l'Institut Universitaire Européen de Florence sur l'histoire de la coopération et de l'intégration européenne', DG X, 4 January 1980.

21. HAEU: Fund EUI-10, 1974–1981, EC, Legal Service, 'Note à l'attention de Monsieur Audland Secrétaire Général Adjoint: Projet de recherche Histoire de l'intégration européenne de l'Institut universitaire européen', 5 December 1979; Letter from Christopher Audland to Walter Lipgens, 31 December 1979; 'Note de dossier: Historique du projet de recherche de l'Institut Universitaire Européen de Florence sur l'histoire de la coopération et de l'intégration européenne', DG X, 4 January 1980.

22. DG X, 'Note de dossier: Historique du projet de recherche de l'Institut Universitaire Européen de Florence sur l'histoire de la coopération et de l'intégration européenne', HAEU, Folder EUI-10, 1974–1981, 4 January 1980.

23. Lipgens and his former student Wilfried Loth carried on several parts of the project at the Saarland University in Saarbrücken, with a subsidy from the Volkswagen Foundation. See W. Loth, 'Preface', in W. Loth (ed.), *Documents on the History of European Integration, vol. III, The Struggle for European Union by Political Parties and Pressure Groups in Western European Countries 1945–1950* (Berlin and New York: W. de Gruyter, 1988), viii.

24. Interview with J. Lastenouse, Brussels, 3 September 2008.

25. J. Lastenouse's Personal Archives (JLPA): DG X/University Information, Report and Papers (April 1982): International Conference of Professors of Contemporary History, Luxembourg, 28–29 January 1982. 'Study of the Beginnings of European Integration: The Value of Source Material and Records', 9; Interview with J. Lastenouse, Brussels, 3 September 2008.

26. JLPA: DG X/University Information, Report and Papers (April 1982): International Conference of Professors of Contemporary History. Gaston Thorn, 'Opening Speech', 29.

27. Ibid., 32.

28. Ibid.

29. Ibid., 51.

30. JLPA: DG X/University Information, Report and Papers (April 1982): International Conference of Professors of Contemporary History. Walter Lipgens, 'Introductory Paper on the Public Archives', 50–51.

31. Ibid., 50.

32. Ibid.

33. Ibid.

34. Interview with A. Marès, by phone, 3 April 2010.

35. Interview with M. Dumoulin, Brussels, 4 September 2009.

36. Ibid.

37. Ibid.

38. Le Boulay, 'Investir l'arène', 114–15.

39. Loth, 'La contribution', 53.

40. HAEU, Fund Emile Noël, EN-1137, 'Groupe de liaison des professeurs d'histoire contemporaine auprès de la Commission Européenne: Rapport des Professeurs A.S. Milward et G. Trausch sur leur mission aux Archives de la Commission des Communautés Européennes', 16 June 1988.

41. Le Boulay, 'Inverstir l'arène', 120.

42. Loth, 'La contribution', 50.

43. JLPA, DG X/University Information, Report and Papers (April 1982): International Conference of Professors of Contemporary History, Programme of the Conference, 4.

44. Interview with A. Marès, by phone, 3 April 2010.

45. M. Dumoulin's personal archives (MDPA), file 'Groupe de Liaison des Historiens', 'Rapport d'Antoine Marès sur les archives orales de la construction européennes', 9 May 1984.

46. Meeting of the Heads of State of Government, Solemn Declaration on European Union, Stuttgart, 19 June 1983. *Bulletin of the EC* 6 (1983), 24–29.

47. See report from the ad hoc committee on a People's Europe, in *Bulletin of the EC* 3 (March 1985), 111–17.

48. MDPA, file 'Groupe de Liaison des Historiens', 'Procès-verbal de la 1057ème session du Conseil des Ministres responsables des affaires culturelles réunis au sein du Conseil du 20 décembre 1985, point Histoire communautaire vécue', 8.

49. HAEU, Fund Emile Noël, EN-1045, Note by Manuel Santarelli to M. Ripa de Maena, Commissioner for Information and Culture, 'Report on the Feasibility of a "Lived History of the Community" as proposed by the Ministers of Culture on 20 December 1985', Brussels, 7 December 1987.

50. MDPA, file 'Groupe de Liaison des Historiens', 'Procès-verbal de la réunion du 30 janvier 1986'; Interview with Michel Dumoulin, Brussels, 4 September 2009.

51. HAEU, Fund Emile Noël, EN-1045, Liaison Committee of Historians, 'Recommendation for the European Commisson on the Project of "Lived History of the Community"', 9 October 1987.

52. Interview with M. Dumoulin, Brussels, 4 September 2009; Loth, 'La contribution', 57.

53. M. Dumoulin, 'Entre mémoire et histoire', in M. Mangenot and S. Schirmann (eds), *Les institutions européennes font leur histoire: Regards croisés soixante ans après le traité de Paris* (Brussels, Peter Lang, 2012), 132.

54. JLPA, Note by Mrs Cauchie, DG X/Audiovisual Production Unit, for the attention of the Liaison Committee of Historians, 'Testimonies on the Beginnings of European Integration Process', Brussels, 5 November 1996.

55. For example, JLPA, Letter from Jacqueline Lastenouse to Gilbert Trausch, Brussels, 12 March 1997; and Note by Jacqueline Lastenouse for the attention of Mrs C. de la Torre, Secreteriat of the Commissioner Oreja, 'Information of the Projects on the History of European Integration', Brussels, 6 May 1999.

56. JLPA, Note by Fabienne Alexandre, DG X/Jean Monnet Unit, 'Project of Oral History of the Jean Monnet Chairs in History', Brussels, 24 July 2000.

57. Varsori, 'From Normative Impetus', 17; Loth, 'La contribution', 57.

58. R. Girault (ed.), *Identité et conscience européennes au XXe siècle* (Paris: Hachette, 1994).

59. HAEU, Fund Emile Noël, EN-1137, Note by René Girault on the Future of the Liaison Committee of Historians and on the Research Projects, Paris, 1 December 1987, 2.

60. Ibid., 3.

61. R. Frank, 'Introduction', in R. Frank (ed.), *Les identités européennes au XXe siècle* (Paris: Editions de la Sorbonne, 2004), 8.

62. MDPA, file 'Groupe de Liaison des Historiens', 'Procès-verbal de la réunion du 16 juin 1988, Florence'.

63. Varsori, 'From Normative Impetus', 17.

64. R. Frank (ed.), *Les identités européennes au XXe siècle: Diversités, convergences et solidarités* (Paris: Publications de la Sorbonne, 2004).

65. Quoted in Le Boulay, 'Investir l'arène', 118.

66. Ibid.

67. JLPA, EC (1998), Note by Spyros A. Pappas, Director-General DG X for the attention of Mr. Calleja, Principal Secretary of the Commissioner for Information and Culture M. Oreja, 22 September 1998.

68. Ibid.

69. Ibid.

70. Ibid.

71. Varsori, 'From Normative Impetus', 21.

72. Loth 'La contribution', 57.

73. See M. Dumoulin et al. (eds), *The European Commission, 1958–72: History and Memories* (Luxembourg: OPOCE, 2007); É. Bussière et al. (eds), *The European Commission, 1973–86: History and Memories* (Luxembourg: OPOCE, 2014).

74. M. Dumoulin, 'Inventing Things as They Went Along', in Dumoulin, *The European Commission*, 26.

Bibliography

Adler-Nissen, R., and K. Kropp. 'A Sociology of Knowledge Approach to European Integration: Four Analytical Principles'. *Journal of European Integration* 37(2) (2015), 155–73.

Audland, C. 'The Historical Archives of the European Union: Their Opening to the Public, Management and Accessibility', *Journal of the Society of Archivists* 8(2) (2007), 177–192.

Bussière, É., et al. (eds). *The European Commission, 1973–86: History and Memories.* Luxembourg: OPOCE, 2014.

Calligaro, O. *Negotiating Europe: EU Promotion of Europeanness since the 1950s.* New York: Palgrave Macmillan, 2013.

Cohen, A. 'Le "père de l'Europe": La construction sociale d'un récit des origines'. *Actes de la recherche en sciences sociales* 166–167 (2007), 14–29.

Dumoulin, M. 'Inventing Things As They Went Along', in M. Dumoulin et al. (eds), *The European Commission, 1958–72: History and Memories* (Luxembourg: OPOCE, 2007), 17–34.

———. 'Entre mémoire et histoire', in M. Mangenot and S. Schirmann (eds), *Les institutions européennes font leur histoire: Regards croisés soixante ans après le traité de Paris* (Brussels: Peter Lang, 2012), 127–42.

Dumoulin, M., et al. (eds). *The European Commission, 1958–72: History and Memories.* Luxembourg: OPOCE, 2007.

Favell, A., and V. Guiraudon. 'The Sociology of the European Union: An Agenda', *European Union Politics* 10(4) (2009), 550–76.

Frank, R. (ed.). *Les identités européennes au XXe siècle: Diversités, convergences et solidarités.* Paris: Publications de la Sorbonne, 2004.

———. 'Introduction', in R. Frank (ed.), *Les identités européennes au XXe siècle: Diversités, convergences et solidarités* (Paris: Editions de la Sorbonne, 2004), 7–12.

Girault, R. (ed.). *Identité et conscience européennes au XXe siècle.* Paris: Hachette, 1984.

Le Boulay, M. 'Investir l'arène européenne de la recherche: Le Groupe de Liaison des historiens auprès de la Commission européenne'. *Politix* 89 (2010), 103–24.

Lipgens, W. *Die Anfänge der europäischen Einigungspolitik 1945–50, Erster Band: 1945–1947.* Stuttgart: Klett, 1977.

Lipgens W. *A History of European Integration, 1945–1947: The Formation of the European Unity Movement.* Oxford: Clarendon Press, 1982.

Loth, W. 'Preface', in W. Loth (ed.), *Documents on the History of European Integration, vol. III, The Struggle for European Union by Political Parties and Pressure Groups in Western European Countries 1945–1950* (Berlin and New York: W. de Gruyter, 1988), i–ix.

———. 'La contribution du Groupe de liaison à l'histoire des institutions européennes', in M. Mangenot and S. Schirmann (eds), *Les institutions européennes font leur histoire: Regards croisés soixante ans après le traité de Paris* (Brussels, Peter Lang, 2012), 47–58.

Ludlow, N.P. 'Widening, Deepening and Opening Out: Towards a Fourth Decade of European Integration History', in W. Loth (ed.), *Experiencing Europe: 50 Years of European Construction 1957–2007* (Baden-Baden: Nomos, 2009), 33–44.

Mudge, S., and A. Vauchez. 'Building Europe on a Weak Field: Law, Economics, and Scholarly Avatars in Transnational Politics'. *American Journal of Sociology* 118(2) (2009), 449–92.

Palayret, J.-M. *A University for Europe: Prehistory of the European University in Florence (1948–1976).* Rome: Presidency of the Council of Ministers, Department of Information and Publishing, 1996.

Palayret, J.-M. 'Des négociations à la création de l'Institut universitaire européen de Florence', Conference 'L'enjeu de la culture dans le champ multilateral'. Lyon: Université Lumière Lyon 2 and Institut d'études politiques, 10–12 May 2001.

Rabier, J.-R. 'L'information des Européens et l'intégration de l'Europe'. Lessons on 17 and 18 February 1965, Complementary course 10, Université libre de Bruxelles, Institut d'Etudes Européennes.

Reinfeldt, A. 'Promoting a Knowledge of Europe: The Youth and European Integration'. History of European Integration Research Society, third conference. Geneva: Graduate Institute of International Studies, 16–17 March 2007.

Torquati, E. 'L'azione Jean Monnet, unicum nelle iniziative della Commissione Europea per l'Università', in A. Varsori (ed.), *Sfide del mercato e identità europea* (Milan: Franco Angeli, 2012), 111–43.

Varsori, A. 'From Normative Impetus to Professionalization: Origins and Operation of Research Networks', in W. Kaiser and A. Varsori (eds), *European Union History Themes and Debates* (Basingstoke: Palgrave Macmillan, 2010), 6–25.

Vauchez, A. 'The Force of a Weak Field: Law and Lawyers in the Government of the European Union'. *International Political Sociology* 20(2) (2008), 128–44.

CHAPTER 3

Representations of National Cultures vis-à-vis the 'European' at the European Union National Institutes for Culture

CLAUDIA SCHNEIDER

Europeanization is a phenomenon that has been seen at the European Union's social and political networks for a while, and it is also visible in cultural policies of the European Union's member states. Aside from the Europeanization of national politics, the Europeanization of national conceptions of European culture and history can be understood as the conjunction between cultural discourses.

The present chapter addresses this question: to what extent do national cultural actors' approaches to European collective identity and memory support further Europeanization? To this end, it concerns itself with the European Union National Institutes for Culture (EUNIC), a network of the cultural institutes of the EU's member states, whose primary aim is 'to expand the role of culture in Europe and to strengthen cultural dialogue'.[1] It discusses the programmatic statements made by the cultural institutes in Berlin, which gave references to national and other projects, and in particular to those that mentioned a common European culture and history. All commemoration projects, which were inaugurated as common EUNIC projects during 2011 and 2012, were investigated. In addition, expert interviews were held with the cultural players in order to reveal their logic of identity and commemoration constructions.[2]

Notes for this section begin on page 60.

Individual Memory Projects Exhibited in EUNIC and their National Contexts

In EUNIC Berlin, national players present their projects, and their first aim is to attract an audience from the same national context. Then, in the presence of EUNIC Berlin, a sort of mutual exclusion between individual projects is already expected. But these individual projects do, in certain instances, give references to other cultural groups with whom they claim to share common histories. For example, the Hungarian project of reminding the past, which was entitled 'German unity at Lake Balaton', features the location at which it combines German and Hungarian cultural interactions and also tells German history from a Hungarian perspective.[3] Similarly, the Slovak Institute often works together with the Federal Association of the Carpathian Germans and with their representation in Slovakia.[4] Austria and Hungary also present a traditional partnership with the former Court of Habsburgs.[5]

The European Union link automatically endows the projects with a 'European' status. The EU is considered to be part and parcel of EUNIC and the exhibiting institutions, and it logically becomes a shared space. Although EUNIC projects in 2011 and 2012 did not broach the European Union in detail, the interviews revealed that they refer to the EU in order to legitimize their narratives. The Finnish Institute of Culture, for instance, stated: 'We do not only act binationally; we should act in the context of Europe or the European Union, as our closest and the most relevant context for represent-ing our pasts'.[6]

A second determining element is Berlin. Individual projects featuring the popular themes such as 'the Cold War' and 'the (Berlin) Wall' also emphasize the importance of the city. The Hungarian delegation states:

> The division is not only of Berlin, but it is most visible here. Not only the great catastrophe, but the reunion is visible here; they play each other geographically and politically in a very interrelated way in Berlin. I can say that Berlin for us is very important and, as I understand it, it is more important than leaving it to the Germans in a national framework. However, this view is also favourable to the Germans. Berlin is the place of the European reflection of European design: ultimately Hungarian interests, but also European interests.[7]

Then it becomes possible to argue that many different national interests overlap ultimately on the Berlin concept and become shared common interests. Take the Slovakian exhibition entitled 'Secret Documents just Discovered', which was entangled with the concept of the fall of the Berlin Wall, or another project about what happened in the country in 1989.[8] The project called '20th Anniversary of the Fall of the Wall' was another example, on which many partners cooperated to underline their shared history.[9] Similarly, the institutions under EUNIC organized a joint event for the sixtieth anniversary of the Second World War,[10] and in another case EUNIC developed a number of projects in 2014 to commemorate the First World War.[11] In these examples, collective memory was extended to an understanding of a greater transnational, European group. And the theme of Berlin evoked common remembrances, especially those between the countries of the former Eastern Bloc. Narrating common events and historical periods, therefore, has the function of reminding Europeans of a common history.

The same is true about Europe as a geographical space. It has already been stated that individual projects of EUNIC regard European space as a unifying element. The removal of borders in Europe is an issue dealt with by all cultural institutes and embassies, as a connecting element between Europe and national memory.[12] In this way, national projects are given a European reference, as argued in the Austrian Cultural Forum: 'This is an Austrian event, but it is also European. Our memory does not differ'.[13] Despite that, constructions of European space sometimes include a geographical limitation, which restricts the channels to other memories. The Slovak Institute therefore expressed: 'This is a Central European theme, so we do not touch upon other countries represented in EUNIC like France or Spain'.[14]

But still, memory is primarily linked to the national reference group and, in this, the national past is constructed with a clear reference to the present state of the national context.[15] The Portuguese Embassy and the Romanian Cultural Institute separately stated that historical memory should have the role of linking the past to the present and the future.[16] In this case, anniversaries, be they about national events or important characters, are critical to the memory representation as the reminder projects of EUNIC featured them.[17] One example is a project of the Romanian Cultural Institute. Their theme was a prison in Romania, where many students charged with political crimes were tortured in the 1950s, and in some cases got killed. The aim of the project was to highlight the mentality of the past socialist regime.[18] Another example is the binational cooperation between Germany and Belgium on the fiftieth anniversary of the Elysée Treaty.[19] These reminder projects broached the past and implied today: they compared today with corresponding historical events and gave the primary reference to the present.

The reminder projects of EUNIC are also considered to be the 'storage' of historical knowledge for generations.[20] The turn of the year 1989 particularly had a transnational importance; strong meanings were (and still are) ascribed to the events of this year, with the rationale of informing the newest generations. The Finnish Institute stated: 'It has been 23 years since the fall of the wall. This is an interesting dialogue, because it means not only a German–Finnish dialogue, but an intergenerational one, especially when it comes to history and identity'.[21] As another example, descriptions of the Elysée Treaty between Germany and France clearly show how much memory is being mobilized in order to address the present generation. The Goethe Institute expressed: 'We now have, for example, the fifty years of the friendship treaty in Franco-German relations. Since the enthusiasm it created for the older generation is gone, we have to re-establish it'.[22]

It needs to be explained how cultural institutes established further connections between national memory and the European category, using their essentialist reminder projects. An important example is the memories of great wars. Some projects about historical wars build on memories represented by contemporary witnesses of a certain group.[23] They are exhibited with the objective of strengthening the new generations' attachment to the national memory, as explained by the Greek Cultural Foundation:

> That was the event 'Europe Tells History', which took place in autumn 2005, and all participating cultural institutions were invited to 'witness' the Second World War. It was the sixtieth anniversary of the end of that war, and it aimed to remind [people] of the war and how it was reflected in the literature at that time – and how it is portrayed today, because viewing angles have changed. We had a witness who actually lived in the time of the war . . . The event was about how different or similar the war memories are that are transmitted.[24]

This partly unexpected war history also influences opinions of the institutes' staff. Many speak of a pan-European culture that emerged in a shared but 'unconscious' past, as did the Portuguese and Finnish institutes: 'We have such a large common base, of which we are often unaware, but we have always been united in a sense'.[25] Without being able to determine in more detail what the historical and cultural unity of Europe looks like, a shared 'European history' is taken for granted in discussions and is thus slightly adapted to the national presentations.[26] The German institute states: 'The self-discovery of Europe in relation to Islamic expansion, this aspect has received far too little attention. Or Europe as the occident, that is indeed a highly topical issue but actually we look to this far too little'.[27] In this regard, many agreed from the beginning that common cultural and universal values and political tendencies arose from a similar 'European' past and they are evidence of a natural cohesion among Europeans.[28] In addition, an almost habitual reference is given to the EUNIC's role in order to concretize the argument of shared history: 'Historically we have something in common with the Europeans and therefore it happens to be very natural that we are members of EUNIC'.[29]

Further, cultural diplomats support their argument on the common European culture and history with transnational cultural forms of expression in literature and art. The German Foreign Ministry stated: 'This starts with the architecture of Europe. Europe is characterized precisely in many parts of churches from Gothic to Baroque and beyond, and with urban planning – for example, the medieval town centres'.[30] The Austrian delegation, on the other hand, gave the example of Europe's musical legacy: 'Neapolitan musicians raised in the courts during the sixteenth and seventeenth centuries – like Mozart and Haydn – went to other European countries and contributed to the cultural foundations of the idea of Europe and the EU'.[31] In addition, connecting elements that were born with the Enlightenment are also found in these statements of the Finnish Institute: 'Whenever you are travelling outside Europe, you can see what makes Europe. Then there are still important, self-evident elements that we have here, such as history, education and the rule of law'.[32]

What is certain in the statements above is that the cultural actors of EUNIC mostly take for granted the pan-European history as the core element of European identity. In these arguments, 'common history', 'common culture', 'traditions' and 'common cultural heritage' are the key terms employed to define a European identity.[33] According to cultural actors, the term 'European history' should therefore be presented abroad as a logical consequence of Europeanness.[34]

Still, the institutions assumed the common European history as a matter of diversity.[35] This all evokes what the European Union adopts today in its official slogan, 'United in Diversity'. Most of the cultural institutes at EUNIC follow this concept uncritically and, within their common and individual projects, they together stress the importance of cultural diversity and the idea of common Europeanness.[36] This is also the case in the representation of European and individual histories. When presenting their national contexts, the cultural institutes still mention their connecting elements shaped in the European history.[37] As the Portuguese Institute expressed it: 'In fact, the history of a single European country cannot be conceived without the others, and today's reality reflects all this'.[38]

Conclusion

Member institutions of EUNIC Berlin give priorities to the presentation of their national contexts, and they do not concretely explain that they are part of a common European culture and history. Remembrance projects serve the common understanding, but they are in the minority at EUNIC Berlin, and the actors involved in remembrance projects still tend to link their memories to their national contexts and their institutes' national works rather than collaborating. In the projects exemplified above, national institutes only refer to a European history when they are to exhibit common concepts and events of European history.

In order to sustain their superficial stress on a broader, European context, the cultural diplomacies of member institutions repeatedly express the EU's famous slogan 'Unity in Diversity'; in this, national identities are assumed to be individual elements but at the same time a part of European identity. Here the mention of European diversity becomes a means to justify the act of presenting national contexts. The main emphasis is laid on national contexts, and the European context becomes only a secondary aspect in the hierarchy of presenting culture and history. Although cultural institutes, through their narratives on common histories, sometimes mention the memory of other national contexts, all these practices do not form systematic references to a common European history. In other words, EUNIC players' approaches to collective identity and memory contribute to the further Europeanization of cultural and historical concepts in a limited sense only.

Claudia Schneider studied political science at the Free University of Berlin and at Maastricht University. She is currently working as an assistant teacher at the University of Potsdam and as a freelance editor. During her doctoral study at the Free University of Berlin, she focused on the Europeanization of EU member states in cultural terms. Her research topics involve Europeanization, the sociology of organizations, and policy analyses.

Notes

The present chapter builds on the methods, interviews and arguments presented in C. Schneider, *Europäisch verbunden national gebunden: Die Europäisierung der Auswärtigen Kulturpolitik der EU-Mitgliedstaaten* (Berlin: Springer, 2016). It was written in German and translated by Caner Tekin with the author's consent.

1. The European Union National Institutes of Culture, Mission Statement, available from http://berlin.eunic-online.eu/?q=content/mission-statement-0 (last accessed 17 September 2016).

2. For more information on the interviews and for detailed explanations, see C. Schneider, *Europäisch verbunden national gebunden: Die Europäisierung der Auswärtigen Kulturpolitik der EU-Mitgliedstaaten* (Berlin: Springer, 2016).

3. P 16 / Collegium Hungaricum 30.04.2012.

4. P 43 / Slovak Institute 27.03.2012.

5. P 16 / Collegium Hungaricum 30.04.2012.

6. P 18 / Finland Institute 17.04.2012.

7. P 16 / Collegium Hungaricum 30.04.2012.

8. P 43 / Slovak Institute 27.03.2012.

9. P 8/ Goethe Institute 18.04.2012; P 22/ Greek Cultural Foundation 02.04.2012; P 26/ Austrian Cultural Forum 22.03.2012; P 31/ Polish Institute 29.03.2012.

10. P 22 / Greek Cultural Foundation 02.04.2012.

11. P 32 / Belgian Embassy / Representation of the German Community, Wallonia and the Federation Wallonia-Brussels 31.05.2012; P 42 / Belgian Embassy Flemish Representation 29.06.2012; P 47 / Embassy of Ireland 21.06.2012.

12. P 31 / Polish Institute 29.03.2012.

13. P 26 / Austrian Cultural Forum 22.03.2012.

14. P 43 / Slovak Institute 27.03.2012.

15. See Maurice Halbwachs, *Das Gedächtnis und seine sozialen Bedingungen* (Berlin and Neuwied: Luchterhand, 1966); Maurice Halbwachs, *Das kollektive Gedächtnis* (Stuttgart: Enke, 1967); Etienne François, 'Pierre Nora und die "Lieux de mémoire"', in P. Nora, *Erinnerungsorte Frankreichs* (Munich: C.H. Beck, 2005), pp. 7–15; Astrid Erll, *Kollektives Gedächtnis und Erinnerungskulturen: Eine Einführung* (Stuttgart: Metzler, 2008); Claus Leggewie, *Der Kampf um Europaeische Erinnerung* (Munich: C.H. Beck, 2001); P 20 / Western Cultural Institute 30.03.2012.

16. P 40/ Embassy of Portugal 23.11.2012; P 28/ Romanian Cultural Institute 02.04.2012.

17. P 16 / Collegium Hungaricum 30.04.2012; P 28 / Romanian Cultural Institute 02.04.2012; P 39 / Swedish Embassy 10/09/2012; EUNIC Berlin; P 43 / Slovak Institute 27.03.2012; P 47 / Embassy of Ireland 21.06.2012.

18. P 28 / Romanian Cultural Institute 02.04.2012.

19. P 34 / Federal Foreign Office 19.06.2012; P 48 / Goethe Institute 09.10.2012.

20. K. Mannheim, 'Das Problem der Generationen', in K. Mannheim (ed.), *Wissenssoziologie* (Berlin: Luchterhand, 1964), 522–555.

21. P 18 / Finnish Institute 17.04.2012.

22. P 48 / Goethe Institute 09.10.2012.

23. P 18/ Finnish Institute 17.04.2012; P 31/ Polish Institute 29.03.2012; P 48/ Goethe Institute 09.10.2012.

24. P 22 / Greek Cultural Foundation 02.04.2012.

25. P 18 / Finnish Institute 17.04.2012; P 40 / Embassy of Portugal 23.11.2012.

26. P 12 / Embassy of Malta 11.06.2012.

27. P 36 / DAAD German Academic Exchange Service 08.06.2012.

28. P 22 / Greek Cultural Foundation 02.04.2012; P 26 / Austrian Cultural Forum 22/03/2012; P 34 / Federal Foreign Office 19.06.2012; P 40 / Embassy of Portugal 23.11.2012; P 44 / Instituto Cervantes 28.03.2012; P 48 / Goethe Institute 09.10.2012.

29. P 28 / Romanian Cultural Institute 02.04.2012.

30. P 34 / Federal Foreign Office 19.06.2012.

31. P 26 / Austrian Cultural Forum 22.03.2012.

32. P 18 / Finnish Institute 17.04.2012.

33. P 12 / Embassy of Malta 11.06.2012; P 39 / Swedish Embassy 10.09.2012).

34. P 34 / Federal Foreign Office 19.06.2012.

35. P 32 / Belgian Embassy / Representation of the German-speaking Community, Wallonia and the Federation Wallonia-Brussels 31.05.2012.

36. P 12/ Embassy of Malta 11.06.2012.

37. P 18 / Finnish Institute 17.04.2012.

38. P 40 / Embassy of Portugal 23.11.2012.

Bibliography

Interviews

P 8/ Goethe Institut (18.04.2012): Interview with the Director. Berlin.

P 10/ British Council (20.03.2012): Interview with the Head of the Society Programme. Berlin.

P 12/ Embassy of Malta (11.06.2012): Interview with the Representative for Press, Culture and Public Relations. Berlin.

P 14/ Bulgarian Cultural Institute (20.03.2012): Interview with the Director. Berlin.

P 16/ Collegium Hungaricum (Hungarian Cultural Institute) (30.04.2012): Interview with the Director. Berlin.

P 18/ Institute of Finland (17.04.2012): Interview with the Director. Berlin.

P 20/ Western Cultural Institute (30.03.2012): Interview with the Director. Berlin.

P 22/ Hellenic Foundation for Culture (02.04.2012): Interview with One of the Representatives. Berlin.

P 24/ Italian Cultural Institute (09.05.2012): Interview with the Director. Berlin.

P 26/ Austrian Cultural Forum (22.03.2012): Interview with the Director. Berlin.

P 28/ Romanian Cultural Institute (02.04.2012): Interview with the Deputy Director of the Institute. Berlin.

P 31/ Institute of Poland (29.03.2012): Interview with the Director. Berlin.

P 32/ Embassy of Belgium / Representation of the German-speaking Community of Wallonia and the Wallonia-Brussels Federation (31.05.2012): Interview with the Head of the Representation.

P 34/ Ministry of Foreign Affairs (19.06.2012): Interview with the Head of Transregional Cultural Projects, Arts, Cultural Heritage Return | Multilateral Cultural and Media Policy. Berlin.

P 36/ DAAD German Academic Exchange Service (08.06.2012): Interview with the head of the Liaison Office DAAD. Berlin.

P 37/ Committee on Culture and Education / EU Parliament (09.11.2012): Interview with the Chair of the Committee on Culture and Education. Brussels, Berlin.

P 39/ Embassy of Sweden (10.09.2012): Interview with the Representative of Culture. Berlin.

P 40/ Embassy of Portugal (23.11.2012): Interview with the Representative of Culture. Berlin.

P 42/ Embassy of Belgium / Flemish representative office (29.06.2012): Interview with the Cultural Officer and the General Delegate of the Government of Flanders in Germany. Berlin.

P 43/ Slowakian Institute (27.03.2012): Interview with the Director. Berlin.

P 44/ Cervantes Institute (28.03.2012): Interview mit the Director. Berlin.

P 45/ Embassy of the Republic of Slowenia (06.06.2012): Interview with the Embassy's Secretary. Berlin.

P 46/ Embassy of the Republic of Estonia (05.07.2012): Interview with the Cultural Attaché. Berlin.

P 47/ Embassy of Ireland (21.06.2012): Interview with Staff from the Department of 'Economic and Cultural Affairs'. Berlin.

P 48/ Goethe Institute (09.10.2012): Interview with the Commissioner and the Head of the Department 'Southwestern Europe'. Brussels.

P 49/ European Commission DG Education and Culture (11.10.2012): Interview Staff, Unit D4 Health Education Research Culture Europe Aid Development and Cooperation. Brussels.

P 50/ European Commission DG Education and Culture Unit Culture Policy, Diversity and Intercultural Dialogue (10.10.2012): Interview with the Head of the Programme 'Sector Globalization, Intellectual Property, Competition'. Brussels.

P 51/ Embassy of the Netherlands (14.11.2012): Interview with the Head of the Department Culture and Communication. Berlin.

P 52/ EUNIC Global (11.11.2012): Interview with Network and Communications Officer. Brussels.

Secondary Sources

Erll, A. *Kollektives Gedächtnis und Erinnerungskulturen: Eine Einführung.* Stuttgart: Metzler, 2008.

François, E. 'Pierre Nora und die "Lieux de mémoire"', in P. Nora, *Erinnerungsorte Frankreichs* (Munich: C.H. Beck, 2005), 7–15.

Halbwachs, M. *Das Gedächtnis und seine sozialen Bedingungen.* Berlin and Neuwied: Luchterhand, 1966.

———. *Das kollektive Gedächtnis.* Stuttgart: Enke, 1967.

Leggewie, C. *Der Kampf um Europaeische Erinnerung.* Munich: C.H. Beck, 2001.

Mannheim, K. 'Das Problem der Generationen', in K. Mannheim (ed.), *Wissenssoziologie* (Berlin: Luchterhand, 1964), 522–555.

Schneider, C.. *Europäisch verbunden national gebunden: Die Europäisierung der Auswärtigen Kulturpolitik der EU-Mitgliedstaaten.* Berlin: Springer, 2016.

CHAPTER 4

Europe – A Concept in its Own Right or an Intermediate State between National Traditions and Global Interrelatedness?

Representations of Europe in Curricula, Textbooks and Surveys

FALK PINGEL

The dissolution of the Soviet Union and the breakdown of the bipolar world order offered Europe the chance to merge its divisions that were two politico-economic blocs inherited from the Cold War period. The Treaty of Maastricht shaped the contours of an expanding and stronger union than before. However, it soon became obvious that the opening up of borders and the (re-)establishment of new states in Europe not only brought about intensified cooperation but also revived old conflicts and triggered new ones. Continuous migration flows from within and without the European Union have transformed European societies into multi-ethnic and multicultural conglomerates. This is felt to be particularly problematic in countries that have become sovereign, more or less homogenous nation states for the first time, such as Poland and Hungary, which now feel threatened by the EU's refugee policy. A Polish history textbook of the late 1990s contends: 'Poland now has the happiest, most advantageous territory of her history, and is basically a homogenous state in regard to culture'. However, in the same book, Poland's cultural and national diversity is seen as an enriching element of life in the past. When the book is dealing with the violent dissolution of Yugoslavia, the ambivalence of cultural diversity is made obvious: because of its ethnically and culturally mixed population, Yugoslavia had to endure a fate from which happy, homogenous Poland has been spared.[1]

Notes for this section begin on page 80.

How have European educational stakeholders – ministries, curriculum experts, textbook authors – coped with these challenges of the changing politico-cultural European landscape since the 1990s? What place do they allot to the concepts of 'nation' and 'Europe' in the teaching of the social sciences? Do we find in textbooks and curricula markers of identification, which should transmit to pupils a feeling of belonging and a recognition of heritage, as well as a commitment to European cooperation? Taking these questions into consideration, this chapter concentrates on the teaching of history, but also takes geography and civics into account.

In view of the variety of national education systems in Europe this chapter can only give an overview of common trends, highlight some characteristic developments, and offer examples of special developments in some countries. It is anyway hard to build clusters of countries. Exceptions can always be found that question rather than corroborate the rule. Nevertheless, some distinct features can be outlined:

- Firstly, the difference between 'West' and 'East' cannot totally be overcome even to this day, and remained indicative for the 1990s.[2]
- Secondly, the economically strong early member countries, such as Germany, France, the Netherlands and Italy, show common features different from some of those in southern European countries that joined later, such as Greece, Portugal and Spain – the latter, however, caught up with some older member states in many regards relatively soon.
- Thirdly, the centre-periphery opposition offers a significant tool to differentiate between countries that set the tone and others that tend to follow educational trends already implemented in the centre. South-eastern European countries are positioned on the rim of developments, whereas the Nordic countries form a more advanced group, with broad international and multicultural orientations.
- Fourthly, Europe is often – implicitly – equated with the European Union. Non-EU-member states are only occasionally referred to in textbooks and curricula, with the exception of Russia, which forms its own centre of gravity and whose European character appears to be questionable.

Overcoming the Legacy of Socialist/Communist Domination – Stages of Reform

Although textbooks and curricula on both sides of the former 'Iron Curtain' have reflected consequences of the changing European and world order since the 1990s, learning objectives and ways of textbook representation signalizing this change only partially overlap in 'East' and 'West'. At least, the chronological orders of alterations in textbooks and curricula differ. Whereas the breaking down of the political, economic and ideological system, accession to the EU and new politico-ethnic conflicts posed the main challenges to curriculum experts and textbook authors in the former socialist countries, their colleagues in the West also felt challenged by the accelerated integration process and the impact of globalization, which is only now gaining ground in textbooks and curricula in countries of the East.[3]

Firstly, the quick withdrawal of socialist/communist content and Marxist theoretic framing of historical explanation and terminology strengthened the importance of the national dimension in history and geography education in most of the former socialist states and newly (re-)founded republics such as the Baltic states and Belorussia. Only in a second phase, starting with the second half of the 1990s, did the European dimension come into the focus of ministerial guidelines and teaching material. Yet, the Europeanization of history curricula did not remain uncontested. Only step by step could the separation between national and international or general history inherited from the socialist/communist system be overcome. In some countries this process triggered fervent debates over whether the increasing significance of the European dimension should decrease the place allotted to national history. In Russia a historiographic debate emerged on Russia's relations with and belonging to Europe in the past and present. Most of the influential textbook authors placed Russia in an overall European context.[4]

Yet, 'Europe' did not play a role in its own right. It owed its new prominence to the rebirth of the nation. Europe was the place the nation state could be anchored in a presumably peaceful world. According to this concept Europe represented, on the one hand, a cultural tradition of which the central and south-east European states had formed a part since the Middle Ages. On the other hand, it represented a promise for the future: it stood for economic growth and social security that should be achieved through future membership in the EU. Institutionally, Europe was – and still is – mainly understood as the European Union. The role of the Council of Europe as the safeguard of civil and human rights and of multicultural approaches in education was considerably less well covered and acknowledged. Textbooks and curricula reflected an expanded model of Western Europe. Consequently, countries not considered eligible for membership in any foreseeable future – such as Belorussia, Moldova and Ukraine – did not form part of this model and were sometimes referred to as a Russia-oriented periphery of Europe. This distancing from the 'Russian East' could particularly but not only be observed in the textbooks of the Baltic countries and Poland. With the expansion of the EU, the 'border of civilization'[5] moved further East. Extra-European history remained marginal in this concept.

A third phase of reform starting around the turn of the century led to a paradigmatic change from the traditional teacher-centred way of teaching and content-oriented textbook writing to a skill- and competency-based approach. Intensive contacts between curriculum experts, teachers and textbook authors from East and West contributed to methodological innovations. Their implementation was already embedded in the European educational reform agenda and supported by European organizations, programmes and scholarly institutions, so contributing to a transfer of modern learning and teaching methods from West to East. Although the 'Bologna'-process is geared at tertiary education, most countries were eager to also reform secondary education accordingly in order to create best conditions for their students, and for educational institutions to advance in the tertiary sector.[6] As a consequence, required skills such as critical thinking and multi-perspective representation of contents questioned the dominance of monocausal explanations, authoritative texts and rote learning. Furthermore, the concept of homogenous and quasi-given nation states could no longer be upheld under these conditions.

However, reform measures were delayed in countries that had achieved sovereignty after forceful (civil) wars, amongst them foremost those states emerging from former Yugoslavia, with the exception of Slovenia, which quickly recovered from a short war.[7]

In Slovenia, engaged teachers and scholars developed new history curricula and textbooks on their own initiative. National and European dimensions were well balanced and also embedded in a global context. As the population supported Slovenia's access to the EU, this professional and civil society-based initiative could be implemented without meeting resistance from ministries or the public. Later revisions under the guidance of the Ministry of Education did not alter the European orientation.[8] In Serbia, in contrast, the relation to Europe remained and still is problematic in view of the after-effects of the Kosovo war. According to the official point of view, shared by most textbook authors well into the first decade of the twentieth century, Serbia has tried to defend not only herself but also European integrity and culture on its borders, from the Middle Ages up to the most recent wars of the 1990s, although her contribution to Europe has never been acknowledged by Europe. Under these circumstances education towards European consciousness could not become a curricular objective. This has not changed considerably since Serbia took up negotiations with the EU. Europe does not represent the smallest common denominator; it is the object of competition between Serbia and her neighbour states. They all want to become members of the EU but they do not want to share Europe with each other. Religion, language and nation bear exclusive identity connotations, and these are stressed in curricula and textbooks. Authors of history textbooks in Serbia, Croatia, Bosnia and Herzegovina, Macedonia and Kosovo who try to deviate from an ethno-cultural national approach trigger public debates and run the risk that their books will be withdrawn from the market.

Between 'Essentialism' and 'Realism' – Europe in the West

In stark contrast to the states and regions formerly under Soviet domination, Europe was already a well-established dimension in the teaching of history and civics in the 'West' of Europe in addition to the still dominant national dimension and a peripheral global perspective. The historical foundations of Europe in Greek–Roman tradition, cultural achievements since the Middle Ages, economic advancement, expansion in Early Modern times and political reforms since the French Revolution were all emphasized. They were presented as civilizational achievements although the costs of many of these processes, and the power with which they were enforced on people, were critically evaluated. German, Italian, French and partly Swiss history and geography textbooks displayed an essentialist approach defining European characteristics, which have constituted European commonalities over centuries.[9] The European Economic Community had mainly been seen as an institution for economic cooperation founded in order to overcome European weakness as a result of the Second World War. Only with its transformation into the EU did the institutionalized Europe establish a firm link to the European politico-cultural heritage. Besides their emphatic, essentialist approach to Europe, Italian history textbooks stood out through an almost worldwide perspective when dealing with contemporary history. More than most textbooks of other European countries, they devoted chapters to continents other than Europe, and did not only concentrate on the big powers such as the United States, China and Japan.

The definition of European characteristics led to a problematic binary concept of inclusion and exclusion. French history curricula of the 1990s called 'liberal democracy' a 'European value', which stands in opposition to the forms of totalitarianism that shaped twentieth-century European history. The question of why Europe produced totalitarian systems has remained unanswered since they are principally regarded as 'non-European'.

Europe was not only conceived as a formative past. It was also understood as a project based on current politico-economic realities, which offer the promise of a bright future of social security, economic prosperity and, last but not least, a peaceful living together of peoples with different national affiliations.[10] Textbooks of the 1980s had shown the first signs of such a positively connoted future dimension based on current economic strength and anchored in rich cultural traditions. With the break-down of the Iron Curtain, the dream could become true. The opening of the Berlin Wall became the symbol of this new Europe of freedom and democracy. Photographs showing young people dancing on the wall were shown in textbooks across Europe, often in prominent places such as on the cover.[11] Together with the authors' texts they transmitted the strong message that Europe was departing to a community of political participation, social justice and recoverable human rights. Faas and O'Connor in their study about Irish curricula conclude: '[I]ndeed, the European narrative is constructed so that EU citizenship and European identity are associated with approved values . . . that are portrayed as triumphant'.[12] In this context, it should be noted that Europe – the EU and partly also the Council of Europe, the European Parliament and other European institutions – is often an obligatory topic in civics curricula,[13] and is treated in separate chapters in civic textbooks.

For a long time, some European countries – often small in size or population – have found a more pragmatic approach to European interrelatedness, on which they feel more dependent than the big politico-economic powers. History and geography lessons emphasize the political, economic and cultural relations with other European countries, and deal less with 'Europe as such' and European characteristics. This applies, for example, to the Nordic countries and the Netherlands. According to the Finnish curriculum of 2004, the teaching of political rights and participation – including European aspects – is part of civic education. History lessons should develop an understanding of the historical conditions that led to European integration and European citizenship rights. As the consumer and mass media societies grew in parallel with economic and political integration, they are also dealt with in history textbooks. In this way, Finnish identity reflects different layers, being part of Nordic as well as European culture. Nation and Europe do not form opposite poles; they complement each other. The social studies curriculum strives to develop 'cultural literacy' revolving around the individual who 'reads' or recognizes his/her social community, is confronted with multicultural encounters and learns about international relations. This pluralistic identity concept includes the individual, national, European and international dimension, starting with the first ones but not prioritizing them theoretically or ideologically over the latter.[14]

Also, the curriculum for the upper secondary level opts for open identity concepts referring to some basic deliberations on the philosophy of history. The 2004 history curriculum stated – in contrast to essentialist positions – that the past does not determine the future but it sets the frame for new developments. The past has its own value and weight, and cannot offer us contemporaries the pedagogy of today. Nevertheless, we can choose a certain perspective, and we derive it from our historical knowledge, moral values and political convictions such as human rights and democracy, to which we now feel committed as active and responsible citizens. It is not history but it is us, here and now, who take the decision.

In spite of the step-by-step expansion of the EU towards central and south-eastern Europe, texts, and in particular maps in geography books, denoted a core zone of economic activity representing European prosperity and well-being that stretches from England through France, the Benelux states and Germany to northern Italy and Spain. Exactly this area also accommodates the highlights of European culture as presented in history textbooks. Whereas history textbooks emphasized cultural achievements of this area, geography books visualized its economic productivity. The centre–periphery scheme, which had already characterized the representation of Europe in the Middle Ages and Early Modern times, also depicted its contemporary features.

History textbooks did and do not conceal that the path towards a Europe with open borders could not always be paved without violence. For example, in an Italian history textbook the chapter on the bloody war in Bosnia and Herzegovina follows immediately after the chapter that deals with the peaceful German reunification.[15] The closeness of an illusionary and a realistic dream of freedom in the textbook narrative represents European contradictions.

However, Europe as an argument in conflict narratives can take on a Janus-face. The Greek-Cypriot Ministry of Education abused 'Europeanness' as an argument to strengthen the Greek cultural traits of Cyprus in past and present against cultural claims of the Turkish-Cypriot community. Ministerial guidelines contended that Cyprus had been shaped by ancient Greek and Christian culture until the advent of the British, and so represents European values and traditions, whereas the population of Turkish origin and Islamic faith is quasi-automatically characterized as foreign or even an adversary to European culture. Philippou summarizes: '[R]eferences to Europe did not occur to teach about Europe as such, but to teach about the [Greek-Cypriot] nation *via* Europe'.[16] In contrast, the new curriculum of Northern Ireland fosters a European orientation in order to offer a way out of the internal conflict. '"Europe" seemed to be a tool to move away from racism and sectarianism'.[17] It does not – like in Cyprus – position the nation within the conflict but provides a dimension to overcome it.

Greek history textbooks transmitted an ambivalent image of Europe. On the one hand, Greece was depicted as the founder of European civilization, while on the other hand, due to its orthodox tradition and as part of the Ottoman Empire until the nineteenth century, it was somewhat detached from 'Western' European culture and economic development. The presentation of the nineteenth and twentieth centuries concentrated heavily on Greek national history, to which the process of European integration was only an annex.[18] The latter did not become – as in most of the 'West' European books – the framework in which the national histories are increasingly embedded.

Also, the development in England omits most of the continental European features. The English National Curriculum for lower secondary classes (key stage 3) concentrated on British history, with only one unit titled 'World Studies after 1900'. No unit was expressly devoted to Europe as a separate topic.[19] As far as textbook authors related British history to Europe, they took a fact-oriented and sceptical approach. They put emphasis on the economic sector and were reluctant to eulogize achievements of political cooperation. The presentation of Europe lacked a historical dimension and was, if at all, characterized by day-to-day culture such as travel and food. The question some authors posed to the pupils reads as if being addressed to the authors themselves: What are the pros and cons of a British membership of the European Union?[20]

Textbooks and curricula have a life span of five to ten years, being moulded by changing governments and adjusted to new political and economic developments. The trends described above have imprinted curricular and textbook developments until well into the twenty-first century. After an initial phase of widespread enthusiasm and an overall positive representation of Europe, the financial crisis of 2007 led to increasing European scepticism, which – for the time being – has peaked in but might not end with the United Kingdom leaving the European Union.

Entangled Histories: Europe, a Net of Relations – an Intersection of National Affiliations and International Aspirations

The European landscape in history textbooks remains shaped by different developmental streams in different regions and countries. One observation may be of general significance although a European-wide comparative enquiry has not existed for the last ten years or so. Taking trendsetters into account, such as Germany, France and Italy, it can be said that the emphatic, essentialist mode of presentation has not expanded but has rather given way to a more sober narrative, which enfolds the increasing complexity of the EU. For example, Blanc has made the revealing observation that French history and geography textbooks occasionally used an explicit 'we' to denote an identity-related affiliation to one's own nation, but only until the early 1990s. After this time, only implicit identification indicators could be found.[21] In this regard, a German upper secondary history textbook stands out. Dealing with the 'Kaiserreich', it defines 'nation' and 'nationalism' as shared instances of giving meaning and legitimation to political action. National feelings would consolidate inner cohesion but they could also be overstated and serve as a substitute for religion. In a later chapter devoted to German history after 1945, the authors pose the question of whether Europe has become part of the identity of its citizens. They do not answer the question because to answer it, they state, one has to know what Europe actually is: 'This is fiercely discussed in Europe and the result is open'.[22] A shorter and more traditional French geography textbook defines 'national culture' as 'the product of history, customs and collective experiences . . . characterized by the practice of language, religion and attachment to a common past . . . Nowadays, Europeans refer first of all to that national culture when defining themselves'.[23]

McKay and Vaupel have observed the trend to a more rational approach in the revised 2007 curriculum of Northern Ireland. Whereas the previous curriculum had dealt with the European dimension in the traditional way, 'to strengthen affective ties to an imagined community knitted together by ethno-cultural, political and economic bonds, this ethno-cultural paradigm . . . is less evident in the revised curriculum, where a more civic-based vision of Citizenship Education appears to have emerged'.[24]

A multilayered approach to collective identity is explicitly built into the Swedish curriculum for upper secondary schools: it should 'encompass Swedish, Nordic, European and global values'.[25] Also, the multilayered internal structure of Swedish society is acknowledged. The description of migrations and mixed societies has become less problem-centred than it was in the past, and is now more value-oriented. 'That contemporary society is "diverse" is a clear starting point', summarize Soysal and Szakács in their overview of European textbooks. Values such as 'respect for the other' and 'tolerance', 'while connected to different national institutions and contexts, are nevertheless embedded in universalistic principles and projected to European and world levels'.[26] Still, there are exceptions to this rule, which transmit a critical undertone or circumvent the topic, such as the Greek social studies curricula[27] and textbooks.

The English National Curriculum of 2007 no longer prescribed specific content units but a range of content issues divided into two categories: 'British history' and 'European and World history'. English textbook authors use the extended freedom in selecting content to prioritize the global dimension when dealing with topics such as immigration, multiculturalism and religious diversity, and they place Europe even more at the rim than in the former curriculum: 'These textbooks [meant for the category 'European and World History'] seem to make an effort to connect Britain more with the world, and thus there are new themes such as Arab civilization, Chinese culture, Jewish and Black communities. With this effort to open up to the world, Europe seems to receive even less attention than it did in the previous textbooks'.[28] One of the books following the 2007 curriculum poses an identity-related question to the pupils. Interestingly, the question serves to stabilize national identity, which seems to be shattered by the impact of 'foreignness'. Pupils are asked: 'What does it mean to be British today?' and to 'explore the idea of Britishness'.[29]

In the East, the often long processes of adjustment to EU market rules disappointed hopes for a quick recovery after the breakdown of the socialist system. It depends to a considerable extent on the determination of the governments, on their will to innovate and accept change, and on whether a positive, future-oriented image of Europe is conceived in textbooks and curricula or whether sceptical undertones prevail, keeping at distance 'Europeanism' and holding on to national values instead. Even neighbouring countries may choose different paths in this regard. Estonia, for example, stands for the first way. The Ministry of Education fosters the development of European awareness in order to support the country's integration into the European Union. This goes hand in hand with methodological innovations, which help to develop critical thinking and to cope with diversity.[30] In contrast, the Latvian government is still afraid of too open an approach to Europe and feels national values are being endangered, not least with a view to the country's minority problem.[31] Slovakia seems to go a middle way, stressing the country's dependence on Europe and its belonging to European culture but neglecting or even rejecting global influences: 'It is a fact that no country and no people outside Europe are dealt with in our secondary history textbooks as carriers of cultural value', states Vajda.[32]

The Polish curriculum has reflected a similar dichotomy since reforms started in the 1990s. Broadly speaking, it discerns five dimensions of history – the global, European, national, regional and individual – with upper secondary classes putting more weight on international, European and global issues. Yet, history curricula define 'Fatherland' and 'Polish heritage' as leading categories for developing pupils' historical consciousness. As a consequence, the chronologically structured narrative concentrates on political, fact-oriented Polish history without neglecting the European and international dimension. However, a concept of European citizenship does not emerge. Pupils learn about the Polish citizen who forms part of European culture and contributes to shaping it. Further reforms since 2010 have aimed at reducing the significance of history in upper secondary classes, which has met with public protest, so obligatory courses in Polish history have been reintegrated into the curriculum.[33]

Bode found in his research about the presentation of the Second World War in school atlases that national patterns of commemoration even inform the space concept as represented in maps depicting the Nazi annihilation policy. German atlases choose a European perspective, with a great number of entries throughout the area of Nazi domination. Maps in Bulgarian, Romanian and Hungarian atlases have only a few entries in restricted areas. Bode speaks of a distanced perspective, which depicts the space of the Holocaust as just a small part of the war theatre. Thus, the atlases reflect the hesitant and reserved coping with the issues of genocide, collaboration and resistance in these countries.[34] In general, atlases of northern, western and southern European countries include maps showing the European space or even the whole globe, whereas national perspectives prevail in atlases of eastern, central and south-eastern Europe.[35]

In the first decade of the twenty-first century, some countries who had favoured a European or even global approach to history were confronted with a backlash, partly induced by conservative politicians and educationalists, and partly supported by parents' organizations and the general public. Dutch history textbooks had given priority to the European and international dimension.[36] However, the new political conservative stream accompanied by xenophobic language led to a critical debate about there being too much internationalism and too little patriotism and national awareness in history education. A canon of compulsory topics was introduced into the curriculum in order to restrict the freedom of textbook authors, who had been suspected of choosing almost arbitrarily too broad a spectrum of contents. The canon favoured – as usual – their own national history over European or world perspectives.[37] A similar debate broke out in Italy on a proposal for a new history curriculum speaking out for a thematic and world-oriented approach. With the advent of the Berlusconi government, the proposal was rejected, and a curriculum that stressed national history and European traditions was implemented. The definition of the overall learning objectives had the aim of balancing out two almost opposite poles: the 'living together' in a globalizing, multicultural world (*convivenza civile*) as a cross-cutting teaching aim in the social studies, and emphasis on nation, Christendom and Christian values as the historical ground on which to base the multicultural orientation.[38] Clearly, these curricular claims were the result of a political compromise and not of historical analysis. However, this conservative approach did not survive the next change of the government. At the end of the struggle a curriculum was introduced in 2012 that mostly went back to the state of affairs as it was before the debate broke out. The curriculum remained Eurocentric in content but abstained from an expressly essentialist language of identification.[39]

Although the Greek curriculum of 2003 has noticeably more references to Europe and follows a more practice-oriented and civic approach than the former one, the Education Ministry felt obliged to emphasize that 'the development of European citizens' awareness' should go hand in hand with the 'preservation of our national identity and our cultural self-knowledge'.[40]

A new curricular development in Switzerland points in the opposite direction. Responsibility for education lies with the cantons. The language of instruction is either German, French or Italian. Correspondingly, the curricula focused on regional and national issues in the past but they have undergone remarkable modernization of methodology and contents in the last decades, influenced by developments in the neighbouring countries Germany and France, and by closer ties Switzerland established with the EU. The new curriculum for the French-speaking cantons ('Plan d'Etudes Romand'), and a corresponding one for the German-speaking cantons, strive partly to establish common standards and so to overcome the language barriers in education. Concerning history, the curriculum favours the concept of 'entangled history',[41] (*histoire croiseê*) emphasizing interrelatedness and interactions on all levels such as local, national, European and global.[42]

Taking most recent curricular changes into account, the Swiss example may signal a new trend. Europe as a cultural, economic and political entity is more and more seen in relation to global developments. The concept of entangled history is particularly applied in French upper secondary textbooks.[43] Already the title of a book on the Middle Ages and Early Modern times sets Europe in a worldwide context: 'The Europeans in World History'.[44] This book chooses a strong social history-oriented approach and builds bridges between ancient and modern times, for example through chapters dealing with 'The Europeans as Part of World Population' and 'The European Population since Ancient Time'. Already the chapter on Ancient History bears a modern title: 'The Invention of Citizenship in the Ancient World'. A sober, informative style replacing former emphatic language describes patterns of economic, social and cultural life typical for larger regions rather than individual states. Here, the social history approach has downgraded political periodization, which traditionally structured history textbooks, to a second order element of the narrative. This result is visualized through the maps – 28 per cent of them show the European space and 22 per cent are world maps or designating the territory of a nation (mostly France), and the rest is devoted to regional aspects. Categorized according to geographical, political and socio-cultural-economic topics, almost half of the maps deal with the last area of topics.

The methodological paradigm of competence- and skill-based learning and the historiographic model of interrelatedness (entangled history) lead to more tasks, questions and references that should enable students to make links across periods and topics. This approach strengthens the concept of European heritage. Thus, a recent German history book concludes the chapter on Ancient Greece with a paragraph titled 'What did the Greek people pass on to us?', mentioning foremost 'democracy' and explaining that 'the constitution of the USA was imprinted by this idea, as was the basic law of the Federal Republic of Germany'.[45] Similarly, the chapter on Ancient Rome finishes with the question 'What is part of the Roman heritage?', and lists the Christian church, influence on the development of European languages, the calendar, and Roman law and script.[46] The latest edition of this series refers more often to Europe than former ones. The European perspective can even take on a universal value orientation when, for example, the treatment of human rights in the French Revolution is followed by a paragraph on 'human rights worldwide' dealing with the UN Charter of 1948 and the violation of human rights today. The chapter titled 'The Heritage of the French Revolution: Which Issues still Have an Impact Today?' is illustrated by a photograph showing demonstrations in Tahir Square in Cairo in 2011.[47]

Chapters comparing European and extra-European features and developments have increased in particular in textbooks for secondary education. The significance of Islam and Islamic countries and culture, and their relation to Europe, have contributed to setting Europe in perspective relative to the outside world. Here again, the European approach is often used to extend it to a global or universal perspective.[48]

In view of the multiplicity of methodological approaches and content dimensions, as well as the lack of explicit markers of collective identities in many textbooks of some EU member states, the paradigm of a history textbook as a 'national autobiography'[49] can only be applied with caveats. Today's textbook authors can no longer be supposed to necessarily follow a strategy 'to produce national, religious and European identity through interpretative reconstruction of historical facts and to bring all facets of identity in a coherent national self-image', as Christophe claims.[50] Such an approach fails to recognize the diversity and often even inconsistencies and incoherent structural patterns of a modern textbook. Direct references to fostering European awareness and identity are more often found in curricula than in textbooks. Curricula, as a rule, are more influenced by current governmental politics than textbooks.

Public Perception of Europe and the Changing Role of Textbooks as Challenges to Teaching European History

Nations and states appear to be clearly defined: they comprise a certain space and population. Even if a nation state's territory was divided or partly annexed by other powers, the former borders are often nevertheless delineated on maps to visualize the claim to a still existent, undividable national territory, as can be seen in Polish textbooks, for example.[51] Europe is less clearly defined. Its political (institutional), cultural and economic borders overlap but do not concur, and are less obviously fixed and stable.

According to a Eurobarometer survey of 2006, 86 per cent of the interviewees in EU member states would accept Switzerland and Norway as new members although their population did not want to enter the EU. In contrast, an overwhelming majority spoke out against membership of south-east European countries such as Romania, Bulgaria and Serbia, which had already been accepted as new members or wanted to become members. Turkey got the lowest number of positive votes, with only 34 per cent. It is interesting that the patterns of peoples' politico-cultural awareness vary widely between EU member states. In Sweden, a majority of 71 per cent voted for accepting south-east European states, whereas Austria showed the lowest ranking in this regard with only 16 per cent.[52] The Swedish government's long-term immigration policy had obviously induced a change in the image of 'otherness', whereas Austrians feared alterations to their still mostly homogenous population through immigration from countries that Austrians regard as economically weak and culturally different, despite being geographically close. Swedish textbooks (similar to the British ones) have integrated migrants in texts and illustrations as normal features of society. They differ in this regard from the problem-oriented depiction of migrants, which is still the dominant approach to the topic in most European civics and history textbooks.[53]

In sum, the evaluation of the EU in the minds of the people has deteriorated dramatically since the financial crisis. After a positive evaluation had peaked in spring 2007, with 52 per cent of the interviewees answering that they had a positive image of the EU, this figure went steadily down to 30 per cent in the years 2011 and 2012, and was at 37 per cent in autumn 2015, being on par with those interviewees who have a neutral (neither positive nor negative) image. The percentage of EU citizens with a negative image increased from 15 per cent in 2007 to 23 per cent in 2015.[54] Interestingly, and in contrast to the time before the crisis, interviewees from the old member states such as Germany, France, the Netherlands and Italy have a more negative image than the EU average, whereas interviewees from central and east European countries still set hope in EU membership and are less sceptical. With the exception of Italy, a vast majority of them speak out against any further enlargement of the EU. They obviously fear that new members could further endanger the economic and political stability of the EU.[55]

Although young people accept multiple identities, the overall majority of them still regard the nation as the main reference point of political identification.[56] The nation is the first concept of an abstract collective identity that pupils are already familiar with when they enter school and when they start to broaden their notion of collective relationship, which had been bound to personal encounters in the first years of their life. This 'natural' concept also imprints their first notion of the nation, which seems to be a given and quasi-eternal. National consciousness is fed by feelings of mutual social attraction, acceptance and cultural similarity. Although these feelings are widely imagined and less anchored in the social and cultural realities of a society, they inform public historical consciousness, national awareness and textbooks. Europe, in contrast, is an artificial construction built by politicians. The concept of Europe requires the ability of abstract thinking. Based on classroom observation in France, Throssell concludes that being a European 'does not refer to a [clearly defined] collective' and 'feeds on knowledge rather than experience and imagination'.[57] With reference to social identity theory, Medrano contends that most respondents in interviews do not feel emotionally attached to Europe because they cannot develop positive feelings for it. Europe is foremost a rational, utilitarian concept, and less an object of socio-cultural identification.[58] Nevertheless, surveys and interviews also show that a rational, argumentative approach to Europe is positively correlated with the level of education. Therefore, a nuanced presentation of European tradition and current developments in school textbooks could contribute to a better European understanding – even if only on a cognitive level.[59]

Wittingly or unwittingly, the standardization and formalization of school examinations across Europe support the fixation on national themes. National topics are regarded as being of higher interest for pupils because they are more often connected to significant public political and historiographic debates than European issues. In addition, the Europe-wide trend towards competency-based curricula may also support the emphasis on the national dimension. Since the stress is no longer laid on content issues that must be covered and should be known by pupils, but on methods of enquiry, teachers tend to choose issues for examinations pertaining to one's own national history, as pupils are expected to have most detailed knowledge in this area.

Against this background, initiatives to develop alternative curricular approaches have a difficult standing. Several projects to produce a 'European history textbook' have failed or their results could not find their way into classroom teaching in any significant quantity.[60] Authors could not find a convincing strategy to integrate the national dimension into a European narrative without either playing down the significance of nation states too much or overstating it.

Partly more successful seem to be history textbooks that – as the first step to a European consciousness – bring together two national histories in order to emphasize each other's relations as well as to overcome long-existing adversary images and stereotypes between nation states that look back to a conflict-ridden history. The prime example is the Franco-German history textbook, which has been written by a Franco-German team of authors. It appeared with identical contents in the two languages and is meant for regular use in history classes of both countries. Although the development of the book was supported by an agreement between the two governments, the initiative came from a meeting organized by the German–French Youth Exchange Service.[61] As a matter of fact, such a book is still based on a national approach to history. However, the German–French relations serve as an example for a basically European conception. The book is not restricted to German and French history but comprises the entire history curricula of both countries, including extra-European and global themes. The most important advancement may be that it proves that school history textbooks can be written by international teams with the explicit objective of giving a voice to authors from the 'other' side. This is still unheard of in many European regions, and unthinkable, for the time being, in Bosnia and Herzegovina and its neighbouring states. Nevertheless, the book has already had an impact reaching beyond France and Germany. University historians and teachers from China, South Korea and Japan took it as an example to develop teaching materials on contested issues of contemporary North East Asian history. To this aim, the book has been translated into the Korean and Japanese languages. Furthermore, a German–Polish team has published the first volume of the German–Polish history textbook, developed with the support of the German Georg-Eckert Institute for International Textbook Research and the Polish Ministry of Education. The first volume addresses a time span from the Stone Age to the Middle Ages under the title 'Europe: Our History', so indicating that it claims to be much more than a binational teaching aid.[62]

Continuous and intensive relations between academic historians and history teachers of both sides, as well as mutual textbook consultations over decades, have paved the way for the production of these textbooks. Even more important may have been the fact that the conflicts between Germany on one side and Poland and France on the other, have been politically settled. In regions of still open conflicts with occurrences of violence, governments hardly feel in a position to back such initiatives. A project launched by the Council of Europe failed to jointly produce a history book for the Caucasus region.[63]

The Internet offers new approaches to make obvious the interrelatedness and commonalities as well as the differences between historical experiences and interpretations across Europe. The Georg-Eckert Institute has launched a portal that makes available images of Europe as presented in textbooks of the twentieth century. Users can compare the different foci and interpretations of the same event, personality or period of history. In this way, a comparative approach to national narratives avoids the monopolization of interpretation, and makes visible any biased interpretations. Pupils are confronted with the multiplicity and variability of perceptions of Europe across regions and time periods without being offered a new master narrative. They can relate their own perceptions of Europe to past views and current perspectives, and can thus clarify and revise their images of Europe, and develop a more profound notion of them.[64]

Falk Pingel is an associate research fellow at the Georg Eckert Institute for International Textbook Research in Brunswick, Germany. He was previously the institute's deputy director for many years. He has been involved in textbook research and revision, dealing with the presentation of conflicting identities, for example in South Africa, the Middle East and East Asia. In 2003/4, he was the first director of the OSCE's education department in Sarajevo, Bosnia and Herzegovina. He also taught contemporary history, as well as theory and didactics of history, at Bielefeld University. He acts as a consultant on issues of textbook and curriculum research and revision to governmental and academic institutions.

Notes

1. M. Wiatr, 'Grenzräume neu vermessen: Multiethnische Raum-Perspektiven in polnischen Schulbüchern' [To survey border areas anew: Multi-ethnic space perspectives in Polish textbooks], *Geschichte in Wissenschaft und Unterricht* 64 (1/2) (2013), 46–60.

2. The terms 'West' and 'East' are used here in a political sense denoting countries in the former West or East European bloc respectively. 'Eastern' and 'western' are used when referring to geographical regions.

3. For a detailed overview, see F. Pingel (ed.), *Insegnare l'Europa: Concetti e rappresentazioni nei libri di testo europei* (Turin: Edizione Fondazione Agnelli, 2003); P.D. Xochellis and F.I. Toloudi (eds), *The Image of the 'Other'/Neighbour in the School Textbooks of the Balkan Countries* (Athens: Dardanos, 2001); F. Pingel, *The European Home: Representations of 20th Century Europe in History Textbooks* (Strasbourg: Council of Europe, 2000).

4. V. Kaplan, 'Alla ricerca di un cammino verso l'Europo: la dimensione europea nei testi di storia del XX secolo della Russia', in Pingel, *Insegnare l'Europa*, 369–400; V. Kaplan, 'The Reform of Education in Russia and the Problem of History Teaching', *Education in Russia, the Independent States and Eastern Europe* 17(1) (1999), 3–19.

5. L. Wolff, *Inventing Eastern Europe: The Map of Civilization on the Mind of the Enlightenment* (Stanford, CA: Stanford University Press, 2000).

6. E. Erdmann and W. Hasberg, 'Bologna – a European or a Global Task? Introduction', in E. Erdmann and W. Hasberg (eds), *History Teacher Education: Global Interrelations* (Schwalbach/Ts: Wochenschau, 2015), 5–10.

7. A. Dimou (ed.) '*Transition' and the Politics of History Education in Southeastern Europe* (Göttingen: Vandenhoeck & Ruprecht, 2009).

8. S. Jazbec, 'Zur europäischen Dimension in den slowenischen Lehrplänen', in R. Seebauer (ed.), *Europäische Dimensionen in der Bildungsarbeit: Intensiv-Programm EURIDENT* (Vienna: LIT, 2010), 77–85.

9. Pingel, *Insegnare l'Europa*; E. Kotte, *In Räume geschriebene Zeiten: Nationale Europabilder im Geschichtsunterricht der Sekundarstufe II* (Idstein: Schulz-Kirchner, 2007); A. Blanc, 'Emergence of the European Union in Upper Secondary Education: A Comparative Analysis of French, English, German and Catalonian History Textbooks', in S. Abendschön (ed.), *Growing into Politics: Contexts and Timing of Political Socialisation* (Colchester: ECPR Press and University of Exeter, 2013), 115–38.

10. W. Hasberg, 'Auf nach Europa? Die europäische Dimension in europäischen Richtlinien und Lehrplänen', in C. Kühberger and C. Sedmark (eds), *Europäische Geschichtskultur – europäische Geschichtspolitik: vom Erfinden, Entdecken, Erarbeiten der Bedeutung von Erinnerung und Geschichte für das Verständnis und Selbstverständnis Europas* (Innsbruck: Studien, 2009).

11. S. Popp, 'Europaweite Konvergenzen in nationalen Lehrwerken für den Geschichtsunterricht?: ein Zugang über den Vergleich von Bildquellen im Schulbuch', *Bildung und Erziehung* 64(1) (2011), 39–52.

12. D. Faas and L. O'Connor, 'Constructions of "Europe", Identity and Citizenship in Post-primary Social Studies Curricula in the Republic of Ireland', in S. Philippou, *'Europe' Turned Local – the Local Turned European?: Constructions of 'Europe' in Social Studies Curricula across Europe* (Münster: LIT, 2012), 186.

13. As an example, see S. Kary and O. Mentz, 'Is "Europe" Getting Lost in German Competence-Oriented Curricula? The Case of Baden-Wurttemberg', in Philippou, *'Europe' Turned Local*, 24–53.

14. A. Virta, 'Recent Developments in History Teaching in Finland', in E. Erdmann, R. Maier and S. Popp (eds), *Geschichtsunterricht international / Worldwide Teaching of History* (Hannover: Hahnsche Buchhandlung, 2006), 323–36.

15. G. Ghiozzi and A. Ruata Pazza, *Tutto Storia 3. Il Novecento* (Turin: Perini editore, 1999).

16. S. Philippou, '"Europe" Turned Local – the Local Turned European? A Discussion of Curricular Issues and Challenges', in Philippou, *'Europe' Turned Local*, 267.

17. Ibid., 285; Faas and O'Connor, 'Constructions of "Europe"'.

18. G. Kokkinos and P. Gatsiotis, 'The Deviation from the Norm: Greek History School Textbooks Withdrawn from Use in Classroom since 1980', *Internationale Schulbuchforschung / International Textbook Research* 30 (2008), 535–46; P. Papoulia-Tzelepi and J.A. Spinthourakis, 'History Teaching and the Educated Citizen: The Case of History Teaching in the Greek Gymnasium', in L. Cajani and A. Ross (eds), *History Teaching, Identities, Citizenship* (Sterling, VA: Trentham Books, 2007), 77–94.

19. Hasberg, 'Auf nach Europa'; E. Karayianni, 'The Place of Europe in English History Textbooks', in N. Mazeikiene, M. Horsley and S.V. Knudsen (eds), *Representations of Otherness. The Eleventh International Conference on Research on Textbooks and Educational Media, September 2011. Kaunas, Lithuania* (IARTEM, 2011), 59–68.

20. Blanc, 'Emergence of the European Union', 133–34.

21. A. Blanc, 'Intégration européenne et évolution du concept de l'état: Réflexion à partir des manuels de l'enseignemnt scolaire de differents pays de l'Union Européenne'. Thesis. (Marseille: Université Paul Cézanne Aix-Marseille III, 2011), 364.

22. *Kursbuch Geschichte. Qualifikation NRW* (Berlin: Cornelsen, 2015), 272–73 and 443.

23. A. Joyeux (ed.), *Géographie* (Paris: Hachette), 24, quoted by Blanc, 'Emergence of the European Union', 128.

24. T. McKay and A. Vaupel, 'The Place of the European Dimension in Post-primary Curricula of Northern Ireland', in Philippou, *'Europe' Turned Local*, 132.

25. L. Niklasson, 'Becoming European: Do National Curricula and Syllabi in Sweden Support Europeanisation?', in Philippou, *'Europe' Turned Local*, 209. These four dimensions are also present in the revised civics curriculum of 2011.

26. Y.N. Soysal and S. Szakács, 'Projections of "Diversity" in Citizenship Education', in C. Hintermann and C. Johansson (eds), *Migration and Memory: Representations of Migration in Europe since 1960* (Innsbruck: Studien, 2010), 88.

27. A. Klonari, '"Europe" in the Secondary School Curricula of Greece', in Philippou, *'Europe' Turned Local*, 161ff.

28. Karayianni, 'The Place of Europe', 63.

29. Ibid. Concerning the significance of the term 'Britishness' in British identity politics, see K. Lunn, 'Reconsidering "Britishness": The Construction and Significance of National Identity in Twentieth-Century Britain', in B. Jenkins (ed.), *Nation and Identity in Contemporary Europe* (London: Routledge, 1996), 83.

30. M. Oja, 'Local, National and Global Level in History Teaching in Estonia', *International Journal of Research on History Didactics* 37 (2016), 119–38.

31. K. Kello and W. Wagner, 'History Teaching as "Propaganda"? Teachers' Communication Styles in Post-transition Societies', in C. Psaltis, M. Carretero and S. Cehajic-Clancyc (eds), *History Education and Conflict Transformation: Social Psychological Theories, History Teaching and Reconciliation* (London: Palgrave Macmillan, 2017), 201–30.

32. B. Vajda, 'On the Global – National – Regional – Local Layers of Slovak Secondary School History Textbooks', *International Journal of Research on History Didactics* 37 (2016), 147.

33. A. Zieliński, 'Geschichtsunterricht in der Republik Polen', in Erdmann, Maier and Popp, *Geschichtsunterricht international*, 357–74; J. Brynkus and P. Trojański, 'Historical Education – Historical Culture – History Didactics in Poland', in E. Erdmann and W. Hasberg (eds), *Facing – Mapping – Bridging Diversity: Foundation of a European Discourse on History Education* (Schwalbach/Ts: Wochenschau, 2011), 142ff.

34. S. Bode, *Die Kartierung der Extreme: Die Darstellung der Zeit der Weltkriege (1914–1945) in aktuellen europäischen Geschichtsatlanten* (Göttingen: V&R unipress, 2015), 357.

35. Ibid., 447.

36. Pingel, *European Home*.

37. K. Wils, 'Dilemmas Galore: History Teaching in Flanders and the Netherlands', in Erdmann, Maier and Popp, *Geschichtsunterricht international*, 337–48; M. Grever, 'Plurality, Narrative and the Historical Canon', in M. Grever and S. Stuurman (eds), *Beyond the Canon: History for the Twenty-First Century* (Basingstoke: Palgrave Macmillan, 2007), 31–47.

38. The Italian history journal *Mundus* 1 (2008) reflects this debate.

39. L. Cajani, 'History Didactics in Italy', in Erdmann and Hasberg, *Facing – Mapping – Bridging Diversity*, 5–30; L. Cajani, 'Nationalism, Europeanism, Cosmopolitanism: Layers of Identity in Italian History Teaching', in Second Series of Meetings of the International Research Association for History and Social Sciences Education. 'Layers of Identities'. Proceedings (Athens: The National and Capodistrian University of Athens, 2016), 13–20.

40. Ibid., 161.

41. A. Ichijo and W. Spohn, *Entangled Identities: Nation and Europe* (Aldershot: Ashgate, 2005).

42. N. Fink, 'Usages du passé et redéfinitions identitaires: Réflexion à propos du nouveau plan d'études en Suisse romande', in Second Series of Meetings of the International Research Association for History and Social Sciences Education. 'Layers of Identities'. Proceedings (Athens: The National and Capodistrian University of Athens, 2016), 61–72.

43. See, for example, the chapters 'How Industrialisation Accelerated Economic Entanglement and Globalization [in French: *mondialisation*]' and 'World Wars and Hopes for Peace', the latter displaying maps of the European and the Asian theatre of war, in *Histoire 1re. Questions pour comprendre le XXe siècle, ES/L/S* (Paris: Hachette, 2015).

44. *Histoire* 2de. *Les Européennes dans l'histoire du monde* (Paris: Hachette, 2014).

45. *Entdecken und verstehen: Geschichte Nordrhein-Westfalen, differenzierende Ausgabe* (Berlin: Cornelsen Schulbuchverlage, 2015), 110.

46. Ibid., 162.

47. Ibid., 132.

48. See, for example, the chapters 'Experiencing "Otherness" in a Worldwide Historical Perspective', 'Images of the Globe in Europe and Asia', 'Self-image and Image of the Other in Early Modern Times', 'The Islamic World and Europe', 'Turkey, a Part of Europe?' and 'Human Rights in Historical Perspective', in *Kursbuch Geschichte. Nordrhein-Westfalen. Einführungsphase* [Course-book history. North-Rhine Westphalia. Introductory phase] (Berlin: Cornelsen Schulbuchverlage, 2014).

49. W. Jacobmeyer, 'Das Schulgeschichtsbuch – Gedächtnis der Gesellschaft oder Autobiographie der Nation' [The history schoolbook – memory of the society or autobiography of the nation], *Geschichte, Politik und ihre Didaktik* 26(1) (1998), 26–34.

50. B. Christophe, 'Religiös oder modern? Nation und Europa in polnischen und türkischen Geschichtsschulbüchern' [Religious or modern? Nation and Europe in Polish and Turkish history textbooks], *Geschichte in Wissenschaft und Unterricht* 64(1/2) (2013), 66.

51. L.F. Garske, 'Geschichte als I Raum I als Geschichte: Dekonstruktion symbolischer Grenzziehungen als Methode des historischen Lernens am Beispiel polnischer und deutscher Geschichtsschulbücher' [History as I space I as history. Deconstruction of the delineation of symbolic borders as a method of historical learning, taking as an example Polish and German history textbooks], *Geschichte in Wissenschaft und Unterricht* 64(1/2) (2013) 13–29; Christophe, 'Religiös oder modern?', 77.

52. G. Ogris and S.Westphal, 'Politisches Verhalten Jugendlicher in Europa', *Aus Politik und Zeitgeschichte* 47 (2006), 7–26.

53. V. Lozic and C. Hintermann, 'Textbooks, Migration and National Narratives: An Introduction', in Hintermann and Johansson, *Migration and Memory*, 13–30.

54. European Commission, Standard Eurobarometer 84. Public Opinion in the European Union. Autumn 2015. First Results. Wave EB84.3. http://ec.europa.eu/COMMFrontOffice/publicopinion/index.cfm/ResultDoc/download/DocumentKy/70297. [accessed 15 Oct. 2016].

55. Ibid. See Annex.

56. A. Ross, *A European Education: Citizenship, Identities and Young People* (Stoke-on-Trent: Trentham, 2008).

57. K. Throssell, 'One Thing Leads to Another: European and National Identities in French School Children', *Politique européenne* 30(1) (2010), 131–52.

58. J.D. Medrano, 'Unpacking European Identity', *Politique européenne* 30(1) (2010), 45–66.

59. S. Duchesne, et al., 'Europe between Integration and Globalization: Social Differences and National Frames in the Analysis of Focus Groups Conducted in France, Francophone Belgium and the United Kingdom', *Politique européenne* 30(1) (2010), 67–105.

60. F. Pingel, 'History as a Project of the Future: The European History Textbook Debate', in K.V. Korostelina and S. Lässig (eds), *History Education and Post-conflict Reconciliation: Reconsidering Joint Textbook Projects* (London: Routledge, 2013), 155–76.

61. C. Defrance and U. Pfeil, 'Symbol or Reality? The Background, Implementation and Development of the Franco-German History Textbook', in Korostelina and Lässig, *History Education*, 52–68.

62. *Europa. Unsere Geschichte*. Vol. 1: *Von der Ur- und Frühgeschichte bis zum Mittelalter/Europa. Nasza historia*. Vol. 1: *Od prahistorii do średniowiecza* (Wiesbaden: Eduversum / Warsaw: Wydawnictwa Szkolne i Pedagigiczne, 2016).

63. K.V. Korostelina, 'The Tbilisi Initiative: The Story of an Unpublished Textbook', in Korostelina and Lässig, *History Education*, 192–208.

64. Eurviews, 'Europa im Schulbuch', http://www.eurviews.eu/nc/start.html [last accessed 11 October 2016].

Bibliography

Archival Sources

European Commission, Standard Eurobarometer 84. Public Opinion in the European Union. Autumn 2015. First Results. Wave EB84.3 http://ec.europa.eu/COMMFrontOffice/publicopinion/index.cfm/ResultDoc/download/DocumentKy/70297 [last accessed 15 October 2016].

Eurviews. 'Europa im Schulbuch'. http://www.eurviews.eu/nc/start.html [last accessed 15 October 2016].

Secondary Sources

Blanc, A. 'Intégration européenne et évolution du concept de l'état: Réflexion à partir des manuels de l'enseignemnt scolaire de differents pays de l'Union Européenne' [European integration and the evolution of the concept of state: Reflections on school textbooks of different EU countries]. Thesis. Marseille: Université Paul Cézanne Aix-Marseille III, 2011.

———. 'Emergence of the European Union in Upper Secondary Education: A Comparative Analysis of French, English, German and Catalonian History Textbooks', in S. Abendschön (ed.), *Growing into Politics: Contexts and Timing of Political Socialisation.* (Colchester: ECPR Press and University of Exeter, 2013), 115–38.

Bode, S. *Die Kartierung der Extreme: Die Darstellung der Zeit der Weltkriege (1914–1945) in aktuellen europäischen Geschichtsatlanten* [Mapping the extremes: The representation of the time of the world wars (1914–1945) in current European history atlases]. Göttingen: V&R unipress, 2015.

Brynkus, J., and P. Trojański. 'Historical Education – Historical Culture – History Didactics in Poland', in Erdmann and Hasberg, *Facing – Mapping – Bridging Diversity*, 117–48.

Cajani, L. 'History Didactics in Italy', in Erdmann and Hasberg, *Facing – Mapping – Bridging Diversity*, 5–30.

———. 'Nationalism, Europeanism, Cosmopolitanism: Layers of Identity in Italian History Teaching', in Second Series of Meetings of the International Research Association for History and Social Sciences Education. 'Layers of Identities'. Proceedings (Athens: The National and Capodistrian University of Athens, 2016), 13–20.

Christophe, B. 'Religiös oder modern? Nation und Europa in polnischen und türkischen Geschichtsschulbüchern' [Religious or modern? Nation and Europe in Polish and Turkish history textbooks]. *Geschichte in Wissenschaft und Unterricht* 64(1/2) (2013), 61–79.

Defrance, C., and U. Pfeil. 'Symbol or Reality? The Background, Implementation and Development of the Franco-German History Textbook', in K.V. Korostelina and S. Lässig, *History Education and Post-conflict Reconciliation: Reconsidering Joint Textbook Projects.* (London: Routledge, 2013), 52–68.

Dimou, A. (ed.). *'Transition' and the Politics of History Education in Southeastern Europe.* Göttingen: Vandenhoeck & Ruprecht, 2009.

Duchesne, S., et al. 'Europe between Integration and Globalization: Social Differences and National Frames in the Analysis of Focus Groups Conducted in France, Francophone Belgium and the United Kingdom'. *Politique européenne* 30(1) (2010), 67–105.

Entdecken und verstehen: Geschichte Nordrhein-Westfalen, differenzierende Ausgabe. T. Berger-v.d. Heide et al. [Discovering and understanding: History for North-Rhine Westphalia, differentiating edition]. Berlin: Cornelsen Schulbuchverlage, 2015.

Erdmann, E., and W. Hasberg (eds). *Facing – Mapping – Bridging Diversity: Foundation of a European Discourse on History Education.* Schwalbach/Ts: Wochenschau, 2011.

———. 'Bologna – a European or a Global Task? Introduction', in E. Erdmann and W. Hasberg (eds), *History Teacher Education: Global Interrelations* (Schwalbach/Ts: Wochenschau, 2015), 5–10.

Erdmann, E., R. Maier and S. Popp (eds). *Geschichtsunterricht international / Worldwide Teaching of History.* Hannover: Hahnsche Buchhandlung, 2006.

Europa: Unsere Geschichte. Vol. 1: *Von der Ur- und Frühgeschichte bis zum Mittelalter/Europa. Nasza historia.* Vol. 1: *Od prahistorii do średniowiecza.* A. Brückmann et al. [Europe. Our history. From prehistoric times to the Middle Ages]. Wiesbaden: Eduversum / Warsaw: Wydawnictwa Szkolne i Pedagigiczne, 2016.

Faas, D., and L. O'Connor. 'Constructions of "Europe", Identity and Citizenship in Postprimary Social Studies Curricula in the Republic of Ireland', in Philippou *'Europe' Turned Local*, 163–89.

Fink, N. 'Usages du passé et redéfinitions identitaires: Réflexion à propos du nouveau plan d'études en Suisse romande' [Making use of the past and redefining identity: Reflections on the new curriculum in Francophone Switzerland], in Second Series of Meetings of the International Research Association for History and Social Sciences Education. 'Layers of Identities'. Proceedings (Athens: The National and Capodistrian University of Athens, 2016), 61–72.

Garske, L.F. 'Geschichte als I Raum I als Geschichte: Dekonstruktion symbolischer Grenzziehungen als Methode des historischen Lernens am Beispiel polnischer und deutscher Geschichtsschulbücher' [History as I space I as history: Deconstruction of the delineation of symbolic borders as a method of historical learning, taking as an example Polish and German history textbooks]. *Geschichte in Wissenschaft und Unterricht* 64(1/2) (2013), 13–29.

Ghiozzi, G., and A. Ruata Pazza. *Tutto Storia 3. Il Novecento* [All history 3. The 20th century]. Turin: Perini editore, 1999.

Grever, M. 'Plurality, Narrative and the Historical Canon', in M. Grever and S. Stuurman (eds), *Beyond the Canon: History for the Twenty-First Century* (Basingstoke: Palgrave Macmillan, 2007), 31–47.

Hasberg, W. 'Auf nach Europa? Die europäische Dimension in europäischen Richtlinien und Lehrplänen' [On the way to Europe? The European dimension in European guidelines and curricula], in C. Kühberger and C. Sedmark (eds), *Europäische Geschichtskultur – europäische Geschichtspolitik: vom Erfinden, Entdecken, Erarbeiten der Bedeutung von Erinnerung und Geschichte für das Verständnis und Selbstverständnis Europas* [European historical culture – European history politics: On inventing, discovering, elaborating the significance of remembrance and history for understanding Europe] (Innsbruck: Studien, 2009), 160–85.

Hintermann, C., and C. Johansson (eds), *Migration and Memory: Representations of Migration in Europe since 1960.* Innsbruck: Studien, 2010.

Histoire 1re: Questions pour comprendre le XXe siècle, ES/L/S [History 1st: Questions to understand the 20th century, ES/L/S]. Paris: Hachette, 2015.

Histoire 2de: Les Européennes dans l'histoire du monde [History 2nd: The Europeans in world history]. Paris: Hachette, 2014.

Ichijo, A., and W. Spohn. *Entangled Identities: Nation and Europe.* Aldershot: Ashgate, 2005.

Jacobmeyer, W. 'Das Schulgeschichtsbuch: Gedächtnis der Gesellschaft oder Autobiographie der Nation' [The history schoolbook: Memory of the society or autobiography of the nation]. *Geschichte, Politik und ihre Didaktik* 26(1) (1998), 26–34.

Jazbec, S. 'Zur europäischen Dimension in den slowenischen Lehrplänen' [On the European dimension in Slovenian curricula], in R. Seebauer (ed.), *Europäische Dimensionen in der Bildungsarbeit: Intensiv-Programm EURIDENT* [European dimensions in educational work: The Intensive Programme EURIDENT] (Vienna: LIT, 2010), 77–85.

Kaplan, V. 'The Reform of Education in Russia and the Problem of History Teaching'. *Education in Russia, the Independent States and Eastern Europe* 17(1) (1999), 3–19.

———. 'Alla ricerca di un cammino verso l'Europo: la dimensione europea nei testi di storia del XX secolo della Russia' [Searching for a path to Europe: The European dimension in Russian history textbooks], in Pingel, *Insegnare l'Europa*, 369–400.

Karayianni, E. 'The Place of Europe in English History Textbooks', in N. Mazeikiene, M. Horsley and S.V. Knudsen (eds), *Representations of Otherness*. The Eleventh International Conference on Research on Textbooks and Educational Media, September 2011, Kaunas, Lithuania (IARTEM, 2011), 59–68.

Kary, S., and O. Mentz. 'Is "Europe" Getting Lost in German Competence-Oriented Curricula? The Case of Baden-Württemberg', in Philippou, *'Europe' Turned Local*, 24–53.

Kello, K., and W. Wagner. 'History Teaching as "Propaganda"? Teachers' Communication Styles in Post-transition Societies', in C. Psaltis, M. Carretero and S. Cehajic-Clancyc (eds), *History Education and Conflict Transformation. Social Psychological Theories, History Teaching and Reconciliation* (London: Palgrave Macmillan, 2017), 201–30.

Klonari, A. '"Europe" in the Secondary School Curricula of Greece', in Philippou, *'Europe' Turned Local*, 136–62.

Kokkinos, G., and P. Gatsiotis. 'The Deviation from the Norm: Greek History School Textbooks Withdrawn from Use in Classroom since 1980'. *Internationale Schulbuchforschung / International Textbook Research* 30 (2008), 535–46.

Korostelina, K.V. 'The Tbilisi Initiative: The Story of an Unpublished Textbook', in Korostelina and Lässig, *History Education*, 192–208.

Korostelina, K.V., and S. Lässig (eds), *History Education and Post-conflict Reconciliation: Reconsidering Joint Textbook Projects*. London: Routledge, 2013.

Kotte, E. *In Räume geschriebene Zeiten: Nationale Europabilder im Geschichtsunterricht der Sekundarstufe II* [Times inscribed into spaces: National images of Europe in the teaching of history in upper secondary schools]. Idstein: Schulz-Kirchner, 2007.

Kursbuch Geschichte. Nordrhein-Westfalen. Einführungsphase [Course-book history. North-Rhine Westphalia. Introductory phase]. Berlin: Cornelsen Schulbuchverlage, 2014.

Kursbuch Geschichte. Qualifikation NRW [Course-book history. Qualification NRW]. Berlin: Cornelsen, 2015.

Lozic, V., and C. Hintermann. 'Textbooks, Migration and National Narratives: An Introduction', in Hintermann and Johansson, *Migration and Memory*, 13–30.

Lunn, K. 'Reconsidering "Britishness": The Construction and Significance of National Identity in Twentieth-Century Britain', in B. Jenkins (ed.), *Nation and Identity in Contemporary Europe* (London: Routledge, 1996), 22–94.

McKay, T., and A. Vaupel. 'The Place of the European Dimension in Post-primary Curricula of Northern Ireland', in Philippou, *'Europe' Turned Local*, 109–35.

Medrano, J.D. 'Unpacking European Identity'. *Politique européenne* 30(1) (2010), 45–66.

Niklasson, L. 'Becoming European: Do National Curricula and Syllabi in Sweden Support Europeanisation?', in Philippou, *Europe' Turned Local*, 191–210.

Ogris, G., and S. Westphal. 'Politisches Verhalten Jugendlicher in Europa' [Political attitudes of young people in Europe]. *Aus Politik und Zeitgeschichte* 47 (2006), 7–26.

Oja, M. 'Local, National and Global Level in History Teaching in Estonia'. *International Journal of Research on History Didactics* 37 (2016), 119–38.

Papoulia-Tzelepi, P., and J.A. Spinthourakis. 'History Teaching and the Educated Citizen: The Case of History Teaching in the Greek Gymnasium', in L. Cajani and A. Ross (eds), *History Teaching, Identities, Citizenship* (Sterling, VA: Trentham Books, 2007), 77–94.

Philippou, S. (ed.), *'Europe' Turned Local – the Local Turned European?: Constructions of 'Europe' in Social Studies Curricula across Europe*. Münster: LIT, 2012.

———. '"Europe" Turned Local – the Local Turned European? A Discussion of Curricular Issues and Challenges', in Philippou, *'Europe' Turned Local*, 271–93.

Pingel, F. *The European Home: Representations of 20th Century Europe in History Textbooks*. Strasbourg: Council of Europe, 2000.

——— (ed.). *Insegnare l'Europa: Concettti e rappresentazioni nei libri di testo europei* [Teaching Europe: Concepts and representations in European textbooks]. Turin: Edizione Fondazione Agnelli, 2003.

———. 'History as a Project of the Future: The European History Textbook Debate', in Korostelina and Lässig, *History Education*, 155–76.

Popp, S. 'Europaweite Konvergenzen in nationalen Lehrwerken für den Geschichtsunterricht? : ein Zugang über den Vergleich von Bildquellen im Schulbuch' [Convergencies of national history textbooks across Europe?: A comparative approach to photographs in textbooks]. *Bildung und Erziehung* 64(1) (2011), 39–52.

Ross, A. *A European Education: Citizenship, Identities and Young People*. Stoke-on-Trent: Trentham, 2008.

Soysal, Y.N., and S. Szakács. 'Projections of "Diversity" in Citizenship Education', in Hintermann and Johansson, *Migration and Memory*, 79–93.

Throssell, K. 'One Thing Leads to Another: European and National Identities in French School Children. *Politique européenne* 30(1) (2010), 131–52.

Vajda, B. 'On the Global – National – Regional – Local Layers of Slovak Secondary School History Textbooks'. *International Journal of Research on History Didactics* 37 (2016), 139–52.

Virta, A. 'Recent Developments in History Teaching in Finland', in Erdmann, Maier and Popp, *Geschichtsunterricht international / Worldwide Teaching of History* (Hannover: Hahnsche Buchhandlung, 2006), 323–36.

Wiatr, M. 'Grenzräume neu vermessen: Multiethnische Raum-Perspektiven in polnischen Schulbüchern' [To survey border areas anew: Multi-ethnic space perspectives in Polish textbooks]. *Geschichte in Wissenschaft und Unterricht* 64 (1/2) (2013), 46–60.

Wils, K. 'Dilemmas Galore: History Teaching in Flanders and the Netherlands', in Erdmann, Maier and Popp, *Geschichtsunterricht international / Worldwide Teaching of History* (Hannover: Hahnsche Buchhandlung, 2006), 337–48.

Wolff, L. *Inventing Eastern Europe: The Map of Civilization on the Mind of the Enlightenment*. Stanford, CA: Stanford University Press, 2000.

Xochellis, P.D., and F.I. Toloudi (eds). *The Image of the 'Other'/Neighbour in the School Textbooks of the Balkan Countries*. Athens: Dardanos, 2001.

Zieliński, A. 'Geschichtsunterricht in der Republik Polen' [History teaching in the Republic of Poland], in Erdmann, Maier and Popp, *Geschichtsunterricht international / Worldwide Teaching of History* (Hannover: Hahnsche Buchhandlung, 2006), 357–74.

CHAPTER 5

The Past in English Euroscepticism

BEN WELLINGS AND CHRIS GIFFORD

Introduction

This chapter argues that the English Eurosceptic view of the past rests on three
'pillars': the long development of representative democracy in England; a
particular view of the benefits of Empire; and memory of twentieth-century
conflict. It illustrates this English Eurosceptic version of the British past by
looking at the political uses to which that narrative has been put since the
formal beginning of the United Kingdom's relationship with the European
Communities in 1961. It will also illustrate the 'embedded persistence' of
this worldview. It will thereby show that English Euroscepticism cannot
be explained solely as an issue of party management, but should instead be
seen as a crucial element of a long-established national tradition that has
been reinvigorated by the politics of European integration. Consequently
this chapter demonstrates the reformulation and maintenance of an identity
distinct from, and in opposition to, European integration.

The chapter is framed around these three 'pillars'. To establish a comparison over time, each of the three sections will take examples from what
we might call the 'accession era', 1961–75; the 'Bruges–Maastricht era',
1988–93 and the 'Lisbon era', 2003–16. English Euroscepticism, with its
emphasis on parliamentary sovereignty and differences from 'Europe' based
on differing historical experiences, comes in 'hard' and 'soft' forms, in a way

similar to Taggart and Szczerbiak's use of these categories.[1] But note that we will not be using these categories to define political parties' attitudes towards European integration, but rather wider narratives within English political culture. Both forms of Eurosceptic narrative inclined the English national imagination away from European integration and back – or forward – to relations with countries outside of Europe. Nevertheless, the 2016 'Brexit' referendum secured the dominance of the 'hard' version, as a majority of voters backed the leave campaign's call to 'take back control from Brussels'. The message was clear: control had existed in the past, and it had been taken away from the British people. The possibility that it could be reclaimed thereby resonated with people's insecurities, particularly the English, in a socially and culturally divided UK.

The Past in European Identity

The past plays a key role in generating collective identities, which applies as much to European identity as to nationalism, two ideologies that have become mutually constitutive in contemporary Europe. This is due to the salience of the past in legitimizing political projects seeking to bind macro-level communities into some form of minimal unity and coherence to allow for redistributive politics.[2] Umut Özkırımlı defined nationalism as a discourse: 'a particular way of seeing and interpreting the world, a frame of reference that helps us make sense of and structure the world around us'.[3] This may be a little too broad as a definition of nationalism per se, but it does help to focus attention onto the role of ideology in legitimizing political projects – in this case, national narratives that draw on the past to transmit a certain view of the world and the nation's place in it.

This is particularly true when rival interpretations of the past are deployed in support of rival political projects. At stake is the legitimacy of one project vis-à-vis the other. As Ashplant, Dawson and Roper argue, 'the power of dominant memories depends not simply on their public visibility, but also on their capacity to connect with and articulate particular popular conceptions, whilst actively silencing or marginalizing others'.[4] Such contestation has been a feature of the relationship between nationalism and Europeanism throughout the twentieth century. Without wishing to overstate the antipathetic nature of that relationship (many nationalists have embraced European integration, and some Europeans can tolerate nationalism) in the immediate post-war years, Europeanism was often presented as an antidote to nationalism.

This version of the past in which Europeans overcame their antagonisms and created institutions that would make further war between them materially impossible, as well as unthinkable, is the European Union's founding myth. This was given its highest profile expression by the award of the Nobel Prize for Peace to the European Union in 2012 – what Ian Manners and Philomena Murray have called the 'Nobel narrative' of Europe integration.[5] For some analysts, this Kantian, universal zone of peace set Europeanism apart from nationalism. Montserrat Guibernau argued that the aim of pro-Europeans in the immediate post-war years was 'to replace the late eighteenth-century nationalist fervour associated with the idea of the nation based on popular sovereignty, and the passionate feelings aroused by romantic nationalism in the mid nineteenth century, with a strong anti-nationalism'.[6]

Such an interpretation, however, draws too sharp a distinction between Europeanism and nationalism, both of which are ideologies that draw heavily on the past in order to legitimize different yet contemporaneous political projects. Certain national narratives, notably the post-war (West) German one, align closely with the 'Nobel narrative'. In contrast, English nationalism was rearticulated in opposition to European integration and in relationship with 'wider categories of belonging' derived from the English-speaking world – a historical tendency that inclined narratives of England away from Europe.[7]

Yet this has been a far from uniform process. In key respects, European integration has been a battleground over competing conceptions of history and how these understandings of the past inform political decisions. The arguments for the UK's membership of the EC/EU were rooted in the discourses of contemporary history and a notion of a break with a past. This was evident in the 1967 Commons debate on membership, which saw 487 to 26 in support of a second application for EEC membership, one of the largest majorities of the twentieth century. In 1967 the arguments in support of membership proved overwhelming. Labour's foreign secretary, George Brown, spoke of 'the reconciliation of deeply felt antagonisms'.[8] He pointed to the decline of Commonwealth trade, alongside the new economic opportunities in Europe. Alternatives to full membership were dismissed: '[W]e would be passengers on the train; but the driving would be done by someone else'.[9] On sovereignty, the then chancellor, James Callaghan, bluntly pointed out that, 'to a very large extent, nations are not free at the moment to take their own decisions'.[10] On this view traditional Anglo-British conceptions of sovereignty and empire were no longer relevant. Moreover, membership meant Britain playing its full part in post-war reconciliation, a final end to the 'standing alone' narrative that had defined the nation at war.

What therefore is extraordinary is the extent to which, by the time of the 2016 Brexit referendum, the break with the past that European membership had implied and that was endorsed by the British people in the 1975 referendum, had lost legitimacy. Indeed, pro-EU arguments were largely focused on the material benefits to the UK of membership of the Single Market and the economic risks of exit. The free trade arguments that had been so central to support for membership on the right, and that were powerfully legitimated by the tradition of economic liberalism within English politics, now favoured those supporting 'Leave'.

Typical of such worldviews were those of David Davis, a senior Conservative Eurosceptic who was elevated to the position of 'Minister for Brexit' in Theresa May's first cabinet. Davis argued in 2016 that 'the European Union was a noble vision'. But, he continued:

> Britain has its own proud tradition of fighting tyranny, of protecting liberty and democracy both at home and abroad. For us, Europe has always been about trade. For the continent, it is about so much more. This does not mean either side is wrong. But the European Project is not right for us. The Global Project is.[11]

Post-imperial British political elites have revised and rearticulated national narratives in ways that project continuity and stability in the face of powerful global forces of social, political and economic change. Yet they have chronically struggled to align these with membership of the European Union. Understanding the dominant English memory of the past, and how this intersects with the political and economic project for European integration, helps to explain why English national narratives sit so uneasily with the drive for European unity.

Representative Democracy

From its very earliest days, it was clear that European integration easily posed a threat to England's continuity with its political past. Precedent is a crucial component of the Common Law tradition, and once the British state had survived the revolutionary challenges of the late eighteenth and early nineteenth centuries, the sense of continuity that was teleologically inclined towards liberty and that stretched back to the reign of King Alfred the Great became lauded as one of its defining features.

Once accession became a realistic prospect in 1961, the incompatibilities of the English past and European integration came into sharp relief. The leader of the Labour Party, Hugh Gaitskell, famously declared his opposition to Britain's entry to the European Communities at the party conference in Brighton in 1962. Gaitskell declared that accession to the Treaties of Rome would spell the end of 'a thousand years of British history', because Parliament would no longer be sovereign. Gaitskell's use of the term 'British history' is revealing. It did not refer to enquiries about the past relating to the archipelago off the north west of the European subcontinent, but

instead was a deployment of a particular understanding of England's constitutional development (that only really became 'British' from the seventeenth
century). The novelty of the European project was presented as a threat to
the defining continuity of the British political system.

In other words, there is no *stunde null* (zero hour) in English history
comparable to 1945 in German history or to the changes of regime in French
history after 1789 that can set a precedent for a radical change associated with
European integration and the subsequent alteration to sovereignty. Even a
rupture such as the 'Glorious Revolution' of 1688, when William of Orange
led an invasion force from the Low Countries to claim the thrones of
England and Scotland, is presented not as an invasion but rather the continuity of Protestant liberties under threat from Catholic despotism. Moreover, it
was this revolution that established the doctrine of parliamentary sovereignty
that was so important to English Euroscepticism. From 1961 to 1975, one
of the most prominent tribunes of this version of English history revivified
by the controversy over European integration came from the outspoken
Conservative MP Enoch Powell. During the 1960s, Powell had eulogized
the mystical qualities of the English constitution, the product of what he
called 'the slow alchemy of centuries'.[12]

A different politician reached the same conclusion about European
integration from the opposite side of British politics. Tony Benn was a senior
figure in the Labour Party in the English radical tradition who sought to
advance socialism in Britain by protecting the British state. Many in the grass
roots of his party shared Benn's view that the European Communities posed
a threat to British socialism from a project closely aligned with Christian
Democracy. Thus in this view of the past, the liberties won from the Crown
by groups such as the Levellers and the Chartists, and subsequently defended
by the Labour Party through the British parliamentary system, were in
jeopardy due to the loss of sovereignty to a big capitalist club.

The 1975 referendum delivered a resounding 'Yes' to EEC membership
but was shot through with ambivalence. Opinion polling for the National
Referendum Campaign, which campaigned for a 'No' vote, suggested that
the main reason for voting 'Yes' was a negative one: that Britain had
nowhere else to go. 'Having lost the Empire,' the pollsters concluded,
'English people were looking for a new role, but not with any conviction'.[13]
The 1975 referendum seemed to endorse the establishment position that
the UK's contemporary history had positioned it firmly as a European
power, and one that would play its full part in the process of European
integration. Yet this governing position had never been consistently or
coherently articulated as a national narrative of transformation and modernization – a defining feature of the Europeanization of many other member
states. Subsequently, Eurosceptics in the 1970s attacked elites for betraying

the people over membership. They claimed that the British people had been asked to endorse an economic community, the 'Common Market', and not a political union – a central argument in 2016 for holding a further referendum on Britain's membership of the EU.

Membership was not secured as part of the national psyche in 1975, and the past as a mobilizer of a distinctive English Eurosceptic worldview never went away. The establishment of the European Union was pivotal for many Eurosceptics, as it firmly demonstrated that European integration was no longer solely about free markets but represented a continental model of state building, which was antithetical to British parliamentary democracy. Governing elites downplayed differences, arguing that the EU remained primarily intergovernmental under the control of sovereign states. Nevertheless, as debates about the Maastricht Treaty and the speed and direction of European integration gathered pace in the 1990s, so too did articulations of political differences conditioned by the past. Writing in *The European Journal*, the publication of the Eurosceptic 'European Foundation', Stephen Hill elaborated a divide between the British and the Germans in relation to sovereignty, the law and rights:

> [O]ur constitution (which has evolved continuously for 781 years) is in an unwritten form and depends on duties. Our monarch is surrounded by an aura of mystery that reflects the ineffable relationship between the metaphysical Form of Sovereignty and the manifest sovereign. In Britain, we believe our liberty is protected in the belief of the Idea of Liberty itself . . . Germans believe the exact opposite. They accept that law is made by the president of the people and is worked out in advance and is written down. Similarly, the constitution (they are on their fifth in 125 years) must be written down. Their liberty, as they see it, is protected by their 'Basic Rights' enshrined in a legal code.[14]

These ideas of difference based on historical development played into the critique of the EU that developed around the so-called 'democratic deficit'. For 'soft' Eurosceptics like David Cameron, this meant reasserting the powers of parliaments in the face of what were seen as increasing EU powers, a step that the EU Act (2011) and the renegotiations ahead of the 2016 referendum were supposed to achieve.[15] For 'hard' Eurosceptics like the MEP Daniel Hannan, the EU was an anti-democratic polity that ideally would collapse through its own internal contradictions – failing that, Britain should leave as soon as possible. Hannan argued that although the European Union was seemingly underpinned by a common 'Western' civilization, the reality was fundamentally different. 'The three precepts that define Western civilization – the rule of law, democratic government and individual liberty – are not equally valued across Europe. When they act collectively, the member states of the EU are quite ready to subordinate all three to political imperatives'.[16]

The British Empire

During the Brexit referendum campaign, Boris Johnson, former London mayor, MP and leading Brexiteer, expressed frustration with arguments about the complexity of renegotiating trade deals if the UK were to withdraw from the EU. This frustration was informed by his view of Britain's imperial past: 'We used to run the biggest empire the world has ever seen, and with a much smaller domestic population and a relatively tiny Civil Service. Are we really unable to do trade deals?'[17] Although the argument about the Commonwealth as an alternative political community to Europe was weak in the 1975 referendum, the idea made a return ahead of the 2016 referendum in the guise of the 'Anglosphere', a concept adopted by the UK Independence Party in its 2015 manifesto and supported by certain figures on the Eurosceptic right of the Conservatives, notably Johnson, Gove and Davis.

Britain's imperial vocation has often been seen as something that has set the United Kingdom apart from continental Europe. This has been as true for committed Europeans as for people in the UK sceptical towards the European project. Count Coudenhove-Kalergi did not include Britain in his original plans for 'Paneuropa' in 1923. When he did approach the British government in 1931 he was told that European integration was for nations 'discontented with their reduced and isolated positions', and that Britain had more in common with Toronto and Sydney that with Paris or Berlin.[18] Thirty years later, General de Gaulle shared this view.[19]

We must be careful, however, not to overstate imperialism as a point of differentiation between Britain and Europe. As Linda Colley argues, 'the claim sometimes made that Britain's empire served to distract and separate it from "Europe" is unsound. Engaging in the overseas empire was actually one of the many things that the British shared with many other European nations'.[20] Despite this, the memory of the British Empire has indeed been used as a means to suggest a difference between England and the European continent. The British Empire is remembered – as it was justified at the time – not merely as an extension of state power but as a universalization of freedoms. This is the role that memory of Empire plays in English Eurosceptic thought.

There was truth to the structural differences between the British economy and the economies of the European states that founded the EEC in 1957, alluded to in this memory of Empire. The UK's role as world banker, underpinned by sterling as a global currency, created a web of financial and commercial dependencies, which formed the economic base of the British formal and informal empire. With the rise of the United States and Germany, the UK's dominance in manufacturing was over by the end of the nineteenth century, replaced by a *rentier* economy that survived by providing finance to the rest of the world. Yet the post-war global economy was driven by large domestic and regional markets for manufactured goods, which suited the newly reconstructed European capitalist economies. In contrast the UK, reliant on Commonwealth trade and the use of sterling, faced relative economic decline. Moreover, this was accompanied by the weakening of British political power and influence. The historic shift within the Conservative Party from Empire to Europe in 1959–60 came after the diplomatic failure at Suez in 1956 and the economic failure of the European Free Trade Association (EFTA) after its launch in 1957. Such were the structural constraints that Gifford argued predisposed the United Kingdom to populist Eurosceptic politics.[21]

By the time of the 'Common Market' referendum in 1975, however, the Commonwealth had virtually disappeared as an alternative political community to the European Communities. Prominent Eurosceptic Barbara Castle was laughed at during an Oxford Union debate during the campaign when she tried to defend the Malaysian pineapple trade with the UK.[22] Even the official government leaflet sent to all households ahead of the vote carried an endorsement from the Australian prime minister Gough Whitlam endorsing Britain's new found role in Europe: 'I do not wish to give any impression', wrote Whitlam, summoning some of the idealism lacking in the debate in Britain, 'that the present Australian government sees any advantage for Australia, for Europe or for the world in Britain leaving the Community – we regard European economic and political integration as one of the great historic forward movements of this century'.[23]

By the 1990s things had changed. This period saw the rehabilitation of Empire as an object of nostalgic greatness. That this was the case can be judged by the reference to Britain's imperial past in Geoffrey Howe's resignation speech of 1990 that ultimately led to Margaret Thatcher's downfall. In this speech Howe cautioned 'not to retreat into a ghetto of sentimentality about our past'.[24] The revival of the memory of Britain's imperial past was a concomitant of the defeat of 'declinism' in British politics.[25] The most visible manifestation of this push against a narrative of managed decline was the Falklands conflict in 1982, after which Thatcher claimed that Britain 'had ceased to be a nation in retreat'.[26] Although Margaret Thatcher praised support from EC member states, at the grass roots different and far more ambivalent conclusions were drawn.[27]

As the 1980s wore on, the European Communities were increasingly seen as another manifestation of decline that needed correction. Memory of Empire played an important role in this re-articulation of Britain's place in Europe and the world. The Eurosceptic manifesto presented in the Bruges

Speech commenced with a version of the past that sought to locate Britain within and *beyond* Europe. Thatcher added to the standard narrative of European unity. 'Too often the history of Europe is described as a series of interminable wars and quarrels,' stated Thatcher, '[y]et from our perspective today, surely what strikes us most is our common experience. For instance, the story of how Europeans explored and colonised and – yes, without apology – civilised much of the world is an extraordinary tale of talent, skill and courage'.[28] In the late 1980s and early 1990s, the rehabilitation of empire had not grown to the full force it would in later years. Regional vocations remained strong. In 1993, John Major underscored to an Australian audience in London the logic of Britain and Australia perusing post-imperial policies of integration in their European and Asian regions respectively.[29]

The reconfiguration of the international order in the wake of the Cold War forced a rehabilitation of empire and the deployment of its memory in Eurosceptic arguments. New Labour's 'ethical foreign policy' implied a more interventionist stance in failing states (especially those that were formerly part of the British Empire), like Sierra Leone. The 2007 commemoration of the bicentenary of the abolition of the slave trade throughout the British Empire and on the high seas was an illuminating choice of commemorative activity, as in that year it trumped the tercentenary of the Act of Union for official support. The academy was anticipating and responding to such events. Simon Schama's characterization of the debate in 2000 as the 'Empire of Good Intentions' was a neat summary of the move away from a notion of Empire as entirely 'bad'. Empire was further re-legitimized as the United States, along with its British and Australian allies, prepared for a ground assault on Iraq in 2002–03. Niall Ferguson's book *Empire*, with its explicit call for the Americans to take up the 'White Man's Burden' of empire, was a further controversial step in the memory and application of imperialism.[30] Importantly, the memory of Empire had been transformed into a new concept of the Anglosphere that appeared to offer English Eurosceptics an alternative to the EU. Importantly, it was an idea that sat well within an English memory of Britain's place in the world, updated for the security and trading needs of the twenty-first century. Crucially it turned Britain's greatest imperial defeat into a post-European inspiration: 'Like the Americans who declared their independence and never looked back,' wrote cabinet minister Michael Gove when declaring his hand for Brexit in February 2016, 'we can become an exemplar of what an inclusive, open and innovative democracy can achieve'.[31] Appointed by the new prime minister, Theresa May, as 'Brexit' minister, David Davies claimed that 'leaving the EU gives us back control of our trade policy, and gives us the opportunity to maximize returns from free trade'.[32] While referring to new global opportunities, former imperial possessions and Commonwealth countries, including

Hong Kong, Canada, Australia and India, were notably singled out to help to rebuild post-EU Britain's global trading relations.

Great Wars

Memory of the wars of the first half of the twentieth century, particularly the Second World War and the Holocaust, played an important part in legitimizing European integration. This memory of the European past was given an important endorsement by the awarding of the Nobel Prize for Peace to the European Union in 2012. In this narrative, Europe went from catastrophe to renaissance. But in English Eurosceptic memory, the trajectory is different. The Second World War was Britain's 'finest hour', and what followed thereafter could only be a decline.[33] The European Communities came to be seen as an institutional monument to such a fall. Thus war memory has been a stalking horse for debates about Britain's place in Europe. In the 1960s and 1970s, the invocation of the wars in debates about accession to the EEC tended to be pro-Commonwealth; by the 1990s the memory of the wars became anti-German. Memory of twentieth-century conflict pulled English Eurosceptics away from European integration by linking a sense of the betrayal of Commonwealth countries to Britain's accession to the European Communities. Memories of these wars shifted over time, but what we might call the 'dominant memories' of these conflicts created an ambivalent relationship between English Eurosceptics and Europe.

The First World War, initially seen as the defeat of Prussian militarism aided by the Empire, was by the 1960s being remembered as a futile conflict caused by continental entanglements. This re-evaluation of the conflict occurred at the same time as Britain's accession negotiations in 1961–63 and 1967. Both Conservative and Labour governments (but especially the former) argued that joining the EEC and Euratom was a way to restore Britain's greatness, which had been temporarily lost following the costly victory in 1939–45. But to some it seemed perverse to prioritize relationships with recent enemies at the expense of those imperial allies who had helped to save the United Kingdom from defeat twice in living memory. The Labour leader Hugh Gaitskell articulated such sentiments when he declared in 1962 that the Labour Party 'did not intend to forget Vimy Ridge [or] Gallipoli'.[34] In the accession era, these battles were not yet in the realm of 'post-memory', but formed leaders' living memories. In campaigning against accession, Lord Baillieu, chairman of Dunlop, reminded his audiences of the two great conflicts between 1914 and 1945, and argued that, '[i]f we are honest, we all know how in both we came near to overthrow and defeat. In both, the balance was tipped in our favour by the unique working partnership which continued throughout, between the peoples of the United States and the British Commonwealth'.[35] During the referendum campaign of 1975, Enoch Powell claimed that the ability to vote for a sovereign parliament to enact laws was 'the fact for which men have fought and died . . . that the laws in their country are made only by the institutions of their country and in Britain that they are made only by the parliamentary institutions of our country'.[36] This may have been a misreading of why individuals fought and died in two world wars, but it powerfully linked war memory and representative democracy, bringing these important themes in English Euroscepticism into alignment.

Churchill helped to fix the Second World War as Britain's 'finest hour' when it 'stood alone' (albeit with the help of the Empire and US Lend-Lease) early in the conflict. Not only was this war the clearest threat to the survival of the United Kingdom since its creation between 1536 and 1801, but the Fall of France, the Royal Navy's attack on French warships at Mers-el-Kebir in 1940, and the experience of the Free French in London all complicated Anglo-French relations, as we have noted above. Two symbolic years – 1940 and 1945 – serve to illustrate the variance in English and European memory of the Second World War. In French memory, '1940' represents a defeat of the most shocking and thorough kind. In England '1940' is the finest hour, a year that produced the 'miracle of Dunkirk' and the Battle of Britain in which defeat was averted and the seeds of victory over Nazism were sown. In German memory '1945' was the *stunde null*: the 'year zero' in which Nazism was defeated by external powers; but it was also the year in which democratic Germany emerged, at least in the West. This contrasted with the dominant English memory of '1945': victory in Europe and Asia, combined with the post-war Labour government's attempts to build a 'New Jerusalem' through the welfare state. But it was tempered by a diminution of prestige through the loss of India, and effective subordination to the USA – rhetoric about the 'Special Relationship' notwithstanding. In English memory, the Second World War was not a catastrophe redeemed by renaissance, but an apogee followed by eclipse.

When what was now dubbed 'Euroscepticism' began to emerge within the Conservative Party in the late 1980s, this 'war debt' was used to assert Britain's place as a reformer of, or brake upon, significant schemes for European integration. At the outset of the Bruges Speech, the British prime minister, Margaret Thatcher, reminded her audience not only of the sacrifice of British soldiers in Belgium between 1914 and 1918, but also the role played by Britain in liberating the Continent from Nazi rule three decades later: 'Had it not been for that willingness to fight and die, Europe would have been united long before now – but not in liberty, not in justice'.[37] Thatcher was a vocal opponent of German reunification, and after 1989 increasingly viewed proposals for further European integration as a mask for German ambitions to dominate Europe, holding a meeting about the 'German national character' in 1990. The strains caused by the growing issue of European union led to a peak of Germanophobia in the 1990s, and was sustained throughout the following decade.[38] This Germanophobia was given expression by the tabloid press in England. The year 1996 stood out in this respect when *The Sun* suggested that John Major had 'declared war on Europe' over the EU's ban on British beef exports, and the *Daily Mirror* planned to send a tank down a German autobahn ahead of the England–Germany semi-final of the UEFA European Football Championships, a game also preceded by the newspaper's infamous headline 'Achtung! Surrender!'[39]

The 'war on terror' and the Iraq war re-emphasized the Atlanticism in the English Eurosceptic view of the past portraying Europe as weak in the face of external threats and capitulating to dictators. John Redwood encapsulated the centrality of history to hard Eurosceptic thought in his 2005 book *Superpower Struggles*. 'Britain is at peace with its past in a way that many continental countries could never be', he claimed, continuing that:

> We do not have to live down the shame that many French people feel regarding the events of 1940–44. We do not have to live . . . with the collective guilt that Germany feels about the Holocaust . . . We do not wake up every morning like Italians, wondering who might be in government today and which government ministers might be charged with corruption tomorrow.[40]

The last point about Italy makes an important link between victory in the twentieth century's conflicts, especially the Second World War, and the endurance of a form of representative democracy superior to anything contrived in post-war Europe, hallowed by its longevity and endorsed by Providence.

As hard Euroscepticism gained ground within the Conservatives, and pushed by the success of the UK Independence Party (UKIP) in the European Parliament elections of 2004, 2009 and 2014, war memory and the idea of 'betrayal' gained ground. In the parliamentary debate about whether to hold an in–out referendum on EU membership, prominent Eurosceptic MP Bill Cash reminded his fellow parliamentarians that his father, who was killed in Normandy, was fighting for freedom and democracy, the very things that would be put at risk by what he saw as the corrupting influence of the European Union.[41] It was this war memory that formed the basis of what Boris Johnson claimed was Britain's betrayal of its Commonwealth allies when it joined the European Communities. In 2013, Boris Johnson spoke of the 'historic and strategic decision that this country took in 1973', whereby 'we betrayed our relationships with Commonwealth countries such as Australia and New Zealand'. This betrayal was the product of specific historical circumstances – domestic, European and global – that no longer pertained. As a result, Johnson argued that was 'perfectly obvious . . . that we need to seek a wider destiny for our country'.[42]

The Eurosceptic push that resulted in Britain's referendum on continued EU membership coincided with the commemoration of the centenary of the First World War. Domestically, the commemorations helped to reinforce a sense of common British endeavour in the face of Scottish secessionism, but also became a vehicle for a critique of 'left-wing' history teaching. Externally, they allowed for links to be made beyond a Franco-German narrative of the war as a precursor to Franco-German reconciliation and ulti-mately European integration.[43] The European tone struck at the ceremony at the St Symphorian cemetery in 2014 and the Anglo-German commemora-tions of Jutland/Skagerrak in 2016 coexisted with a re-emphasis on Empire and Commonwealth in centenary commemorations at Gallipoli in 2015 and on the Somme in 2016. These commemorative activities showed that in English Eurosceptic memory, 'Post-War' operates as a period of time rather than a state of being. The memory of twentieth-century conflict does not link Britain with Europe in a project of Kantian peace, but instead continues to link England with former Commonwealth countries, thereby asserting an English distinctiveness from Europe.

Conclusions

The English Eurosceptic version of the past rests on three pillars: representa-tive democracy, empire, and twentieth-century conflict. The soft version of English Euroscepticism suggests that England was the home of representative democracy, which helped to create the conditions necessary for an empire of free trade – and that, in turn, helped to rid Europe of militarism and totali-tarianism. Hence, British governments have been strong advocates of the Single Market, and opening it up to the wider global economy, while resist-ant to further political integration. Hard English Euroscepticism presents the development of representative democracy in England as being incompatible with what its supporters see as the 'anti-democratic' development of the EU since 1992, which means that the UK should turn away from Europe and embrace the opportunities of global markets and reinvigorate relationships with traditional allies. This reorientation includes re-emphasizing ties with its former Empire and Commonwealth that helped it to win two world wars, but was then betrayed by a political class in 1973 that had lost confidence in Britain's abilities as a global actor. Both versions of England's history have crowded out a Europhilic version of the past, and were deployed by their political supporters to legitimize their projects in the referendum campaign of 2016. The result demonstrated the Leave campaign's success in mobilizing support for a view of the English past that was antithetical to European integration. Leaving the EU meant reclaiming a version of the nation's history that had been tainted by membership. On this view, the soft Eurosceptic attempts to accommodate the English political tradition with European integration were a betrayal of that history.

Ben Wellings is senior lecturer in politics and international relations at Monash University in Melbourne, Australia. He is the author of *English Nationalism and Euroscepticism: Losing the Peace* (Peter Lang, 2012); 'Euroscepticism and the Anglosphere: Traditions and Dilemmas in Contemporary English Nationalism' (with Helen Baxendale), *Journal of Common Market Studies* 53(1) (2015), 123–39; and 'Euro-myth: Nationalism, War and the Legitimacy of the European Union' (with Ben Power), *National Identities* 18(2) (2016), 157–77.

Chris Gifford is the director of Postgraduate Taught Programmes at the University of Huddersfield. He is a political sociologist and has presented and published widely on British Euroscepticism. He is the author of *The Making of Eurosceptic Britain* (2014, Second Edition), and co-edited *The UK Challenge to Europeanization* (2015).

Notes

1. P. Taggart and A. Szczerbiak, 'Supporting the Union? Euroscepticism and the Politics of European Integration', in M. Green Cowles and D. Dinan (eds), *Developments in the European Union 2* (Basingstoke: Palgrave Macmillan, 2004), 67.

2. D. Miller, *On Nationality* (Oxford: Oxford University Press, 1995), 62–63.

3. U. Özkırımlı, *Contemporary Debates on Nationalism: A Critical Engagement* (Basingstoke: Palgrave, 2005), 30.

4. T.G. Ashplant, G. Dawson and M. Roper, 'The Politics of War Commemoration: Contexts, Structures and Dynamics', in Ashplant, Dawson and Roper (eds), *The Politics of War Commemoration* (Abingdon: Routledge, 2000), 13.

5. I. Manners and P. Murray, 'The End of a Noble Narrative? European Integration Narratives after the Nobel Peace Prize', *Journal of Common Market Studies* 54(1) (2015), 185.

6. M. Guibernau 'The Birth of a United Europe: On Why the EU has Generated a Non-emotional Identity', *Nations and Nationalism* 17(2) (2011), 305.

7. B. Wellings, 'Our Island Story: England, Europe and the Anglosphere Alternative', *Political Studies Review* 14(3) (2016), 369.

8. *Hansard's Parliamentary Record*, 10 May 1967, col. 1506.

9. *Hansard's Parliamentary Record*, 10 May 1967, col. 1513.

10. *Hansard's Parliamentary Record*, 9 May 1967, col. 1302.

11. D. Davis. 2016. 'Britain would be better off out of the EU – and here's why', *Conservative Home*, 4 February 2016. http://www.conservativehome.com/platform/2016/02/david-davis-britain-would-be-better-off-out-of-the-eu-and-heres-why.html (last accessed 16 March 2016).

12. S. Heffer, *Like the Roman: The Life of Enoch Powell* (London: Weidenfeld & Nicolson, 1998), 336.

13. British Library of Political and Economic Sciences (BLPES), SHORE/10/45 [EEC, 1974–75], 'Summary of qualitative research findings on attitudes and beliefs towards the EEC, carried out for the National Referendum Campaign', Boase Massimi Pollitt Partnership, 1975, 13.

14. S. Hill, 'Memo to Major, Copy to Blair, re: The Image Thing', in *The European Journal: The Journal of the European Foundation*, May 1996, 13–14.

15. B. Wellings and E. Vines, 'Populism and Sovereignty: The EU Act and the In–Out Referendum'. *Parliamentary Affairs* 69(2) (2016), 310.

16. D. Hannan, *Inventing Freedom: How the English-Speaking Peoples Made the Modern World* (New York: HarperCollins Books, 2013), 4–5.

17. B. Johnson, 'There is only one way to get the change we want – vote to leave the EU', *Telegraph*, 21 February 2016. http://www.telegraph.co.uk/news/newstopics/eureferendum/12167643/Boris-Johnson-there-is-only-one-way-to-get-the-change-we-want-vote-to-leave-the-EU.html (last accessed 22 February 2016).

18. Historical Archives of the European Union, 'Minutes of meeting "Public Interest in European Union": A Meeting in the Commons to Consider Measures', 17 February 1931, PAN/EU 000007.

19. J. Alsop, 'General de Gaulle's Europe', *Manchester Guardian*, 9 May 1962.

20. L. Colley, *Acts of Union and Disunion: What has Held the United Kingdom Together – and What is Dividing It?* (London: Profile Books, 2014), 132.

21. C. Gifford, *The Making of Eurosceptic Britain*, second edition (Farnham: Ashgate, 2014), 6.

22. B. Castle, *The Castle Diaries, 1974–76* (London: Weidenfeld & Nicolson, 1976), 406.

23. Britain in Europe, 'Referendum on the European Community (Common Market): Why You Should Vote Yes' (London: HMSO, 1975), 3.

24. Cited in R. Tombs, *The English and Their History* (London: Penguin, 2014), 824.

25. R. Ovendale, 'The End of Empire', in R. English and M. Kenny (eds), *Rethinking British Decline* (Basingstoke: Palgrave, 2000), 274.

26. Margaret Thatcher Foundation, 'Speech to the Conservative Rally at Cheltenham', 3 July 1982. http://www.margaretthatcher.org/speeches/displaydocument.asp?docid=104989 (last accessed 1 April 2016).

27. Mass Observation Archive. Special Directive 1982, EEC Special: Tenth Anniversary of British Entry into Europe, Box 42 – Report on Material.

28. Margaret Thatcher Foundation, 'Speech to the College of Europe', 20 September 1988. http://www.margaretthatcher.org/speeches/displaydocument.asp?docid=107332 (last accessed 1 April 2016).

29. J. Major, 'Australia and Britain: A Relationship which Matters'. Speech by the Prime Minister, the Right Honourable John Major MP, to the Britain–Australia Society, 21 January 1993, in M. Kooyman and P. Beckingham (eds), *Australia and Britain: The Evolving Relationship* (Melbourne: Monash ANZ Centre for International Briefing, 1993).

30. N. Ferguson, *Empire: How Britain Made the Modern World* (London: Penguin, 2003), 366.

31. Cited in N. Watt, 'Michael Gove and five other cabinet members break ranks with the PM over EU', *Guardian*, 21 February 2016. http://www.theguardian.com/politics/2016/

feb/20/michael-gove-and-five-other-cabinet-members-break-ranks-with-pm-over-eu (last accessed 23 February 2016).

32. D. Davis, 'Trade Deals. Tax Cuts. And Taking Time before Triggering Article 50. A Brexit Economic Strategy for Britain'. *Conservativehome*, 14 July 2016. http://www. conservativehome.com/platform/2016/07/david-davis-trade-deals-tax-cuts-and-taking-time-before-triggering-article-50-a-brexit-economic-strategy-for-britain.html (last accessed 15 July 2016).

33. B. Wellings, *English Nationalism and Euroscepticism: Losing the Peace* (Bern: Peter Lang, 2012), 48.

34. Cited in D. Healey, *The Time of My Life* (London: Penguin Books, 1989), 211.

35. National Archives of Australia. M2576/88, Personal papers of Prime Minister Menzies. Conference papers (re Commonwealth Prime Ministers' Conference, includes correspondence, speeches and notes on Britain's entry into the Common Market). Text of speech sent by Lord Baillieu to R.G. Menzies, 2 July 1962.

36. British Library of Political and Economic Sciences, SHORE/10/59, 'The Great Debate', BBC Radio Three.

37. Thatcher, 'Speech to the College of Europe'.

38. J. Ramsden, *Don't Mention the War: The British and the Germans since 1890* (London: Abacus, 2006), 363–65.

39. C. Midgley, 'Wakeham tells papers to curb jingoism', *The Times*, 14 May 1998.

40. J. Redwood, *Superpower Struggles: Mighty America, Faltering Europe, Rising Asia* (Basingstoke: Palgrave Macmillan, 2005), 12.

41. *Hansard's Parliamentary Record*, 23 October 2011, col. 80.

42. B. Johnson, 'The Aussies are just like us, so let's stop kicking them out', *Telegraph*, 24 August 2013. http://www.telegraph.co.uk/news/politics/10265619/The-Aussies-are-just-like-us-so-lets-stop-kicking-them-out.html (last accessed 29 August 2013).

43. C. Cadot, 'Wars Afterwards: The Repression of the Great War in European Collective Memory', in S. Sumartojo and B. Wellings (eds), *Nation, Memory and Great War Commemoration: Mobilizing the Past in Europe, Australia and New Zealand* (Bern: Peter Lang, 2014), 260.

Bibliography

Archival Sources

Britain in Europe. 'Referendum on the European Community (Common Market): Why You Should Vote Yes'. London: HMSO, 1975.

British Library of Political and Economic Sciences (BLPES). SHORE/10/45 [EEC, 1974–75], 'Summary of Qualitative Research Findings on Attitudes and Beliefs towards the EEC, Carried Out for the National Referendum Campaign'. Boase Massimi Pollitt Partnership, 1975.

———. SHORE/10/59, 'The Great Debate', BBC Radio Three.

Hansard's Parliamentary Record, 9 May 1967, col. 1302.

Hansard's Parliamentary Record, 10 May 1967, col. 1506–13.

Hansard's Parliamentary Record, 23 October 2011, col. 80.

Historical Archives of the European Union. 'Minutes of meeting "Public Interest in European Union": A Meeting in the Commons to Consider Measures', 17 February 1931, PAN/EU 000007.

Margaret Thatcher Foundation. 'Speech to the Conservative Rally at Cheltenham', 3 July 1982. http://www.margaretthatcher.org/speeches/displaydocument.asp?docid=104989 (last accessed 1 April 2016).

———. 'Speech to the College of Europe', 20 September 1988. http://www.margaretthatcher. org/speeches/displaydocument.asp?docid=107332 (last accessed 1 April 2016).

Mass Observation Archive. Special Directive 1982, EEC Special: Tenth Anniversary of British Entry into Europe, Box 42 – Report on Material.

National Archives of Australia. M2576/88, Personal papers of Prime Minister Menzies. Conference papers (re Commonwealth Prime Ministers' Conference, includes correspondence, speeches and notes on Britain's entry into the Common Market). Text of speech sent by Lord Baillieu to R.G. Menzies, 2 July 1962.

Secondary Sources

Alsop, J. 'General de Gaulle's Europe', *Manchester Guardian*, 9 May 1962.

Ashplant, T.G., G. Dawson and M. Roper. 'The Politics of War Memory and Commemoration: Context, Structures and Dynamics', in Ashplant, Dawson and Roper (eds), *The Politics of War Memory and Commemoration*. Abingdon: Routledge, 2000.

Cadot, C. 'Wars Afterwards: The Repression of the Great War in European Collective Memory', in S. Sumartojo and B. Wellings (eds), *Nation, Memory and Great War Commemoration: Mobilizing the Past in Europe, Australia and New Zealand*. Bern: Peter Lang, 2014.

Castle, B. *The Castle Diaries, 1974–76*. London: Weidenfeld & Nicolson, 1976.

Colley, L. *Acts of Union and Disunion: What has Held the United Kingdom Together – and What is Dividing It?* London: Profile Books, 2014.

Davis, D. 'Britain would be better off out of the EU – and here's why', *Conservative Home*, 4 February 2016. http://www.conservativehome.com/platform/2016/02/david-davis-britain-would-be-better-off-out-of-the-eu-and-heres-why.html (last accessed 16 March 2016).

———. 'Trade Deals. Tax Cuts. And Taking Time before Triggering Article 50: A Brexit Economic Strategy for Britain'. *Conservativehome*, 14 July 2016. http://www.conservativehome.com/platform/2016/07/david-davis-trade-deals-tax-cuts-and-taking-time-before-triggering-article-50-a-brexit-economic-strategy-for-britain.html (last accessed 15 July 2016).

Ferguson, N. *Empire: How Britain Made the Modern World*. London: Penguin, 2003.

Gifford, C. *The Making of Eurosceptic Britain*, second edition. Farnham: Ashgate, 2014.

Guibernau, M. 'The Birth of a United Europe: On Why the EU has Generated a Nonemotional Identity'. *Nations and Nationalism* 17(2) (2011), 302–15.

Hannan, D. *Inventing Freedom: How the English-Speaking Peoples Made the Modern World*. New York: HarperCollins, 2013.

Healey, D. *The Time of My Life*. London: Penguin Books, 1989.

Heffer, S. *Like the Roman: The Life of Enoch Powell*. London: Weidenfeld & Nicolson, 1998.

Hill, S. 'Memo to Major, Copy to Blair, re: The Image Thing', *The European Journal: The Journal of the European Foundation*, May 1996, 13–14.

Johnson, B. 'The Aussies are just like us, so let's stop kicking them out', *Telegraph*, 24 August 2013. http://www.telegraph.co.uk/news/politics/10265619/The-Aussies-are-just-like-us-so-lets-stop-kicking-them-out.html (last accessed 29 August 2013).

———. 'There is only one way to get the change we want – vote to leave the EU', *Telegraph*, 21 February 2016. http://www.telegraph.co.uk/news/newstopics/eureferendum/1216 7643/Boris-Johnson-there-is-only-one-way-to-get-the-change-we-want-vote-to-leave-the-EU.html (last accessed 22 February 2016).

Major, J. 'Australia and Britain: A Relationship which Matters'. Speech by the Prime Minister, the Right Honourable John Major MP, to the Britain–Australia Society, 21 January 1993, in M. Kooyman and P. Beckingham (eds), *Australia and Britain: The Evolving Relationship*. Melbourne: Monash ANZ Centre for International Briefing, 1993.

Manners, I., and P. Murray. 'The End of a Noble Narrative? European Integration Narratives after the Nobel Peace Prize'. *Journal of Common Market Studies* 54(1) (2015), 185–202.

Midgley, C. 'Wakeham tells papers to curb jingoism', *The Times*, 14 May 1998.

Miller, D. *On Nationality*. Oxford: Oxford University Press, 1995.

Ovendale, R. 'The End of Empire', in R. English and M. Kenny (eds), *Rethinking British Decline*. Basingstoke: Palgrave, 2000.

Özkırımlı, U. *Contemporary Debates on Nationalism: A Critical Engagement*. Basingstoke: Palgrave, 2005.

Ramsden, J. *Don't Mention the War: The British and the Germans since 1890*. London: Abacus, 2006.

Redwood, J. *Superpower Struggles: Mighty America, Faltering Europe, Rising Asia*. Basingstoke: Palgrave Macmillan, 2005.

Taggart, P., and A. Szczerbiak. 'Supporting the Union? Euroscepticism and the Politics of European Integration', in M. Green Cowles and D. Dinan (eds), *Developments in the European Union 2*. Basingstoke: Palgrave Macmillan, 2004.

Tombs, R. *The English and Their History*. London: Penguin, 2014.

Watt, N. 'Michael Gove and five other cabinet members break ranks with the PM over EU', *Guardian*, 21 February 2016. http://www.theguardian.com/politics/2016/feb/20/michael-gove-and-five-other-cabinet-members-break-ranks-with-pm-over-eu (last accessed 23 February 2016).

Wellings, B. *English Nationalism and Euroscepticism: Losing the Peace*. Bern: Peter Lang, 2012.

———. 'Our Island Story: England, Europe and the Anglosphere Alternative'. *Political Studies Review* 14(3) (2016), 368–77.

Wellings, B., and E. Vines. 'Populism and Sovereignty: The EU Act and the In–Out Referendum'. *Parliamentary Affairs* 69(2) (2016), 309–26.

CHAPTER 6

(Trans)national Memories of the Common Past in the Post-Yugoslav Space

JELENA ĐUREINOVIĆ

In October 2014, the city of Belgrade was celebrating the seventieth anniversary of its liberation. The president of the Russian Federation, Vladimir Putin, visited Belgrade on the occasion of the Victors' March, a large military parade held that year on 16 October – four days before the actual liberation day – so that he could attend it. The first military parade in Belgrade since 1985, it involved thousands of soldiers of the Serbian Army showcasing the air force, the river fleet, infantry units and equipment. The whole event lasted several hours and was broadcast live on Serbian national television. Twelve years before this event, following the fall of Slobodan Milošević, the Day of the Liberation of Belgrade was removed from the official calendar, while numerous street names commemorating the Partisan or the Red Army soldiers were also changed. Subsequently, the Cemetery of the Belgrade Liberators memorial park was neglected and left to decay. However, contrary to the dominant narrative of the end of the Second World War as an occupation rather than a liberation, the local authorities and the Serbian government started modestly commemorating liberation day from 2007 on, culminating in 2014 with the parade and week-long celebrations. The year before this parade, the Day of the Liberation of Belgrade was returned to the official state calendar, which prescribes the dates to be commemorated, and it has had the status of an official holiday ever since.

The military parade and the events surrounding it might have created the impression that Serbia embraced its Yugoslav and antifascist past, rather than sought to disassociate itself from socialist Yugoslavia and everything related to it. The official politics of memory after the fall of Slobodan Milošević in 2000 had been founded upon this narrative of separation from socialism. However, the military parade managed to appropriate the Yugoslav memory narrative, transforming it into the narrative of Serbian antifascism. In the speeches of Serbia's highest officials, the liberation of the capital city by the joint forces of the Yugoslav Partisans and the Red Army was framed as the common struggle of the Serbian and Russian people. Although the flags of the different battalions were displayed, the participation of Croatian, Italian and other partisan units, as well as the Ukrainian Red Army units, in the liberation was left out from the commemoration narrative. Moreover, the communist nature of the resistance movement, the Yugoslav state that had emerged from it, and even the army leader Josip Broz Tito, were not referred to or visible. Framed as an episode in the long history of the brotherhood of the Serbian and Russian nations, and taken out of the wider historical and political context, the liberation of Belgrade was nationalized and 'de-Yugoslavized'.

The Day of the Liberation of Belgrade represents an example of 'transnationalism in reverse', which has been the dominant paradigm in the post-Yugoslav space since the establishment of the nation states in the early 1990s.[1] The Yugoslav memory culture was founded on a transnational narrative that interpreted the Second World War through the lens of the common struggle of all Yugoslav states against the occupation and for the liberation of their country. Various vernacular memories celebrating the memory of the forces who had fought against the Yugoslav Partisans, excluded from the official politics of memory of socialist Yugoslavia, naturally existed in society, but they were most prominent and openly promoted in the publications and mnemonic practices of the political emigration. These opposing narratives became more evident within Yugoslavia during the legitimacy crisis of the 1980s, parallel to the growing interpretation of the Second World War in national terms in the different Yugoslav republics. Since the dissolution of Yugoslavia and the beginning of the transformation of the states from the socialist order to liberal democracy, these nation-centred narratives became central to hegemonic national memory cultures. Within this hegemony, the past common to all former Yugoslav republics has been predominantly reinterpreted in national terms, with the Second World War, the post-war period and socialism being the most evident objects of revision.

Transnational and National Memory

Following similar trends in the social sciences and humanities, the field
of memory studies has taken a 'transcultural turn' during the last decade.
Exploring memory through the 'transnational lens' has become the mainstream paradigm of the field, displacing the long-standing interest in the
nation as the most important unit of analysis.[2] Transcultural memory studies
is founded upon a critique of methodological nationalism, and moves
beyond the nation as the core category of the social and political order, and
thus memory. It questions the assumption that 'a national ontology can no
longer serve as a self-evident point of departure'.[3] Reviewing the development of memory studies, Astrid Erll asks whether, after gaining a deeper
insight into the invention of tradition, politics of memory, the issues of
war, trauma, genocide and reconciliation, 'memory became a mere stencil,
and memory studies an additive project', where we add yet another site of
memory and address yet another historical injustice.[4] In this regard, many
scholars of memory in the last decade have understood that the time had
come to develop new theoretical frameworks and methodologies, while
turning to new sites and resources for examining collective memory beyond
the nation state.[5] In the context of globalization and transnationalization,
national frames are seen as less relevant to current realities. We could ask
whether national frameworks still retain their relevance, firstly, in exploring
historical memory cultures, and secondly, in conditions where we fragment
the homogenizing global perspective and take an empirical approach to
memory cultures and practices.

A full description of the transnational turn would require a separate
study. Because of the limited scope of this chapter, just a few notable
concepts that illustrate the research paradigm will be addressed here. The
mass atrocities, above all of the twentieth century, have inspired the majority of the contributions to this field, often involving some sort of ethical,
normative or utopian vision. The Holocaust memory and 'the globalization
of the Holocaust discourse' have generated a considerable research interest.[6]
In this way, the concept of cosmopolitan memory, coined by Levy and
Sznaider, perceives the Holocaust as a transnational symbol that has enabled
and empowered the articulation of memories about genocide and human
rights in different parts of the world.[7] Similarly, Rothberg examines the ways
in which the Holocaust discourse enables the discourses of colonialism and
slavery. He traces the phenomenon that he terms multidirectional memory
back to the 1960s, and sees it as a mode of memory that is opposed to the
idea of competitive memory. Rothberg suggests that we consider memory
as 'subject to ongoing negotiation, cross-referencing and borrowing, as

productive and not privative'.[8] Multidirectional memory should thus engender solidarity and common visions of justice. Another similarly idealistic vision of transnational memory is evident in Assmann's model of dialogic memory as a recipe for dealing with the past. According to this model, two or more states that share histories of mutual violence engage in a dialogic memory by 'mutually acknowledging their own guilt and empathy with the suffering they have inflicted on others'.[9]

Although it might seem so in the existing literature, the turn to the transcultural in memory studies does not necessarily imply negation or replacement but rather complementing the research on national memory, which remains equally relevant. Even in the age of globalization and within unifying Europe, it is still the nation state that plays a major role in the creation of memory culture by 'initiating rituals of public commemoration, setting up memorials, financing museums, conceiving of educational agendas'.[10] The nation state remains a central actor in Assmann's dialogic model, too. However, as Bond and Rapson point out, the transcultural approach is about recognition that memories exist in relation to each other, but it does not mean that 'particular communities do not possess important specificities in their approach to, and articulation of, the past'.[11] It is precisely this locatedness of memory that should not be left out when examining memory through the transnational lens. The focus on the specific sites and contexts and 'on the locatedness of engagements with memories on the move' could prevent 'the abstract detachments of a superficial "non-location" of theories and studies'.[12]

It is evident that most of the scholars of this strand of memory studies do recognize the importance of the national framework as one container of memory, but they nevertheless argue for memory studies moving beyond it. Bond and Rapson rightfully raise the issue of whether 'we are right to think about the past as "memory without borders", without rigorously questioning whether the most idealistic aspects of memory theory actually reflect the complexity of how commemoration works in practice'.[13] The conceptual frameworks of transcultural memory studies could be rethought when examining particular case studies by asking whether shared mnemonic practices represent a genuinely novel transnational circulation of memory, or whether they might perhaps be thought of in terms of the existing concepts of cultural transfer or transfer of knowledge. Thinking in this direction, this chapter is concerned with the tensions between the national and transnational level. More precisely, the chapter examines national memory cultures in Croatia and Serbia from the perspective of their relation to each other and the wider paradigms in memory politics in the postsocialist states. In other words, while acknowledging transnational perspectives of European or postsocialist politics of memory, a comparative approach encompassing the national specificities, which often entail competitiveness rather than multidirectionality, remains useful. This chapter thus examines a time and a space where the very definition of the nation changed, as the nation state of Yugoslavia fragmented into smaller but still national units. Thus the ultimately homogenizing theories of transnational memory studies, sometimes positioned in 'non-locations', are reterritorialized here.

This chapter is primarily interested in the nationalization of memory within the borders of the states that emerged after the dissolution of Yugoslavia. Taking the above-mentioned concepts of transnational and transcultural memory into consideration, the chapter is also concerned with the travelling of mnemonic carriers, media, contents, forms and practices, as well as their appropriation and transformations in the national contexts. This travelling can be understood as happening through both time and space. The temporal perspective encompasses the process of the national fragmentation of memory in the post-Yugoslav space, which inverted the transnational memory culture of socialist Yugoslavia to place a singular national interpretation of the common past at its core. The processes that occurred in the memory politics of the post-Yugoslav nations took similar forms, and this thus enables a comparative approach to the newly prevalent, mutually exclusive and competitive narratives of the common past. Alongside the collapse of old transnational forms, new modes of transnational memory have travelled into and between the countries of former Yugoslavia, with this process replicated across the broader East European space, or even across the whole of Europe when it comes to memory politics and the Second World War. This sense of travelling of memory is also transnationally constituted as it entails the transplantation of the discourses from the European Union and postsocialist countries of Central and Eastern Europe to the post-Yugoslav context.

The Yugoslav Memory Culture and its Downfall

After the attack of the Axis forces in April 1941, the territory of the Kingdom of Yugoslavia was dismembered into a diverse mosaic of annexed, occupied and quasi-independent entities.[14] The Second World War in Yugoslavia was not only a war of occupation and liberation, but also a civil war, where Yugoslav people, divided along political, ethnic and regional lines, fought with or against the Axis forces and against each other.[15] The destruction of the Jewish population, mass atrocities and ethnic violence against civilians were committed both by the occupation forces and different domestic groups. The People's Liberation Army (more commonly known as the Partisans) represented the greatest challenge to the Axis occupation and the quisling regimes of the Ustasha in the Independent State of Croatia and Milan Nedić in occupied Serbia. The Partisans, under the leadership of the Communist Party, got organized in 1941, and the movement grew rapidly and massively as the war continued. The Second World War had the characteristics of a class war as well, because, alongside the liberation war and the civil war against the domestic collaboration forces, the Partisans – who were mostly peasants – also fought against the socioeconomic order of the Kingdom of Yugoslavia and for the transformation of the society.[16]

Towards the end of the war and in the immediate post-war period, the Partisans and the newly established Yugoslav socialist regime were settling accounts with their enemies, mostly directed at those considered responsible for war crimes and collaboration. This process of dealing with collaboration reflected the wider European context at the time, where the first retributions, usually meaning extrajudicial executions, happened before and immediately after the war officially ended, and were followed by the institutionalization through the establishment of commissions and military tribunals in the post-war period.[17] Already before the end of the war, amnesty was possible for the members of the quisling forces who had not committed war crimes. After all, almost half of the members of the Chetnik movement and members of the Croatian and Slovenian Home Guards had changed sides in 1944 and continued fighting together with the Partisans.[18]

The Second World War was the founding event and the main source of legitimacy for post-war Yugoslavia, framed as 'the common struggle against the occupiers and the domestic traitors'.[19] The narrative of the People's Liberation War was the central foundation myth of the state, encompassing both the antifascist struggle and the victory of the Partisans, as well as the socialist revolution. Emphasizing the size and the authentic nature of the People's Liberation War, as opposed to the other socialist states liberated by the Red Army as the external power, also served as a strong emancipatory factor.[20] The very complex and many-sided conflict was interpreted in a simplified way through the prism of unconditional collaboration and unconditional resistance, without anything in between.[21]

The narrative of the united resistance in the Second World War was based on multinational or transnational solidarity that was the core of new socialist Yugoslavia.[22] The simplified interpretation of the war included placing armed conflicts and mass crimes of the Yugoslav people against each other within a transnational narrative, or alternatively, leaving it out completely. The violence inflicted by the Partisans upon their enemies, especially at the end of the war, was not included in the narrative of the pure Partisan war. The variations in the representation of the nations in the People's Liberation Army on the one hand, and the support which, for instance, the Ustasha in Croatia had among the people on the other, were also adjusted to fit the dominant narrative framework. Thus, the inter-Yugoslav conflicts and national hatred were blamed on the Axis occupation forces, the ruling class and the bourgeoisie, and not on the working people.[23] Additionally, domestic 'enemies of the people' were to blame – in other words, those who had fought against the Partisans and collaborated with the occupation, encompassing most notably the Ustasha in Croatia, the Chetnik movement, the Slovenian Home Guard and the military and police apparatus of the Serbian quisling government of Milan Nedić. In the dualistic interpretation of the war, which was based on its ethnic neutralization, all Yugoslav nations were said to have contributed equally to the antifascist struggle, while they all contributed to the collaboration as well, but without any group being blamed any more or less than any other for the inter-Yugoslav atrocities. Both glory and guilt were distributed to all nations equally.[24] In short, the legitimization of the Yugoslav regime was not the only purpose of the official politics of memory and the constant foregrounding of the National Liberation War, but the consolidation of the multinational state – and the people's identification with it was equally crucial.

Counternarratives did exist during the Yugoslav period but they were only expressed publicly among the emigration. At the end of the Second World War and in the post-war period, many collaborators managed to escape Yugoslavia. It was among political émigrés in different countries that publications and events promoting a view of the war opposed to the Yugoslav interpretation were blossoming, celebrating the anticommunist movements of the war regardless of their complicity in the mass atrocities and the Holocaust. The war narratives from the emigration started gaining more significance within Yugoslavia in the 1980s after the death of Josip Broz Tito, while Yugoslavia was facing an economic and a legitimacy crisis. In this period, the nationalization of the victims of the Second World War became more dominant, when the groups, previously framed in general terms as victims of fascism, were given back their nationality and religious belonging, and were instrumentalized in the political debates and number games such as on the victims of Jasenovac concentration camp. The perpetrators, until then also ethnically neutralized, became clearly defined in a similar way. The challenges to the official war narrative, namely the re-evaluation of the anticommunist movements of the Second World War through the justification of their wartime activities, and the relativization of collaboration and crimes, appeared in the spheres of historiography and literature. Parallel to that, post-war executions and trials not discussed before slowly emerged in the society.

The Yugoslav attempt to neutralize the negative aspects of its past was severely jeopardized as the country went towards the wars and dissolution. The confrontations about the interpretation of history outgrew the sphere of academic debate and transformed into 'verbal wars full of bigotry and national exclusivity'.[25] The replacement of the socialist paradigm with a nationalist one meant separation from two positive values of Yugoslav socialism: firstly, the idea of Yugoslavism as an effort towards multiculturalism and overcoming the animosities, and secondly, the idea of antifascism as a liberating and emancipating movement.[26] This tendency grew stronger and transitioned to the level of official historical narratives after the dissolution of Yugoslavia. During the wars of the Yugoslav succession in the 1990s and continuing into the decade afterwards, the history of the Yugoslav state became an unnecessary burden. It was an outfit that was uncomfortable, too tight and not fashionable anymore, and it was restricting the movement of the growing ethnocentric and nationalist tendencies. It thus had to be thrown away.[27]

Contemporary Debates in Croatia and Serbia

In parallel to the dissolution of the state, the Yugoslav community of memory fell apart. The national fragmentation of memory that went hand in hand with the dissolution of Yugoslavia and the wars that ensued, ended in the creation of new national regimes of memory. As Sundhaussen explains, with the exception of Slovenia, the transformation processes started around ten years later than in other postsocialist countries because of the wars and lasting authoritarian regimes.[28] It was only after the death of the president of Croatia, Franjo Tuđman, and the overthrow of Slobodan Milošević in Serbia in 2000, that these two countries started their delayed transitions. The dominant tendencies in politics of memory in contemporary Croatia and Serbia follow the similar lines and share very similar mnemonic practices and discourses about their common past. In both countries, the Second World War is the central theme of the contemporary debates and it is the main object of revision. This is directly linked to the memory of Yugoslavia as the war provided legitimacy to the socialist state, which implies that its revision is an important part of the process of the delegitimation of Yugoslavia. The war is observed not only through the national lens, but also through the prism of its final period with the particular focus on the revolutionary terror by the Partisans and the communist repression. Through the focus on the 'crimes of the liberators', the year 1945 as the year of the liberation of Yugoslavia is framed rather as the year of the defeat of the nations.

The idea and the movement of Yugoslav antifascism is equated with communism and thus interpreted negatively since it was led by the communists as 'the power struggle of the communist criminals' and collaboration with fascism becomes the positive past, interpreted as 'the legitimate struggle against the criminal communists'.[29] Milosavljević argues that the revival of the collaborationist movements had the goal of switching value positions: the parallel rejection of antifascism as a communist crime and social accept-ance of collaborators as the defenders of the nation.[30] The forces defeated in the Second World War were politically and legally rehabilitated without concern for the fact that they fought on the side of the Axis forces. The Ustasha movement and the Independent State of Croatia represent the focal point in Croatia, while Serbian memory politics has constructed the Chetnik movement as the national antifascist force, also relativizing the nature of the Milan Nedić regime of occupied Serbia. In both countries, the crimes and collaboration of these groups as well as their complicity in the Holocaust are justified and whitewashed, since they are seen as representing a more suitable point of reference for the consolidating nation states than the antinationalist and communist-led Partisans. Because of the fact that many of the members of these movements and regimes went into exile at the end of the war and those who stayed faced retributions, they are not only framed as the victims of communism, but through the criminalization of the Partisan movement and socialist Yugoslavia, they merge into the narrative of the innocent victims of politically and ideologically motivated repression and violence. In this process of the reinterpretation of the past, the victims of fascism are marginalized and replaced by the victims of communist violence.[31]

It should be noted that the paradox of the post-Yugoslav politics of memory is that, on the rare commemorative occasions when antifascism is not ignored or completely discredited through its equation with com-munism, it is nationalized and cleansed from communism. Already in the 1980s, the controversy about the representation of certain Yugoslav nations in the People's Liberation Army was a part of the debates on the Second World War, when Croatian and Serbian intellectuals strived to prove that their nation was more antifascist than the other. According to Kuljić, this competition marks the beginning of the nationalization of antifascism.[32] On the occasions of important anniversaries such as the Day of the Liberation of Belgrade, described at the beginning of the chapter, the Partisan memory is commemorated in national terms, 'de-Yugoslavized', cleansed from its transnational and communist nature.

As seen above, the dominant interpretations of the Second World War and Yugoslavia in Croatia and Serbia revolve around commonplaces related to the notions of resistance, collaboration and victimhood. If we look at how both countries deal with the legacy of the 1990s wars, there are also some similarities. However, in the context of the 1990s when Croatia and Serbia were on the opposing sides of the armed conflict, and regardless of the similar view on the war and Yugoslavia that prevails on both sides, the dominant narratives are not compatible, but instead prove mutually exclusive and competitive. Although the two countries share a common past, having spent most of the twentieth century in one state, the mnemonic content, as opposed to the general forms and practices of memory politics, cannot be described in transnational or multidirectional terms. An approach that proves valuable is the comparative one, examining the general paradigm, correlations and potential transfer of ideas, but at the same time focusing on the specificities of the historical and political context. The nationalization of memory in Croatia and Serbia has two perspectives: one is the above-mentioned nationalization or ethnification of antifascism, if it is addressed at all, and the other entails an exclusive focus on one's own national victims, which encompasses both civilian victims of the Second World War and the victims of the post-war retributions. The narrative of the nation being the largest victim of the Yugoslav regime not only excludes the people from other Yugoslav republics, but also the ethnic minorities from within the country.

It can be concluded that the politics of memory in Croatia and Serbia entails some sort of consensus about the condemnation of the post-war executions and trials by the Yugoslav Partisans, striving for political and legal rehabilitation of victims, regardless of their wartime activities. There is a common understanding that they were innocent victims of political repression and violence, and that the post-war trials and courts were ideologically motivated. However, the media discourses that followed the rehabilitations of Dragoljub Mihailović, the leader of the Chetnik movement, in Serbia in 2015 and of Alojzije Stepinac in Croatia in 2016 revealed another paradox in the relation of the national interpretations of the common past. Extremely negative reactions to these rehabilitations coming from the other country represent the same Yugoslav courts as right and objective when sentencing Stepinac, but wrong and ideologically motivated when sentencing Dragoljub Mihailović and when pronouncing Milan Nedić as an enemy of the people. This argumentation exists the other way around as well.

The rehabilitation of the above-mentioned people and the movements they represented or supported is linked to another issue in the dynamics of memory politics between Croatia and Serbia, which is based on the usage of the other country as the most relevant point of comparison and its discursive construction as the 'significant other'. As already mentioned, the rehabilitation process of Dragoljub Mihailović sparked a wave of negative reactions from Croatia, especially in 2012 when it was expected that he would soon be rehabilitated. The critiques coming from the political parties and government officials emphasized that it was historical revisionism and that his rehabilitation was especially problematic, bearing in mind the Chetnik revival in the wars in the 1990s. The response to these concerns came from Serbia, mostly from the proponents of the rehabilitation of the Chetnik movement, arguing that Croatia did not have any right to complain, having rehabilitated the Ustasha in the 1990s and being founded on their legacy and emphasizing the difference between the Chetniks and the Ustasha. Similarly, any step taken in politics of memory that is deemed controversial is usually justified by pointing out to the other country that what is going on there is much worse. This has its roots in the debates in the 1980s between Croatian and Serbian intellectuals about the Second World War, in which the Serbian side accused the Croatian nation of being genocidal because of the crimes of the Ustasha regime against the Serbian population, and the attempts to picture the Chetnik movement in a more positive light met with criticism from Croatia because of the war crimes they had committed.

Postsocialist Politics of Memory in Relation to Eastern Europe

The main themes and dynamics of the postsocialist politics of memory in Croatia and Serbia can be examined not only in relation to each other but also to the wider context of memory in postsocialist Central and Eastern Europe, where the fall of communism generated an instant need to address the communist past in the politics of memory, even if this involved drawing a 'thick line' of forgetting under the period, as was the case in the first postsocialist years in Poland. Drawing on the study by Clarke, I argue that in this context, as with the post-Yugoslav space, memory of the Second World War and communism has some transnational characteristics but it is nevertheless based in the realm of national history and memory.[33] He argues that Central and East European states have pushed for greater recognition of the crimes of communism at the European Union level as an apparently united front, but these efforts have always been related to domestic politics and national contexts.[34] In the existing research about memory of the Second World War in Europe in general, similar conclusions have been drawn.[35]

Without a doubt, there are similarities in the majority of the postsocialist states, where memory of communism is intertwined with memory of the Second World War, as it was instrumentalized for decades, providing legitimacy to the communist rule. After the fall of communism, 'a new cleansing of the past took place in which the formerly dominant class approaches to "resistance" and "collaboration" was replaced with a focus that often reflected revisionist tendencies'.[36] In most of these countries, the powerful institutions have forged a unitary interpretation of the past from above, instead of the expected democratic pluralization of memory that would follow the fall of communism.[37] In that sense, there are commonplaces defined by the decades of communism. Nevertheless, as Troebst points out, the dictatorial experience connects these countries to the European South, and the collaboration and occupation experience of the Second World War links them to West European countries such as Norway, Denmark and France.[38]

The European Union memory politics has acknowledged the strivings of the postsocialist countries for a recognition of the crimes of communism, most notably by the adoption of the Resolution on European Conscience and Totalitarianism by the European Parliament, but in particular prioritizing the crimes of National Socialism. This resolution is understood as not only equating communism and fascism, but it is framed as emphasizing the condemnation of communism in many postsocialist states. In the context of the post-Yugoslav space, and taking into consideration that Slovenia was one of the states initiating it, the resolution validates historical revisionism, proponents of which look up to the European discourses about the condemnation of totalitarian regimes, and apply them in the contemporary debates on the contemporary history of Yugoslavia. This is problematic, and not only because it ignores the specificity of Yugoslav socialism which was established by the movement massively supported by the people of Yugoslavia.[39] The (post-)Yugoslav context has another specificity, which is the way the country dissolved, through the armed conflicts between the independent states that came out of Yugoslavia, and that continued even into the twenty-first century in Macedonia and Kosovo. Furthermore, the process of reverse transnationalism from a large-scale multinational state to smaller (mostly) nation states parallel to the national fragmentation of memory makes the post-Yugoslav context different. Nevertheless, this chapter does not intend to argue that there is exceptionalism in the Yugoslav case, separating it from all other postsocialist countries. It is, rather, an example of the need for memory studies to fragment and be located, where Central, South Eastern or Eastern Europe represent a non-location, which is often too broad and requires effacement of local specificities.

Conclusion

The process of reverse transnationalism from Yugoslav memory culture to its fragmentation into divided and divisive national memories, summarized in this chapter, encompasses the dominant discourses and the official memory politics in Croatia and Serbia. History writing in these countries often reflects it as well. As opposed to the Yugoslav memory culture based on the transnational narrative that strived for the inclusion of all Yugoslav people, the memory cultures that became dominant during and in the aftermath of the dissolution of the common state are founded on the nation-centred historical narratives. What represents the common past for Croatia and Serbia has been interpreted in national terms, the most prominent objects of revision being the Second World War, the post-war period, and the period of Yugoslav state socialism.

This chapter has argued that, in the context of the transcultural turn that dominates the field of memory studies, nation-centred, often mutually exclusive and competitive memory cultures as well as the locatedness of memory and specificities of national frameworks nevertheless remain relevant. Understanding travelling of memory and its carriers, modes, contents, forms and practices as transnationally constituted does not imply a homogenizing approach that moves away from the locatedness of memory. Examining the national memory cultures in Croatia and Serbia in the comparative perspective thus entails equal attention being given to the relations among them as to their place in the wider postsocialist and European context, where travelling of memory happens and from where certain aspects of national memory cultures are transplanted.

Jelena Đureinović is a doctoral candidate in the Department of History at Justus Liebig University in Giessen, Germany. She holds an MA degree in nationalism studies from Central European University in Budapest. Her current research explores the memory of the Second World War and state socialism in contemporary Serbia, examining specifically the process of the reinterpretation of the Yugoslav Army in the Homeland. Her general research interests lie in the fields of contemporary history and memory studies, with a particular focus on socialist Yugoslavia and the post-Yugoslav space.

Notes

        1. G. Kirn, 'Transnationalism in Reverse: From Yugoslav to Post-Yugoslav Memorial Sites', in C. De Cesari and A. Rigney (eds), *Transnational Memory: Circulation, Articulation, Scales* (Berlin: De Gruyter, 2014), 313–38.
        2. C. De Cesari and A. Rigney (eds), *Transnational Memory: Circulation, Articulation, Scales* (Berlin: De Gruyter, 2014).
        3. D. Levy, 'Changing Temporalities and the Internationalization of Memory Cultures', in Y. Gutman, A. Sodaro and A. Brown (eds), *Memory and the Future: Transnational Politics, Ethics, and Society* (Basingstoke: Palgrave Macmillan, 2010), 17–18.
        4. A. Erll, 'Travelling Memory', *Parallax* 17(4) (2011), 4.
        5. De Cesari and Rigney, *Transnational Memory*, 2.
        6. A. Huyssen, 'Present Pasts: Media, Politics, Amnesia', *Public Culture* 12(1) (2000), 23.
        7. D. Levy and N. Sznaider, *The Holocaust and Memory in the Global Age* (Philadelphia, PA: Temple University Press, 2006).

8. M. Rothberg, *Multidirectional Memory: Remembering the Holocaust in the Age of Decolonization* (Stanford, CA: Stanford University Press, 2009), 3.

9. A. Assmann, 'From Collective Violence to a Common Future: Four Models for Dealing with a Traumatic Past', in H. Gonçalves da Silva et al. (eds), *Conflict, Memory Transfers and the Reshaping of Europe* (Newcastle upon Tyne: Cambridge Scholars Publishing, 2010), 17.

10. Erll, 'Travelling Memory', 7.

11. L. Bond and J. Rapson (eds), *The Transcultural Turn: Interrogating Memory Between and Beyond Borders* (Berlin: De Gruyter, 2014), 19.

12. S. Radstone, 'What Place Is This? Transcultural Memory and the Locations of Memory Studies', *Parallax* 17(4) (2011), 111.

13. Bond and Rapson, *The Transcultural Turn*, 18.

14. H. Sundhaussen, *Jugoslawien und seine Nachfolgestaaten 1943–2011: Eine ungewöhnliche Geschichte des Gewöhnlichen* (Vienna, Cologne and Weimar: Böhlau, 2012), 371.

15. See the introduction to T. Sinbaek, *Usable Histories? Representations of Yugoslavia's Difficult Past from 1945 to 2002* (Aarhus: Aarhus University Press, 2012).

16. K. Stojaković, 'Uvod: Revolucionarno nasilje u Narodnooslobodilačkom ratu', in M. Radanović, *Kazna i zločin: Snage kolaboracije u Srbiji* (Belgrade: Rosa Luxemburg Stiftung, 2015), 21.

17. See I. Deak, J.T. Gross and Tony Judt (eds), *The Politics of Retribution: World War II and its Aftermath* (Princeton, NJ: Princeton University Press, 2000).

18. For a very detailed factual account of the collaboration forces within the territory of Serbia, see M. Radanović, *Kazna i zločin: Snage kolaboracije u Srbiji* (Belgrade: Rosa Luxemburg Stiftung, 2015).

19. J. Dragovic-Soso, *'Saviors of the Nation': Serbia's Intellectual Opposition and the Revival of Nationalism* (London: Hurst, 2002), 70.

20. S. Koren, *Politika povijesti u Jugoslaviji (1945–1960): Komunistička partija Jugoslavije, nastava povijesti, istoriografija* (Zagreb: Srednja Evropa, 2012), 509.

21. H. Sundhaussen, 'Jugoslawien und seine Nachfolgestaaten: Konstruktion, Dekonstruktion und Neukonstruktion von "Erinnerungen" und Mythen', in M. Flacke (ed.), *Mythen der Nationen: 1945 Arena der Erinnerungen* (Berlin: Deutsches Historisches Museum, 2004), 378.

22. Kirn, 'Transnationalism in Reverse', 315.

23. Sindbaek, *Usable Histories?*, 75.

24. W. Höpken, 'Vergangenheitspolitik im sozialistischen Vielvölkerstaat: Jugoslawien 1944–1991', in P. Bock (ed.), *Umkämpfte Vergangenheit: Geschichtsbilder, Erinnerung und Vergangenheitspolitik im internationalen Vergleich* (Göttingen: Vandenhoeck & Ruprecht, 1999), 224.

25. M. Ristović, 'Kome pripada istorija Jugoslavije?', *Godišnjak za društvenu istoriju* 1 (2013), 139.

26. O. Milosavljević, 'Geschichtsrevisionismus und der Zweite Weltkrieg', in Đ. Tomić et al. (eds), *Mythos Partizan. (Dis-)Kontinuitäten der jugoslawischen Linken: Geschichte, Erinnerungen und Perspektiven* (Münster: Unrast, 2013), 226–27.

27. Ristović, 'Kome pripada', 133.

28. Sundhaussen, *Jugoslawien*, 444.

29. Milosavljević, 'Geschichtsrevisionismus', 227.

30. Ibid.

31. T. Kuljić, 'Anti-antifašizam', *Godišnjak za društvenu istoriju* 1(3) (2006), 181.

32. Ibid., 174.

33. D.J. Clarke, 'Communism and Memory Politics in the European Union', *Central Europe* 12(1) (2014), 99–114.

34. Ibid.

35. S. Berger, 'Remembering the Second World War in Western Europe, 1945–2005', in M. Pakier and B. Stråth (eds), *A European Memory? Contested Histories and Politics of Remembrance* (New York: Berghahn Books, 2010), 119–37. R.N. Lebow, W. Kansteiner and C. Fogu (eds), *The Politics of Memory in Postwar Europe* (Durham, NC: Duke University Press, 2006).

36. H. Karge, 'Practices and Politics of Second World War Remembrance: (Trans-) national Perspectives from Eastern and Southeastern Europe', in M. Pakier and B. Stråth (eds), *A European Memory? Contested Histories and Politics of Remembrance* (New York: Berghahn Books, 2010), 138.

37. J. Mark, *The Unfinished Revolution: Making Sense of the Communist Past in Central-Eastern Europe* (New Haven, CT: Yale University Press, 2010), 59.

38. S. Troebst, 'Was für ein Teppich? Postkommunistische Erinnerungskulturen in Ost(mittel)europa', in V. Knigge and U. Mahlert (eds), *Der Kommunismus im Museum: Formen der Auseinandersetzung in Deutschland und Ostmitteleuropa* (Vienna, Cologne and Weimar: Böhlau, 2005), 35.

39. Kirn, 'Transnationalism in Reverse', 334.

Bibliography

Assmann, A. 'From Collective Violence to a Common Future: Four Models for Dealing with a Traumatic Past', in H. Gonçalves da Silva et al. (eds), *Conflict, Memory Transfers and the Reshaping of Europe* (Newcastle upon Tyne: Cambridge Scholars Publishing, 2010), 8–24.

Berger, S. 'Remembering the Second World War in Western Europe, 1945–2005', in M. Pakier and B. Stråth (eds), *A European Memory? Contested Histories and Politics of Remembrance* (New York: Berghahn Books, 2010), 119–37.

Bond, L., and J. Rapson (eds). *The Transcultural Turn: Interrogating Memory Between and Beyond Borders*. Berlin: De Gruyter, 2014.

Clarke, D.J. 'Communism and Memory Politics in the European Union', *Central Europe* 12(1) (2014), 99–114.

Deak, I., J.T. Gross and Tony Judt (eds). *The Politics of Retribution: World War II and its Aftermath*. Princeton, NJ: Princeton University Press, 2000.

De Cesari, C., and A. Rigney. *Transnational Memory: Circulation, Articulation, Scales*. Berlin: De Gruyter, 2014.

Dragovic-Soso, J. *'Saviors of the Nation': Serbia's Intellectual Opposition and the Revival of Nationalism*. London: Hurst, 2002.

Erll, A. 'Travelling Memory'. *Parallax* 17(4) (2011), 4–18.

Höpken, W. 'Vergangenheitspolitik im sozialistischen Vielvölkerstaat: Jugoslawien 1944–1991', in P. Bock (ed.), *Umkämpfte Vergangenheit: Geschichtsbilder, Erinnerung und Vergangenheitspolitik im internationalen Vergleich* (Göttingen: Vandenhoeck & Ruprecht, 1999), 210–47.

Huyssen, A. 'Present Pasts: Media, Politics, Amnesia'. *Public Culture* 12(1) (2000), 21–38.

Karge, H. 'Practices and Politics of Second World War Remembrance: (Trans-)national Perspectives from Eastern and Southeastern Europe', in M. Pakier and B. Stråth (eds), *A European Memory? Contested Histories and Politics of Remembrance* (New York: Berghahn Books, 2010), 137–47.

Kirn, G. 'Transnationalism in Reverse: From Yugoslav to Post-Yugoslav Memorial Sites', in C. De Cesari and A. Rigney (eds), *Transnational Memory: Circulation, Articulation, Scales* (Berlin: De Gruyter, 2014), 313–38.

Koren, S. *Politika povijesti u Jugoslaviji (1945–1960): Komunistička partija Jugoslavije, nastava povijesti, istoriografija*. Zagreb: Srednja Evropa, 2012.

Kuljić, T. 'Anti-antifašizam', *Godišnjak za društvenu istoriju* 1(3) (2006), 171–84.

Lebow, R.N, W. Kansteiner and C. Fogu (eds). *The Politics of Memory in Postwar Europe* Durham, NC: Duke University Press, 2006.

Levy, D. 'Changing Temporalities and the Internationalization of Memory Cultures', in Y. Gutman, A. Sodaro and A. Brown (eds), *Memory and the Future: Transnational Politics, Ethics, and Society* (Basingstoke: Palgrave Macmillan, 2010), 15–30.

Levy, D., and N. Sznaider. *The Holocaust and Memory in the Global Age*. Philadelphia, PA: Temple University Press, 2006.

Mark, J. *The Unfinished Revolution: Making Sense of the Communist Past in Central-Eastern Europe*. New Haven, CT: Yale University Press, 2010.

Milosavljević, O. 'Geschichtsrevisionismus und der Zweite Weltkrieg', in Đ. Tomić et al. (eds), *Mythos Partizan. (Dis-)Kontinuitäten der jugoslawischen Linken: Geschichte, Erinnerungen und Perspektiven* (Münster: Unrast, 2013), 222–34.

Radstone, S. 'What Place Is This? Transcultural Memory and the Locations of Memory Studies'. *Parallax* 17(4) (2011), 109–23.

Ristović, M. 'Kome pripada istorija Jugoslavije?'. *Godišnjak za društvenu istoriju* 1 (2013), 132–43.

Rothberg, M. *Multidirectional Memory: Remembering the Holocaust in the Age of Decolonization*. Stanford, CA: Stanford University Press, 2009.

Sinbaek, T. *Usable Histories? Representations of Yugoslavia's Difficult Past from 1945 to 2002*. Aarhus: Aarhus University Press, 2012.

Stojaković, K. 'Uvod: Revolucionarno nasilje u Narodnooslobodilačkom ratu', in M. Radanović, *Kazna i zločin: Snage kolaboracije u Srbiji* (Belgrade: Rosa Luxemburg Stiftung, 2015), 11–28.

Sundhaussen, H. 'Jugoslawien und seine Nachfolgestaaten: Konstruktion, Dekonstruktion und Neukonstruktion von "Erinnerungen" und Mythen', in M. Flacke (ed.), *Mythen der Nationen: 1945 Arena der Erinnerungen* (Berlin: Deutsches Historisches Museum, 2004), 373–426.

———. *Jugoslawien und seine Nachfolgestaaten 1943–2011: Eine ungewöhnliche Geschichte des Gewöhnlichen*. Vienna, Cologne and Weimar: Böhlau, 2012.

Troebst, S. 'Was für ein Teppich? Postkommunistische Erinnerungskulturen in Ost(mittel) europa', in V. Knigge and U. Mahlert (eds), *Der Kommunismus im Museum: Formen der Auseinandersetzung in Deutschland und Ostmitteleuropa* (Vienna, Cologne and Weimar: Böhlau, 2005), 31–55.

CHAPTER 7

Disturbing Memories

Coming to Terms with the Stalinist History of Europe

CLAUDIA WEBER

I carried everything I had. It wasn't actually mine. It was either intended for a different purpose or somebody else's. The pigskin suitcase was a gramophone box. The dust coat was from my father. The town coat with the velvet neckband from my grandfather. The breeches from my Uncle Edwin. The leather puttees from our neighbour, Herr Carp. The green gloves from my Auntie Fini. Only the claret silk scarf and the toilet bag were mine, gifts from recent Christmases. The war was still on in January 1945.

—Herta Müller, *The Hunger Angel*[1]

With these much-quoted lines, Herta Müller begins *The Hunger Angel*, a novel that honours the memory of her close friend Oskar Pastior, and that of others. *The Hunger Angel* describes the fate of the so-called Banat Germans – among them Uncle Edwin, Mr Cap, and Auntie Fini – in Sovietized Romania, and subsequently during the Ceaușescu dictatorship. As someone who admonished others not to forget the injustices of communism, state repression, and the constant threat of Romania's infamous Securitate, Herta Müller was both eyed with suspicion and celebrated following the announcement, in October 2009, that she was to be awarded the Nobel Prize for literature. The German news magazine *Der Spiegel* perceived the Nobel Prize for Müller as a dramatic signal that such memories should not be suppressed. Ilija Trojanow, a writer like Müller, viewed the award as a sign that warned against trivializing communist injustices. And the *Süddeutsche Zeitung* lauded the laureate as a 'virtuoso in the horrific process of recollection' of the harrowing realities in the camps and the humiliation of daily life under totalitarian state socialism.[2]

There can be no doubt that, for Herta Müller, her life and work centres on the dramatic confrontation with the existential experience of living in a dictatorship, as well as on the abysmal pain of losing one's home. But that is not the reason I have chosen to begin my chapter with a quotation from her book. *The Hunger Angel* focuses on the Stalinist deportation policies implemented against the Germans in Romania. The novel illuminates a chapter of the European history of Stalinist violence that for a long time seemed to have disappeared both from academia and from peoples' memories. Stalin's terror has remained for the most part an inner-Soviet issue, since it was seen as synonymous with the 'Great Terror' of 1935–38, both among contemporaries and with respect to reflections on the past. But this perspective was never accurate, not even in the era of *Ezhovshina*, during which the NKVD massacred large numbers of international communists, citizens of other states, and members of other ethnic-national groups. Stalin's terror was not inner-Soviet violence; in terms of its justifications and implementation, it was always directed at the world outside the Soviet Union and at Europe – and that was the case even before the Red Army marched into Poland on 17 September 1939. Only in recent years has it become possible to study the extent to which even the Spanish Civil War was defined by the terror of the NKVD. But in the memories of the Second World War that prevailed during the Cold War, the international dimension of Stalinism had retreated into the background. On this historical backdrop, Herta Müller has written a history of Europe that renders it impossible to continue to assign the story of Stalinist mass annihilation and expulsion a place in Russian and Soviet memory alone.

The Hunger Angel confronts readers with Europe's disturbing history of violence and dictatorships that manifests itself in the biographies of the continent's inhabitants. Unintentionally, and with all the personal tragedy this entailed, the author became a master of this 'horrific recollection'. Then, in autumn of 2010, it was revealed that the life of the poet Oskar Pastior, upon which *The Hunger Angel* was based, involved more than the experience of life in a Stalinist camp. Under the cover name 'Stein Otto', Pastior was an informal collaborator of the Romanian secret police, the Securitate. Evidence shows that he actively wrote reports for the Securitate; one former colleague has charged that his reports led to the suicide of the young Romanian-German poet Georg Hoprich in 1969. Oskar Pastior's biographical entanglements, which shocked Herta Müller and caught her completely unaware, are not only a further, devastating example of how transient the categories of 'victim' and 'perpetrator' are. They also reveal how these ascriptions fail to grasp the realities of life in a dictatorship and in a society shaped by violence. Pastior's life and the most recent revelations about it demonstrate – and on a personal level this is quite simply tragic – how the ambivalences of the history of violence in Europe hold abominable lessons in store, even for the 'virtuoso in the horrific process of recollection'. These are lessons that historians will be forced to address, as well.

For historians, at least two questions emerge from the confrontation with this case and its lessons. The first revolves around the issue of an adequate and appropriate academic narrative. How can scholars, in writing about history, do justice to the disturbing truths about Europe's history of violence, to the blurred boundaries between victims and perpetrators, and to the grey zones of war? Can historians, who have reached a conscious decision not to employ a poetic or fictional language, successfully confront these questions in a scholarly narrative? The problem of approaching, with the process of writing, the 'coexistence and co-presence of the disparate' has increasingly preoccupied scholars of East European history like Karl Schlögel, formerly a professor at the European University Viadrina in Frankfurt (Oder), since the Soviet archives were opened. In his book *Moscow, 1937* (first published in German in 2008 as *Terror und Traum: Moskau 1937*), Schlögel attempted – most successfully, I think – to create a narrative of simultaneity, in terms of space and time, that draws together the extremes of life under the regime of violence in Stalin's Moscow.[3] An approach to the study of history that refers to space and time is, without a doubt, a method for recollecting and grasping disparate history, as if in a prism.[4] This kind of approach would lend itself equally to addressing, by writing, the confrontation with the European experience of dictatorship – Schlögel's topic is Stalinism. It seems to me that a further possibility is a biographical approach, a method that is not new within the tool kit of historiography. The aim of this approach would be to open up the prism of historical contradictions through the description of contemporary lives such as that of Oskar Pastior. At times, biographical methods have been subject to criticism – criticism that is at times justified – because they lead to speculation on psychological factors. But this is not the kind of biographical method I am referring to here. My aim is not to explain biographical twists and turns; rather, I would like to take them as a starting point for elaborating on and condensing the historic 'co-presence of the disparate'. The Dutch writer Harry Mulisch, who died in 2010, once summarized this biographical approach with a typical sweeping gesture in the words 'I am World War II'. Mulisch was referring indirectly to the biographical tension between his Jewish mother and his father, who collaborated with the Nazis. This tension shaped the literary work of Mulisch, and also reflected the reality of the Second World War. But now I would like to end my remarks on methods, despite their unfinished nature, because they are not the central topic of my chapter.

The second question also pertains to the academic discipline of historiography. However, it is one that is much more intensely connected with current public and political discussions centring on European cultures of memory. These discussions have largely emerged since the process of EU enlargement started in Eastern Europe. They centre mostly on debates about the peculiar competition between the experience of National Socialist and Stalinist violence, an East–West conflict over the politics of memory, which becomes apparent especially in the context of the search for and establishment of symbols and sites of memory and commemoration. The establishment of the Holocaust as the founding myth of European or Western civilization at the Holocaust conference in Sweden in 2000 triggered a demand to establish, after the accession of the East European and East-Central European states to the EU, 23 August as a European day of commemoration, it being the date on which the Molotov-Ribbentrop Pact had been signed. The question is whether – with a backdrop of the contradictions of ascriptions of the victim and perpetrator roles, competing referential narratives, and the ideological heritage of the memories of violence in the Cold War – a European culture of memory is even conceivable. Can Europe be based on a common history, and who are the actors in shaping this 'invention of tradition'? I would like to approach these questions by reviewing the past, and while I will not be able to supply final answers, I hope to offer some perspectives for further consideration.

Nowhere: Eastern Europe

After the end of the Second World War, a Europe that preserved the memory of Stalinism did not exist. In the East, any confrontation with the terror of the 1930s and the Stalinist violence perpetrated during the war was a highly political taboo. Calling that taboo into question was linked, at least in certain periods, to life-threatening consequences. Despite the various political cycles and turns of the ensuing decades, the taboo attached to the Soviet Union's own history of terror and violence remained in place until the Gorbachev era. The taboo was juxtaposed by the monstrous myth of the Great Patriotic War; in its shadow, the Great Terror and all contradictory memories of the war disappeared. When Stalin's huge victory parade took place on 24 June 1945, elite troops that had never seen the trenches, rather than former front soldiers, marched through Red Square in Moscow. These steely *molodzi* (great fellows), who threw down Nazi flags in front of the

Lenin Mausoleum, symbolized not only the myth of the victorious Red
Army but also presented the image of a shining victory and an illustrious
victor – Stalin. Addressing issues like terror and violence in the presence of
such greatness could only seem like blasphemy.[5]

Nikita Khrushchev's 'Thaw', which has been described correctly, if
often somewhat too schematically, as an antipode to Stalinism, did not bring
about a fundamental shift in the politics of history. Of course, the critique
of Stalin's cult of personality and of the purges changed the configuration
of the myth: Stalin disappeared and actual front soldiers, who told a less
glorious story of dirt, hunger and death in the trenches, replaced the steely
elite soldiers. Parallel to the developments in Western Europe, in Germany,
and in the United States, the Soviet Union also carefully began addressing the Holocaust in the 1960s. Perceiving the Jewish population of the
Soviet Union as victims of the war had been unthinkable while political
anti-Semitism reigned in the late Stalin era. Yevgeny Yevtushenko's poem
Babi Yar was published and was used by Dimitri Shostakovich as the basis
for his thirteenth symphony. When debates emerged in Kiev over whether
a monument commemorating the victims of Babi Yar should be erected,
however, Khrushchev quickly put an end to them, asserting: 'Russians also
died in Babi Yar. Who else? If we deal with this, then we will generate a
conflict'.[6] This conflict, which would have involved the confrontation with
Stalin's anti-Semitic policies and with popular resentments, was avoided
by the official Soviet politics of history until Perestroika set in. As under
Stalin, in the Brezhnev era, the murder of Soviet Jews disappeared from
view behind the general slogan that referred to the 'annihilation of peace-
able Soviet citizens'. In the course of the 1970s, however, the myth of the
'Great Patriotic War' solidified to become part of a monolithic culture of
monuments and commemoration, with clichés, rituals, military honours,
and special rights that stifled veterans' personal memories – especially the
undesirable ones.

For lack of time, I have only outlined very briefly the history of memories of violence in the Soviet Union, which is, for the most part, a history of
the mythologized memory of the 'Great Patriotic War'. My main concern
was to indicate what was possible, and in doing so reveal what was *impossible*.
For despite all the modifications that occurred, Stalinist violence and Soviet
terror remained excluded from collective memory in Europe. Publication
of Aleksandr Solzhenitsyn's novel *One Day in the Life of Ivan Denisovich* in
1962 did not bring any real change. Precisely because Denisovich, the hero
of Solzhenitsyn's novel, was a soldier who was sent to the gulag after being
held as a prisoner of war by the Germans, opening up political debates about
the book would have meant that the war myths might have been called
into question. If Stalinist terror was addressed at all, then it was only in the

context of critique of Stalin as an individual, and the personality cult that he fostered – this had nothing to do with a confrontation with the Soviet history of violence. There was not even a small niche here in which the European dimension of Stalinism could find its place. Topics like the purges of the NKVD in Spain, Stalinist violence in Eastern and South Eastern Europe, the policies of expulsion and annihilation during occupations by the Red Army, and the various forms of collaboration with the Nazi regime during the period of the Molotov-Ribbentrop Pact remained untouched until the end of the Cold War.

The deep-seated fear of addressing these issues had, above all, one key motive. Any form of dealing with the ethnic-national policies of expulsion, with sexual violence, and with the purges during the Sovietization of Eastern Europe – including those that used literature or the other arts – would have fundamentally called into question the legitimacy of Moscow's hegemonic position with respect to the satellite states. History and memory were perceived by all Soviet leaders – including Stalin, Khrushchev and Brezhnev, as well as Gorbachev – as existential threats to the cohesion of the Soviet empire in the period after the Second World War. Gorbachev's refusal to finally publish, in 1990, the order set down by Stalin and the Politburo to kill twenty-two thousand Polish prisoners of war in 1940 is one especially telling example. Although the Soviet foreign minister at the time, Eduard Shevardnadze, the chairman of the International Department of the Communist Party's Central Committee, Valentin Falin, and even KGB head Vladimir Kryuchkov had made it unmistakably clear in late March 1989 that 'in this case, time is not our ally', and the inner-Soviet debate about the Great Terror was already underway, Gorbachev hesitated to begin addressing Soviet war crimes.

A further factor that is a key to explaining the decades in which the taboo surrounding Stalinist crimes and the hesitance to address the international dimensions of Stalinism emerged pertains to the satellite states themselves. The leaders of these states – from Bulgaria's Todor Zhivkov to Poland's Wojciech Jaruzelski to East Germany's Erich Honecker – feared the erosion of their own power if they permitted a discussion of how their parties had acquired it. This applied to both a focus on the Stalinist repression of the international communist movement – Poland's Communist Party had been almost completely obliterated in the 1930s – and to the violent seizure of power after the Second World War. The communist parties' dependence on Moscow rendered them apologists of the Soviet historical myths. Memory in Eastern Europe was subordinated under a 'master narrative' that was merely extended to include the topoi of liberation and the antifascist resistance movements. As in the Soviet Union, the commemoration of the Holocaust was not possible in the East European states, especially since that would have meant confronting the anti-Semitism manifested in Hungary, Romania, Poland and elsewhere, and would have turned victims into collaborators and perpetrators.

Memories of the experience of violence that ran counter to the official historical myths of state socialism survived in niches. Memories of wartime sexual violence, such as the mass rape by Red Army soldiers, were represented in coded language, for example in sentences that did not have to be ended to nonetheless be complete: 'Then, when the Russians came. . .'. Also present in coded language in family memories were the experiences of expulsion or the gulag; such memories were passed on in the form of social behaviour, as well. Herta Müller describes how much her mother's years in the camp shaped her own life. Müller was given the first name of her mother's friend, who died while imprisoned. And the sentence 'There was nothing to eat in the camp' accompanied the meals of her childhood.[7] The third space in which the memories of the Sovietization of Western Europe survived that contradicted the myth of liberation was in dissident circles and in Samizdat publications. In the People's Republic of Poland, to refer to just one example, Andrzej Wajda's early films *Kanał* (Sewer, 1956) and *Popiół i diament* (Ashes and Diamond, 1958), which centre on the tragic fate of the Poles in the Second World War and the violent suppression of the Warsaw uprising under the eyes of the Red Army, reveal the fractures in the image of the Soviet liberator.

Nowhere: Western Europe

Now I would like to turn to Western Europe. In the period after the Second World War , a common market was established as well as a common legal framework and, gradually, a political community, which is today called the European Union. Today, the memory that shapes this union's identity is based on the Holocaust. The Holocaust is the historical reference point for European self-understanding. It is an appellative, negatively framed site of memory, from which emanates a mission – the conviction that the sole protection against history repeating itself is the fostering of a European democratic society.[8] This is seen as both the task for the present and the design for the future that underlies memories of the Holocaust. But in a manner similar to what historian Peter Novick once described for the United States, the Holocaust did not become this unquestionable topos of history in the Federal Republic of Germany or in the rest of Europe until the late 1960s. A European memory of the Holocaust that is not only based on narratives of resistance and identification with the victims but also incorporates the confrontation with the role of Europe as a perpetrator did not emerge until the

1990s. In Western Europe, publications such as Henry Rousso's *Le Syndrome de Vichy*, which appeared in 1987, played a key role in deconstructing the myth of a French nation united in the *Résistance* and described collaboration practices in the Nazis' annihilation of the European Jews. (Note that the US historian Robert O. Paxton had undertaken a similar attempt with his study *Vichy France: Old Guard and New Order*, published in 1972, but it had met with rejection in France's public arena. In the 1990s, French scholars themselves began questioning their country's master narrative.) In Eastern Europe, and especially in Poland, a book published by US historian Jan T. Gross, *Neighbors: The Destruction of the Jewish Community in Jedwabne, Poland*, unleashed an impassioned debate about Polish complicity in the murder of the Jewish population.[9] The confrontation with its role in the annihilation of the Jews, which was based on structural anti-Semitism in society, is an especially painful process in Poland. Myths of victimhood – which are founded in the memory of the partitions of Poland in history and the double or even triple occupation by the Nazi regime and the Soviet Union during the Second World War, and then again by the Soviet Union in the post-war period – form the sacrosanct core of a national identity that has always positioned itself as a strong counterweight to the system of state socialism.

But where, then, is the site of remembrance of the violence of Stalinism? In a striking parallelism to the East European mode of dealing with the topic, there also existed in Western Europe a way of remembering Stalinism that concentrated mainly on the inner-Soviet dimension of terror. Stalin's policies and practices of repression and annihilation were not treated as a taboo, as long as they could be dealt with as a problem of Soviet history. Arthur Koestler's novel *Darkness at Noon*, which appeared in the United Kingdom in 1940 (while the Molotov-Ribbentrop Pact was still in effect) and became an international bestseller, described the atmosphere of the first show trials and political purges that targeted the old Bolsheviks. This is a book about the gradual eclipse (to use the title of the German edition, *Sonnenfinsternis*) over the Soviet Union, not over Europe. The same holds for Solzhenitsyn's epic novel, *The Gulag Archipelago*. Published for the first time in Paris in December 1973 in Russian, it is no doubt one of the most influential books about twentieth-century history. The book exposes the Stalinist system of justice and the camp system within the Soviet Union, but Solzhenitsyn did not take up Soviet terror perpetrated outside the USSR. Both books, to be sure, were the target of abrasive attacks on the part of European, and in particular French, leftists when they were released in 1940 and 1973 respectively. In Great Britain and the USA, in contrast, they strengthened the anticommunism of the Cold War. The chapter has very limited space to dwell on these debates, but the argument should be stressed in this context, namely, that both the possible remembrance of Stalinism and the political and ideological ways it was dealt with, ignored – or at least marginalized – topics such as the Stalinist terror in the Second World War and the ethnically and nationally motivated policies of expulsion.

In Western Europe, memories of Stalin's war crimes and of the expulsion policies – this again reveals a remarkable parallel to Eastern Europe – were also relegated to niches. Memories of Stalin's terror, if they existed at all, were saved in the personal or family realm, and once again this generally occurred in coded language. The niches that existed in the Cold War were devoted not so much to the memories of violence but instead served to deal with the experience of loss. Organizations like the Federation of Expellees (Bund der Vertriebenen) in West Germany focused on the loss of their former homeland and dedicated themselves to the exterritorial maintenance of regional identity and traditions. The work of this and similar organizations centred, furthermore, on demands for restitution to offset at least in part what they had suffered and to recognize and compensate for losses on a material level. The Association of Victims of Stalinism (Vereinigung der Opfer des Stalinismus), founded in West Berlin in 1950 to represent the interests of people who had been detained in the so-called Soviet special camps in Germany, also focused mainly on practical issues of rehabilitation and material aid. The denial of Stalinist terror in the politics of history fit well with these survival strategies of adaptation, caring for traditions, and compensation for material losses. For a long period, West Germany's official policies regarding remembrance ignored Stalinist violence and did not begin addressing the issues involved until after the end of the Cold War. In the ideological force fields of the Cold War, however, the activities of associations representing the interests of expellees and victims of Stalinist violence were never unpolitical. Their rhetoric and their actions were marked by a radical brand of anticommunism that aligned itself with the right or even extreme right within the political spectrum. In the course of public debates about the Holocaust and Nazi crimes that began to surface in the late 1960s in West Germany, memories focusing on the flight from Eastern Europe, the expulsion of Germans from the East, and the violence associated with liberation from the Nazis by the Soviets were interlinked with political revanchism. The official West German politics of history had to draw a clear boundary separating itself from such tendencies. That Stalinist violence was instrumentalized by historical revanchism from the right-wing margins has rendered it much more difficult to deal with this violence in the cultures of memory. Survival of such memories 'on the right-wing margins' is a further factor that has contributed to suppressing Stalinism in West European memories of the Second World War.

During the Cold War, the memory of Stalinist crimes was caught between the political right's desire to relativize Nazi crimes and charges from the left regarding this kind of relativism. Moreover, the status of such memories was defined by a hierarchy of violence and memories of violence. Addressing Stalinism – which was generally left to right-wing groups, East European emigrants, and the so-called renegades – was frequently viewed as an attack on the singularity of the Holocaust. At this point, I must briefly address the *Historikerstreit* of the late 1980s, a debate over the politics of history that was rooted in the issue of the comparability of National Socialism and Stalinism. Those who argued in favour of the comparability of the two dictatorships, such as Joachim Fest, the prominent historian and journalist, were accused by those who fundamentally rejected the idea – including philosopher Jürgen Habermas and historian Wolfgang Wippermann – of aiming to relativize Nazi crimes and questioning their unique nature. The hierarchization of violence that determined that the Holocaust is to be perceived as the 'crime of all crimes' was written into every comparison of dictatorships; this hierarchization preceded any comparison. The comparison between National Socialism and Stalinism was only possible under the dictum of this singularity, a dictum that confirmed itself in the act of comparing. Despite a number of outstanding studies that have emerged from historical work comparing dictatorships in recent decades, this precondition of any comparison has become its problem. It reproduces a hierarchy of violence that frequently means that the historical method almost unavoidably but unintentionally ends in a heuristic vacuum.

For if National Socialism was 'evil itself', then Stalinism could not be as evil, much less 'more' evil. This hierarchy shaped memories of Stalinism in Western Europe during the Cold War. It meant that Stalin's crimes always appeared to be less extreme, because they were, as Hannah Arendt argued, more old-fashioned in their moral legitimation. In contrast to National Socialism, Arendt asserted, Stalinism did not require the complete collapse of all valid moral norms. Stalin acted like a common criminal, who could never admit his crimes, but who hypocritically justified them on the basis of a traditional canon of values. National Socialism, which did not, in contrast, have need of moral norms, could do this without hypocrisy. The Nazi regime was, as Arendt wrote, 'morally, not in societal terms, more extreme than Stalin's regime in its worst form'. And elsewhere in the same text: 'From a strictly moral perspective, Stalin's crimes were, in a manner of speaking, old-fashioned'.[10]

But the opposite argument was also possible. So-called revisionist Soviet research, which emerged in the 1970s especially in the United States, considered Stalin's crimes less extreme – not because they were based on an old-fashioned moral code but because their foundation was moral radicalism.[11] Belief in an egalitarian design of a communist society and the utopia of the new human being were the preconditions for this shift, which set the terror in motion. The utopian vision was its justification. Both explanations, which I have sketched here very briefly and extrapolated, do not view Stalinism as 'evil itself'. Stalinism was either the collateral damage of a radical process of modernization and a utopian vision of society, or it was the effect of backwardness and tradition, which was at times also rooted in culturalism.

Nowhere: Europe

Eastern Europe is dead. With this pronouncement, Berlin historian Jörg Baberowski triggered an intense debate in the 1990s about the state of East European history and research on Eastern Europe after the end of the Cold War.[12] Baberowski, who charged that his colleagues had cultivated a decades-long self-isolation and methodological provincialism, called on them to over-come ingrained political and ideological ways of thinking. He articulated the hope that, when East European research ended its comfortable self-absorp-tion, then (and only then) would its focus, the history of Eastern Europe, be incorporated into the broader field of European history. The artificial division that was the product of the Iron Curtain would then only have to itself be historicized within the scope of a historiography of Europe as a whole, a historiography structured along the lines of different epochs and methods.

The crises of recent years suggest, however, that today Western Europe may also be dead. In contrast to the end of Eastern Europe, manifested at the end of the Soviet Union and the ensuing establishment of new nation states, the erosion of Western Europe has been unfolding in much more subtle ways. Nearly three decades after the fall of the Berlin Wall, Eastern and Western Europe as political-ideological units are becoming a thing of the past. Their history now again appears to be unrestrained; old certainties and the rhetoric of relativization provoke discontent, and the coordinate system of memory and remembrance seem to have shifted. A European memory calls for a con-frontation with the European dimension of Stalinist violence and its absence in the Cold War's cultures of memory. If I were to call for incorporating the history of Stalinist violence into Europe's culture of memory solely on the grounds that it belongs to Europe geographically, historically and culturally, then this justification would be inadequate. But my intention is instead to show that Stalinism is a part of European memory because Stalinist violence occurred here. This violence shaped the continent's history and its culture of memory, in the East and the West. The European dimension of Stalinism, the confrontation with Stalinist war crimes, and Stalinism's influence on the ideological trench warfare of the Cold War continue to be, for the most part, lacunae in historical research. These gaps are derived, on the one hand, from the difficulties in accessing relevant archive documents; on the other hand, they are also the result of the hesitancy of researchers when it comes to exposing themselves to the disturbing dimensions of history.

The real challenge for a European history of memory is to allow the historical entanglements of the twentieth century to become a part of representations of its history of contradictions. This would involve portraying contradictions like the ones we encounter in the life and literary work of Herta Müller and Oskar Pastior. Life in societies shaped by violence is a nervous balancing act, in which the slightest shift of weight can have fatal impacts. To reconstruct historically this balance that is needed to survive – and to allow it to surface in memory – is a difficult undertaking. To do both is all the more difficult, since those who were born when the occurrences in question were over know what their outcome was. We have become accustomed to referring to the situation of people in historical periods under consideration as tragic, since they lack knowledge of how things ended. The historian's gaze, in contrast, has been called privileged, precisely because of that knowledge. I am not certain whether this distinction is correct or whether we might not be closer to the truth if we turned it around. The painstaking and precise efforts of the historical profession accept the tragedy of those who know. Our supposed privilege is deceptive if we all too quickly read the possibilities of human life from their known end. Life in violence is one possible mode of human coexistence. It cannot be a desired form, but it is a possibility that exists historically and, in some places, in the present. It is a disturbing form of existence that historians, writers, and those who shape the politics of history must approach. Whether a European culture of memory will emerge from this approach is something I cannot predict. I am not at all certain that Europe will ever produce a European memory that also remembers the 'co-presence of the disparate'. That this co-presence is perceived can hardly be considered adequate.

Claudia Weber is professor of European contemporary history and focuses on the history of East and South East Europe, as well as the cultural dimensions of Europeanization in the twentieth century. She has recently authored the monograph *Krieg der Täter: Die Massenerschießungen von Katyń* [War of the perpetrators: The mass shootings of Katyń] (Hamburg: Hamburger Edition, 2015).

Notes

1. Quote from excerpt online at http://www.signandsight.com/service/1925.html (last accessed 4 September 2015).

2. Der Spiegel Online, 'Fanal gegen den Furor des Vertuschens', http://www.spiegel. de/kultur/literatur/ (last accessed 26 February 2011). Thomas Steinfeld, 'Der Hunger – nur er frisst immer weiter' [The hunger – it simply eats on and on], http://www.sueddeutsche.de/ kultur/, 8 October 2009 (last accessed 26 February 2011).

3. Karl Schlögel, *Moscow, 1937* (Cambridge: Polity Press, 2012).

4. Ibid.

5. Irina Scherbakowa, *Zerrissene Erinnerung: Der Umgang mit Stalinismus und Zweitem Weltkrieg im heutigen Russland* (Göttingen: Wallstein, 2010), 14.

6. Scherbakowa, *Zerrissene Erinnerung*, 26.

7. Von Festenberg et al., 'Die Waffe Poesie', *Der Spiegel* 42 (2009), 147.

8. Since the 2000 Holocaust conference in Sweden, European states have committed themselves to commemorating the Holocaust. The declaration is available at https://www. holocaustremembrance.com/about-us/stockholm-declaration (last accessed 4 September 2015).

9. Jan T. Gross, *Neighbors: The Destruction of the Jewish Community in Jedwabne, Poland* (Princeton, NJ: Princeton University Press, 2001).

10. 'moralisch, nicht gesellschaftlich, extremer als das Stalin-Regime in seiner schlimmsten Gestalt. . . . Von einem streng moralischen Standpunkt aus waren Stalins Verbrechen sozusagen altmodisch'. From a lecture delivered in 1965 at the New School for Social Research in New York, 'Some Questions of Moral Philosophy', published in German in the following volume: Hannah Arendt, *Über das Böse: Eine Vorlesung zur Fragen der Ethik* (Munich: Piper, 2006), first sentence p. 15, second sentence p. 14. An edited version in English was published in the collection Hannah Arendt, *Responsibility and Judgment* (New York: Schocken Books, 2005).

11. See Sheila Fitzpatrick, 'Revisionism in Soviet History', *History and Theory* 46 (December 2007), 77–91; and from the same author, 'Revisionism in Retrospect: A Personal View', *Slavic Review* 67 (Fall 2008) 3, 682–704.

12. For a summary of the controversy with the articles published by Jörg Baberowski and others, see Stefan Creuzberger et al. (eds), *Wohin steuert die Osteuropaforschung? Eine Diskussion* [Where does the East European research go? A discussion] (Cologne: Bibliothek Wissenschaft und Politik, 2000).

Bibliography

Archival Sources

Der Spiegel Online. 'Fanal gegen den Furor des Vertuschens', http://www.spiegel.de/kultur/ literatur/ (last accessed 26 February 2011).

Secondary Sources

Arendt, H. *Über das Böse: Eine Vorlesung zur Fragen der Ethik.* Munich: Piper, 2006 (English version: Arendt, H. *Responsibility and Judgment.* New York: Schocken Books, 2005).

Creuzberger, S., et al., (eds). *Wohin steuert die Osteuropaforschung? Eine Diskussion.* Cologne: Bibliothek Wissenschaft und Politik, 2000.

Festenberg, N. von, et al. 'Die Waffe Poesie' [The poetry as a weapon], *Der Spiegel* 42 (2009), 146–49.

Fitzpatrick, S. 'Revisionism in Soviet History'. *History and Theory* 46 (December 2007), 77–91.

————. 'Revisionism in Retrospect: A Personal View'. *Slavic Review* 67 (Fall 2008), 682–704.

Gross, J.T. *Neighbors: The Destruction of the Jewish Community in Jedwabne, Poland*. Princeton, NJ: Princeton University Press, 2001.

Müller, H. *The Hunger Angel*. New York: Metropolitan Books, 2012.

Scherbakowa, I. *Zerrissene Erinnerung: Der Umgang mit Stalinismus und Zweitem Weltkrieg im heutigen Russland* [Torn memory: Dealing with Stalinism and the Second World War in present-day Russia]. Göttingen: Wallstein, 2010.

Schlögel, K. *Moscow, 1937*. Cambridge: Polity Press, 2012.

Steinfeld, T. 'Der Hunger – nur er frisst immer weiter' [The hunger – it simply eats on and on], *Süddeutsche Zeitung*, 8 October 2009. http://www.sueddeutsche.de/kultur/ (last accessed 26 February 2011).

CHAPTER 8

'Glorious, Accursed Europe'

A Fictional Historian, Transcultural Holocaust Memory and the Quest for a European Identity

JUDITH MÜLLER

Introduction

In his well-known essay on Jewish history and Jewish memory, Yoseph Hayim Yerushalmi not only reflects on the crucial role that memory has played in Jewish life and tradition throughout the centuries and how it influenced the canonical texts, but he also distinguishes between historiography in the modern understanding and the concept that is called memory. This distinction between the two is essential, especially in modern times, since the interest in history only emerged with the decline of Jewish memory in its traditional – meaning religious – sense:

> The modern effort to reconstruct the Jewish past begins at a time that witnesses a sharp break in the continuity of Jewish living and hence also an ever-growing decay of Jewish group memory. In this sense, if for no other, history becomes what it had never been before – the faith of fallen Jews. For the first time in history, not a sacred text, becomes the arbiter of Judaism.[1]

Moreover, 'only in the modern era do we really find, for the first time, a Jewish historiography divorced from Jewish collective memory, and in crucial respects, thoroughly at odds with it'.[2] From both quotes we hear the actual message, that historiography was not something completely new to Judaism in the nineteenth century. On the contrary, many of the religious scriptures contain historiographic information, and the memory books of the Middle Ages testify to pogroms and other events in great detail. In addition, when we think of the Jewish holidays alone we encounter commemorations of traumatic events from biblical times onwards. However, this Jewish memory did not depend on historians; rather, it was embedded in the common faith as well as in religious and social institutions.[3] Moreover, historiography goes beyond the past that religious communities want to commemorate, and thus 'memory and modern historiography stand, by their nature, in radically different relations to the past'.[4] Memory is rather selective, whereas the historian not only tries to fill the gaps that memory leaves open, but 'constantly challenges even those memories that have survived intact'.[5] Constructed communal memory, by contrast, does not challenge the communities understanding of the past, nor does it try to ask difficult questions; instead the opposite is true. Memory as constructed from historic events is often full of myths, and its task is to build a communal identity, especially in 'imagined communities'.[6]

Traditional Jewish memory – for example, the already mentioned commemoration of events on Jewish holidays – originated from a time when memory worked differently. As Jan Assmann elaborates, memorization through repetition, the very essence of human learning, is also the basis for what is today called cultural memory. As Assmann further explains, neurology and psychology posit that memory is a phenomenon solely connected to an individual's brain, but cultural studies put it in a social context: 'The question [of] what content this memory can receive, how it organizes these contents and how long it is able to keep them is not a question of inner capacity and control, but rather of external social and cultural circumstances'.[7] Whereas the cultural memory is passed on through rituals and symbols, the significance of social connectivity and dependence on communication with others is discussed under the term communicative memory.[8] Aleida Assmann sees a significant connection between the two: 'There is a parallel between the *cultural* memory that spans vast time periods and is based on normative texts and the *communicative* memory that encompasses three generations and consists of orally transmitted memories'.[9] Both aspects, the cultural and the communicative, are suggestible, and thus collective memory is often used for specific politics of remembrance and forgetting.[10] Yerushalmi, as well as Jan and Aleida Assmann, show the development from a traditional, ritualized memorization to different contemporary concepts and debates. However, Yerushalmi then turns to modern history and historiography whereas Assmann and Assmann focus on the concept of collective memory and its difficulties. Both directions are of relevance in the context of this chapter.

It has been seen as crucial for the construction of a community's identity that the individuals living in it share what has often been called a collective memory, a term that is obviously very controversial. The concept of collective memory is already problematic regarding, for instance, a nation or a similar community. Thus, it is even more relevant to subject it to critical examination when it comes to events like the Holocaust, which is claimed by different communities as an identity constructing crisis and part of their history. Although the 'geography of Holocaust memory is located in Europe',[11] and the commemoration from a victim's perspective is with the Jewish communities around the world, it is now remembered on a global level.[12] One example for the Holocaust as transcultural memory is the Chinese novel *A Jewish Piano* by Beila (2007).[13] This demonstrates two trends as elucidated by Aleida Assmann: the tendency to commemorate mostly negative events, and the preference for the perspective of the victims rather than the perpetrators.[14] Assmann elaborates: 'Indeed, today this historical event is not only remembered by the survivors and the families of the Jewish victims in the mode of a (victim identified) self-victimization, but also by a growing transnational non-Jewish community of remembrance in the mode of victim-empathy'.[15]

In the context of this chapter, the Holocaust as European history that turned later on into a founding myth of the European Union, and thus, the construction of a European memory of the Holocaust, is a crucial transcultural aspect worthy of query. Generally, memory is supposed to have a unifying effect – an aim that many politicians, intellectuals and public figures have in a Europe that was once torn apart by wars and conflicts among its nations. However, the neighbours that were once enemies still do not get along easily, especially because the victims' narrative is at the centre of memory. Thus, memory conflicts within Europe are almost unavoidable:

> The one-sided commemorations by the victims of crimes committed in neighbouring countries, that are blotted out in the memory there [the neighbouring countries] due to another national narrative of victimhood, lead to strong tensions along internal European borders. These tensions can only be overcome through a common form of transnational remembrance and on the basis of mutual respect and restored trust.[16]

As Assmann and many others have discussed, the biggest discrepancy when it comes to the discussion about the role of the Holocaust in European memory is between East and West:[17] 'When generally talking about the Holocaust as "European founding myth" it has been widely ignored that only in the West the Holocaust plays a role as a connecting memory icon'.[18] Moreover, only after the Stockholm conference in 2000 was a guideline for its remembrance and perception established in writing, and acknowledged by its member countries. In addition, it was not until 2005 that the date of 27 January was marked for the first time as the official day of remembrance in the European Parliament.[19] Assmann stresses the relevance of the changed perception in this context: 'In this sense, the public commitment to Holocaust memory and its institutionalization were the answer to a changing historical sensibility that came with a widened European responsibility for these crimes'.[20] In addition to the fact that in the EU as a whole, not solely the East, this memory culture appeared very late, it should be remembered that the eastern member states only joined in 2004, decades after the EC and EU were founded as a union of peace in order to avoid war and genocide on the continent.

Whereas the Holocaust functions as a negative founding myth, the European cultural heritage and its values are often characterized as positive and, in many cases, have been idealized. Interestingly, this paradox or double-faced perception of Europe can be found in Israel as well, and has shaped European Jewish history and memory. In 2006 the monograph *Glorious, Accursed Europe* by Yaacov Shavit and Jehuda Reinharz was published in Tel Aviv. In the subheading, the book was defined as an 'essay on Jews, Israelis, Europe and Western Culture'. In their preface, Shavit and Reinharz emphasize that the Jews of Europe did see themselves as Europeans. The authors then stress the Jews' relation to Europe and Europeanness: 'Also in the new Jewish centres outside of Europe – in Eretz Israel and the United States – and for the ones that did not come from Europe, Europe still had an important role in constructing the memory of Jews, in setting their expectations for the future and in conducting the struggles for their cultural orientation and identity'. The perception of Europe in Israel today, especially the Europe of the past, is dominated by two major images. The first is drawn from an idealized remembrance of the long nineteenth century, of a humanistic and cultural Europe in which assimilation was possible, as is often represented by European immigrants in Israel. The second is the Europe of nationalism, of two devastating world wars and the Holocaust.

The nostalgia and the yearning for a lost Europe that does not exist anymore is what leads to an idealization of cultural and national coexistence. This can be demonstrated in an exemplary fashion in Central Europe and the former Habsburg monarchy. One autobiography, especially in vogue for its positive attitude towards Europe, is Stefan Zweig's *The World of Yesterday*. However, it has to be taken into consideration that Zweig's description of Vienna consists of memories of his childhood and youth, and that the historical facts do not present us with a tolerant and problem-free imperial capital. Although, since Zweig attested that the Feuilleton was the Viennese's preferred section of the newspaper, it is no surprise that he left out politics. Moreover, it has been argued, nostalgia and a nostalgic mode of writing existed way back and was present in Habsburgian culture long before the empire disintegrated.[21]

Today it appears as if Europe is dragged into this ambiguous past again and again. Politicians and public characters remind the Europeans of their values and their 'common' culture, while simultaneously telling them which past horrors they should never deign to return. The roots of both these narratives unfold between the enlightenment and the Second World War – the period when historiography in the modern sense was established and when history became more and more relevant to the public discourse.

In this chapter I aim to question the construction of a collective European memory that is based on the Holocaust. In reading Lizzie Doron's *On the Brink of Something Beautiful* (2007), not only in the context of second generation narratives but in discussing one specific character, the historian Hesi Sonnenschaijn, it is the purpose of this chapter to elaborate on the role of historiography in creating individual, national and European narratives. Furthermore, the interrelation of the character's personal traumatization and his profession will be discussed. Hesi himself crosses from the victims' memory into the multilayered sphere of European memory by first studying and teaching history at the Sorbonne and then engaging in a memory project in Poland. How does he shape the 'memory' of his French students and his European colleagues? Are there differences between the different countries represented in Hesi's narrative? To what extent is the victim's perspective included in building a European narrative, or is the European memory of the Holocaust different? Or, is the obsession with memory in the media, in public discussions about Europe and in literature, as well as the obsession of the second generation and Hesi, caused by the same mutual feeling? At least the factors that Iris Milner names do not only apply to people with a second-generation trauma. Milner describes an 'acute feeling of a lost belonging to a tradition and roots, a past that has been violently stolen . . ., that is expectedly accompanied by a sense of loneliness and alienation, and thus produces an obsession with memory which is the shared foundation of the whole modern culture and literature in general'.[22]

Between Fiction and History

Holocaust literature is first and foremost written by the survivors of the catastrophe and appears all over the globe – mainly in Israel, the United States and Europe, and in many different languages – Hebrew and English, but also French, German, Yiddish and others. Moreover, the texts are composed in a variety of genres, from the poetry of Paul Celan, to the fictional prose of Aharon Appelfeld, the autobiographical accounts of Primo Levi and the essayistic texts of Jean Améry. The literature of the second generation is mostly centred in Israel and the United States and is written in prose.

But there are, of course, exceptions; for example, Art Spiegelman's graphic novel *Maus*. The perception of Europe differs when we look at the fictional descriptions of the two generations, for example in Israel. Whereas the survivors had spent part of their lives or at least their childhoods in Europe, their children never got to know the former home of their parents as it was. Thus, the parents' perception is rather ambiguous and includes positive childhood memories, whereas their children often draw a singularly negative image.

Second-generation literature started to appear in Israel in the 1980s. Lizzie Doron published her first book at the end of the 1990s. She was raised by a survivor mother who played a rather large role in the development of Doron's writing. After her mother died, too many questions were left open, and thus Doron – who had been born in 1953 and had studied sociology, criminology and linguistics – started to process her memories and the trauma of her mother in writing.[23] Iris Milner states that many second-generation authors ask similar questions in their books or try to find the missing link to their family's past through writing. Milner's monograph *Past Present: Biography, Identity and Memory in Second Generation Literature* presents the reader with an overview of the central aspects of second-generation literature in general, and in Israel in particular. Moreover, she identifies and analyses central topics and narratological strategies. The term 'second generation' has cultural aspects, but it derives first and foremost from a clinical and therapeutic context.[24] Therefore, Milner uses psychoanalytical tools in her reading process and to interpret the second-generation literature that focuses first and foremost on the (childhood) trauma of the next generation after the events themselves occurred. In addition 'to the decision of those authors who are children of the survivors to put "their Holocaust" at the centre of their literary work, came young Israeli authors who were not the sons and daughters of survivors, but who, like the survivors' children themselves, grew up in the shadow of a silenced secret'.[25] Although the writers are constantly torn between 'speechlessness and talking', this literature not only puts an end to the silence in general, but to the Holocaust narrative as a private narrative in particular.[26]

On the Brink of Something Beautiful is Lizzie Doron's fourth book. In her first texts she deals primarily with the second generation, its trauma and the Holocaust in general. In contrast, later texts like *Who the Fuck is Kafka* (2015) evolve around other issues in Israeli society as well. *On the Brink of Something Beautiful* is structured in three parts, each of them dedicated to one specific character: Amalia, Hesi and Gadi respectively. The three characters lived in the same neighbourhood when they were little and they all have survivor parents. Although not constructed in chronological order, short text pieces tell the stories of their lives from their childhood into their fifties. In this paper the focus will be on Hesi, a character who is confronted

with different European narratives of the Holocaust and who combines his
identity as a survivor child with the one of a professional historian. In other
words, his narrative is shaped by a personal and traumatic memory as well as
by historical facts.

The boy whose parents survived Auschwitz is introduced as 'Hesi
Holocauster' (103), a nickname given to him by his first Parisian lover and
the woman in whose house he lives after arriving in the French capital for his
studies. The onomatopoeia hints at a constant up and down in Hesi's life that
is caused by the Holocaust and especially his parents' experiences. Moreover,
the tonal connection to the word 'rollercoaster' lets the reader picture a
character who follows a fixed track he cannot escape from. Obviously, this
is the case in Hesi's childhood, however his obsession starts to grow with
his studies, and later with his research in Paris. The Holocaust dominates
his professional life and his relationship with his parents, as well as the
short-lived dream that he could have a future with Amalia. In a way, the
nickname Holocauster suits Hesi much better than the bright family name
'Sonnenschaijn' ('sunshine' in German), given to him by his parents.

As a child, Hesi moved with his parents and their friend Wolf
Katzenelnbogen to the north of the city. Thus, they leave behind the neighbourhood in south Tel Aviv where many other Holocaust survivors, mostly
Yiddish-speaking people from Eastern Europe, lived. Hesi's mother misses
her community and struggles in her daily life. Suddenly, her memories and
her trauma seem to reappear: 'Mum was sitting next to the entrance door
and remained silent. When I asked her for whom she was waiting, she said
that she was waiting for Ischo, Tscheska, Etel and other people I did not
know' (112). Later on, Hesi understands that these are friends and relatives
his mother lost in the Holocaust. She develops a coping mechanism and
a way to commemorate her loved ones: 'The same night, Mum sat in the
kitchen and drew with a pencil on little slips of paper from the grocery store.
I had goose bumps from the scratching of the pencil' (114). Hesi's mother
draws houses, shops and the details of graves at the graveyard in her former
hometown in Poland (114). The drawings get a lively touch when she adds
people: her family, her friends and other people from her daily life over
'there'. However, at the same time she loses contact with the present world.
She speaks less and less until she stops communicating at all, except for her
drawings and the sentences and explanations she adds to them in Yiddish.
When Hesi moves to Paris she sends them to him, week after week, and after
she dies he finds many more drawings at his parents' house.

Those people whom Hesi knows only from the drafts become his own
obsession, and it is their world that Hesi wants to recreate. This 'imagined
reality'[27] dominates his thinking when he visits Poland for the first time. At
this point he already teaches at the Sorbonne, and he comes to Auschwitz

on the occasion of the March of the Living as an expert for a French television broadcasting company. When Hesi is at the 'heart of the darkness'[28]
he suddenly looks for the people he knows from the drawings: 'I looked
for Estherke Katzenelnbogen, the mother of Tonishka, for Tscheska, the
funny sister, for Eyna who was gone and for Jenia who might come back,
but when I lifted my gaze from the earth I saw only flags, the flags of
Israel' (159–60). The flags that remind him of the existence of the Jewish
state do seem to be misplaced in the bygone world Hesi is trying to stay
focused on. Before he flies back to Paris he takes one step further, leaves
the crowds, and travels to the town his mother was born in: Ustrzyki. Hesi
tries to identify the houses and to figure out which family had lived where
(163). He sees the stains the Mesusot had left on the doors (164) and he
feels that this is where he comes from – and where he wants to be. After
these realizations about his mother's past, we then learn about another of
Hesi's grandiose thoughts: he wants to marry Amalia like his grandfather
had married his grandmother, and bring back joy to the place where his
mother had been born (164).

As Iris Milner elaborates, many of the second generation wish to learn
about the traumatic past their parents did not talk about. Some do go on a
journey to the epicentre of their parents' experiences, just like Hesi does.
On those journeys the children try to understand missing connections in
their own stories. They do not always go to the actual geographical places
of their parent's past horrors, but to the silenced realms, and in some cases
their travels are not even physical journeys but rather complex psychological
journeys into the past.[29] Hesi's journey includes both concepts; he travels
geographically in space but mentally back in time. Furthermore, his explora-
tion of Ustrzyki goes far beyond a journey: he aims to convince Amalia that
they belong there (130). Belonging implies a deep emotional connectivity to
a place. Hesi may indeed have this sense of connection, after all the people
in his mother's drawings seem almost alive to him. Moreover, both their
families have a history there: 'Our families were here for four hundred years.
This is the smell they smelled, the air they inhaled, those are the trees, the
streets and the sky they saw' (120). However, in contrast to him, this connection is not enough for Amalia. She dreams of a life with Hesi in Paris,
having tried to forget about her family history for years by submerging into
her Sabra identity and the kibbutz and military communities in Israel. Hesi,
on the other hand, does not understand her decision and dream, and he does
not see Israel as a permanent solution: 'She needs to understand that the State
of Israel is not the true victory over the Nazis; the State of Israel does not
give us back what we lost. After the war the Frenchmen stayed in France, the
Dutch in the Netherlands, the Romanians in Romania, and only the Jews
did not stay here, exactly like Hitler wanted it' (131).

In many cases, the survivors' children realize that the places they want to reconnect to are now occupied by someone or something else.[30] Hesi, however, does not seem to see and to understand and to him, the places are a void that needs to be filled with life, wherein his imagination and fantasy can fully flourish.[31] However, there are Poles mentioned from time to time, and the fact that Hesi chooses the greyness of Poland over the city of light is a subconscious reminder that the places he wants to refill with joy are also the places of death: 'An autumn morning in Krakow, cold rain fell down and dropped on the windowpane' (105).

Commemoration Here and There

Lizzie Doron is a well-known fiction author in Germany, and her books have been translated not only into German, but other European languages as well. In a wider, philosophical definition, her readership in Europe also belongs to the second generation: 'According to this approach, which examines the universal cultural influences of the Holocaust, the term "second generation" is not exclusive to one sector or another, and not even to one nation or another. It constitutes an inclusive cultural concept that reflects the historical break the Holocaust left in Western culture'.[32]

In her working paper 'Does Literature Matter? On the Reception of Israeli Literature in Germany after 1989', Karin Neuburger suggests that 'the boom in Israeli literature in Germany has started to wane'.[33] Nevertheless, it is remarkable that sales figures and the general interest in translation of Israeli fiction rose in the 1990s, the decade after the Zionist narrative in Israeli literature lost its central role and gave way to a pluralist spectrum of narratives, among them the one of the second generation: 'The interest may be conceived as part of the process of rapprochement between Jews and Germans in general, and Israelis and Germans in particular, in the aftermath of the Holocaust'.[34] Moreover, David Grossman's novel *See Under: Love* (1986), which deals with the long-term impact of the Holocaust on many levels, has been overwhelmingly received in Europe.[35] Moscati Steindler states that Israeli books with a connection to the Holocaust are 'enthusiastically acclaimed' in Italy since they are somehow 'liberating'.[36] Nevertheless, Neuburger does not find any indicators that there might be a link between the topic of the Holocaust and the interest in Israeli literature among German critiques:

> Interestingly enough, the fact that Israeli culture is to some extent the culture of the survivors of the Shoah and their offspring is not mentioned in the reviews discussed in this paper. And yet it seems plausible that the vivid interest in Israeli literature during the period in question has to do with the

intensive involvement with the memory of the Shoah and the lost Jewish life in Germany.[37]

However, Anat Feinberg does indeed see a connection to the past among publishers, one that goes far beyond interest and has a rather negative aspect: 'I have never witnessed anti-Jewish or anti-Israel feelings among publishers, but I have experienced great embarrassment, reasoning based on guilt, and even destructive philo-Semitism'.[38] Our protagonist Hesi is confronted with similar problems in his life, and especially when it comes to the project to rebuild Ustrzyki. One of his most important supporters is Ursula, an Argentinian-born German he first meets when he starts studying in Paris. He is suspicious of her family background, but she tells him over and over again that she does not know anything about her family history, and starts to lament how her mother had not liked living in Argentina. Finally, Hesi answers sarcastically: '"You sound like a Jew." I interrupted her and I was angry at myself that I even listened to her. I asked the waiter for the bill and told Ursula that our meeting was over' (154). Interestingly, Hesi identifies her with the Jewish suffering, yet she herself seemingly does not. Unconsciously she apparently feels guilt that possibly leads to her unconditional and seemingly zealous interest and support.

Whereas Ursula is the only German Hesi encounters, working at the Sorbonne and growing up with his parents' close friend Wolf Katzenelnbogen, he is from the start familiar with the French narrative of *résistance*. But when he comes to Paris and begins studying with Professor Lucien, he experiences a different perspective. His mentor reminds him that 'history . . . is not only a collection of events and dates. At the end, history is a story about human beings' (138–39). The professor admits that the French history during the Second World War is still full of black holes – all of which could be potential PhD theses (139) – a path that Hesi subsequently chooses. Years later, after taking over teaching from his late professor, Hesi tells his students:

> 'In the Second World War, France fought with the allied forces against the Germans . . .' I began the first class as lecturer with a quote from a history book. 'This is written in all your history books. But France and the Second World War, they are not what you think they are!' In a blow I closed the book and put it at the end of the table. 'In the days of the Second World War the French government collaborated with the Nazis. France agreed to a military cooperation with the Germans that led to the defeat of Britain. Racial laws against the Jews were established in France; French citizens and policemen handed over French Jews to Nazi officials' (145).

This paragraph hints at an interesting aspect in the European memory debate: Claus Leggewie sees in the collaboration with the Nazi regime in many countries all over Europe one of the reasons that leads him to the conclusion that the Holocaust stands indeed at the centre of a common European memory.[39]

A Plurality of Memories

One of the major issues in the discussions about a European memory and the crucial role of the Holocaust is the discrepancy between East and West. The Holocaust does not play the same role in the East European countries as in the West, whereas Stalinism and Communism, which inevitably also evoke horrific memories for their victims, are not remembered in the West as they are in the East. Tony Judt explains the differences between the West that embarked on the 'European adventure'[40] and the East that lived under communist rule until 1990 as follows: 'If the problem in Western Europe has been a shortage of memory, in the continent's other half the problem is reversed. Here there is too much memory, too many pasts on which people can draw, usually as a weapon against the past of someone else'.[41] Whereas the events of the Holocaust gained more and more importance and attention in the West – the Historikerstreit and the Singularitätsthese are not the only examples for lively debates – anti-Semitism and the history that comes with it was buried under communist rule, and even the Jews did not want to admit to its existence.[42]

As a child, Hesi knew primarily people who came from what Timothy Snyder called the bloodlands[43] – although they were first and foremost Holocaust survivors and not survivors of the Stalinist regime: 'I knew people from abroad like from Poland, Romania, Hungary, Czechia and a few from Germany, and that's it' (106). In Europe, however, the people from the eastern countries seem to have minor roles. The Poles are familiar with the places in their country, and Hesi needs them to find squares, streets and buildings. They know where the old synagogue was, and which graveyards still exist, because they live within the memory landscape – but Hesi does not know their narrative. He listens to Ursuala's story and works with French colleagues and students, although it does not seem as if the Holocaust is part of their memory either. He told Solange, his Parisian girlfriend: 'You are another people; you are a people wrapped in crème brûlée and spread in butter and chocolate, a people that covers up its sins with make-up and powder' (141).

As Lewis P. Hinchman and Sandra K. Hinchman argue in their introduction to *Memory, Identity, Community*, the reappearance of narrative in the humanities in the 1990s gives power to personal identity and reaffirms plurality,[44] or 'personal identity, the answer to the riddle of "who" people are, takes shape in the stories we tell about ourselves'.[45] Although, the concept of narrative is often used in the context of communities and collectives, the individual remains right in the centre of the theory: 'The stories that individuals create often strike variation upon a repertoire of socially available narratives that in turn legitimize the community and guarantee its continued existence'.[46] The individual's voice within a community should also be taken into account when discussing memory, and even more so when talking about Europe. Although there might be a way into a common European future, the rather pluralistic voices of the past and the present are not to be silenced. In other words, Europe has – if at all – a collected but not a collective memory.[47]

Towards a Conclusion

In Holocaust literature, as in other genres that aim to stay close to a historical reality, the difference between fiction and documentary became blurry.[48] However, the 'distinction between historiography representing undiluted facticity on the one hand, and literariness, the fact including its interpretation and the response of the writer on the other hand, is itself a fairly modern one'.[49] Hesi's narrative in On the Brink of Something Beautiful plays with this distinction: he is a historian but only a fictional character. Furthermore, the separation between memory, history and historiography is not as clear as discussed above. Leon Yudkin adds that the unclear division between fiction and documentary makes it difficult to distinguish between the facts and their interpretation.[50] The facts are first and foremost what can help humankind to find the path to its future – or to put it in the words of Hesi's mentor: 'There is no room for myths in history, there is room for facts though. Only when we know the facts . . . will there be a future that is a bit better' (144).

On his journey from Tel Aviv, to Paris and the Sorbonne, to Krakow and Ustrzyki, Hesi encounters myths, but he keeps to himself. The myths of others do not have any influence on him except for the fact that he develops the need to deconstruct them, as becomes obvious by the example of the French résistance narrative. When comparing Hesi's individual narrative to the one of Amalia and Gadi we can find similarities. However, each narrative stands for itself and not for the collective of the second generation. It is Hesi's personal history and the memory of his mother that lead him on his path. Furthermore, the character of Hesi and his European counterparts not only show that memory is collected rather than collective, but his example also shows the thin and vague boundaries between factual history and subjective memory. When his profession turns into an obsession and his mother's drawings are taken as historical facts, he loses the ability to build a future that does not drown in the past. Additionally, he is not able to see other identities, memories and histories anymore.

Hesi mourns the loss of European Jewish culture: 'Yesterday I understood that there aren't and won't be a Marx, Freud or Einstein anymore;

there aren't and won't be a Heine, Mendelssohn or Kafka' (165). Hesi not only mentions West European Jewish culture, he laments on the death of Yiddish, the Jewish language, and its literature. Except for the fact that Europe has a common history of collaborating with the Nazi regime – in the cases of some countries more, of others less – this cultural loss and the feeling that the Jews were 'European' are part of the construction of a European memory as well. There is no doubt that the Holocaust has to play a crucial role in Europe's commemoration of its past, and nor can there be any doubt that a way towards a more pluralistic memory needs to be found. However, as the fictional character of Hesi shows, the facts of history can shape an identity, but those facts are not the single key to a better future. The identity of an individual is multilayered, and connected to more than one narrative. It is thus neither the past of a glorious Europe nor the past of an accursed Europe that is the sole cornerstone for a European identity. Rather it is the multitude of histories that have, together with dreams and plans for the present and the future, an impact not only on European identity but on identities in Europe.

Judith Müller is a doctoral candidate at the Department of Hebrew Literature at Ben Gurion University of the Negev, Beer Sheva. In her dissertation project she focuses on the perception of Europe in Hebrew Literature from 1890 to 1938, but her general research interests include Jewish literatures and history of the nineteenth and twentieth centuries, as well as the changing conceptualization of Central Europe. Müller has presented her research at various conferences in Israel, Europe and the United States. Her paper on literary characters from a world of yesterday in Judith Katzir's novel *Matisse has the Sun in his Belly* was published in *Germanica Revues* in 2015.

Notes

1. Y.H. Yerushalmi, *Zakhor: Jewish History and Jewish Memory* (Seattle, WA and London: University of Washington Press, 1982), 86.

2. Ibid., 93.

3. Ibid., 94.

4. Ibid.

5. Ibid.

6. In the context of the emergence of the national, Benedict Anderson spoke of 'imagined communities'. B. Anderson, *Imagined Communities: Reflections on the Origin and Spread of Nationalism* (London: Verso, 1983).

7. J. Assmann, *Das kulturelle Gedächtnis: Schrift, Erinnerung und politische Identität in frühen Hochkulturen*, 2nd edition (Munich: C.H. Beck, 1999), 19–20. Translation from German by J.M., if not noted otherwise. The first modern theory about memory and society was written

by M. Halbwachs, *On Collective Memory* (Chicago, IL and London: University of Chicago Press, 1992).

8. Assmann, *Das kulturelle Gedächtnis*, 20–21.

9. A. Assmann, *Erinnerungsräume: Formen und Wandlungen des kulturellen Gedächtnisses* (Munich: C.H. Beck, 1999), 13.

10. Ibid., 15.

11. Z. Wei and A. Erll, 'Notes from the Periphery of Globalizing Memory: The Jewish Exile in Shanghai', *Hagar* 12 (2014), 150.

12. I. Milner, קרעי עבר. ביוגרפיה, זהות וזיכרון בסיפורת הדור השני [Past present: Biography, identity and memory in second generation literature] (Tel Aviv: Am Oved, 2003), 9–10.

13. Wei and Erll, 'Notes from the Periphery', 151.

14. A. Assmann, *Das neue Unbehagen an der Erinnerungskultur: Eine Intervention* (Munich: C.H. Beck, 2013), 143.

15. Ibid., 146.

16. Ibid., 150.

17. See, for example, Assmann, *Das neue Unbehagen*; T. Judt, 'The Past is Another Country: Myth and Memory in Postwar Europe', *Daedalus* 121(4) (1992), 83–118; C. Leggewie, *Der Kampf um die europäische Erinnerung: ein Schlachtfeld wird besichtigt* (Munich: C.H. Beck, 2011).

18. Assmann, *Das neue Unbehagen*, 158.

19. Ibid., 156–57.

20. Ibid., 158–59.

21. S. Beller, 'The World of Yesterday Revisited: Nostalgia, Memory, and the Jews of Fin-de-Siècle Vienna', *Jewish Social Studies* 2(2) (1996), 37–53.

22. Milner, קרעי עבר [*Past Present*], 93.

23. A. Jackont, '*Doron, Lizzie*': *The Heksherim Lexicon of Israeli Authors* (Or Yehuda: Dvir, 2014), 309.

24. Milner, קרעי עבר [*Past Present*], 11.

25. Ibid., 17.

26. Ibid., 13.

27. Ibid., 98.

28. Ibid., 95.

29. Ibid., 95–96.

30. Ibid., 126.

31. According to Milner, the emptiness that the destruction left in many places leads indeed to imagination. Ibid., 122.

32. Ibid., 25.

33. K. Neuburger, 'Does Literature Matter? On the Reception of Israeli Literature in Germany after 1989'. European Forum at the Hebrew University. Working Paper 136 (Jerusalem, 2014), 3.

34. Ibid., 4.

35. According to Gabriela Moscati Steindler, Grossman has been seen as the Israeli Marquez in Italy. G. Moscati Steindler, 'A New Understanding', *Modern Hebrew Literature* 7 (1991), 11. The seventh volume of Modern Hebrew Literature collects short articles on the reception and translation of Israeli literature in the United States and several European countries.

36. Steindler, 'A New Understanding', 12.

37. Neuburger, 'Does Literature Matter?', 15.

38. A. Feinberg, 'Rays of Light and the Shadows of History', *Modern Hebrew Literature* 7 (1991), 9.

39. Leggewie, *Der Kampf um die europäische Erinnerung*, 15–16.

40. Judt, 'The Past is Another Country', 95.
41. Ibid., 99.
42. Ibid., 106. For the developments in the West, see Assmann, *Das neue Unbehagen*, 161.
43. T. Snyder, *Bloodlands: Europe between Hitler and Stalin* (New York: Basic Books, 2010).
44. L.P. Hinchman and S.K. Hinchman, 'Introduction' to *Memory, Identity, Community: The Idea of Narrative in the Human Sciences* (Albany, NY: State University of New York Press, 1997), xv.
45. Ibid., xvii.
46. Ibid.
47. J.K. Olick, 'Collective Memory: The Two Cultures', *Sociological Theory* 17(3) (1999), 333–48.
48. L.I. Yudkin, 'Memorialization in New Fiction', *World Literature Today* 72(3) (1998), 485.
49. Ibid.
50. Ibid.

Bibliography

Anderson, B. *Imagined Communities: Reflections on the Origin and Spread of Nationalism*. London: Verso, 1983.

Assmann, A. *Erinnerungsräume: Formen und Wandlungen des kulturellen Gedächtnisses* [Realms of remembrance and the transformation of cultural memory]. Munich: C.H. Beck, 1999.

———. *Das neue Unbehagen an der Erinnerungskultur: Eine Intervention* [The new unease towards the culture of remembrance: An intervention]. Munich: C.H. Beck, 2013.

Assmann, J. *Das kulturelle Gedächtnis: Schrift, Erinnerung und politische Identität in frühen Hochkulturen* [The cultural memory: Writing, remembrance, and political identity in early civilization], 2nd edition. Munich: C.H. Beck, 1999.

Beller, S. 'The World of Yesterday Revisited: Nostalgia, Memory, and the Jews of Fin-de-Siècle Vienna'. *Jewish Social Studies* 2(2) (1996), 37–53.

Doron, L. ‫התחלה של משהו יפה‬ [On the brink of something beautiful] (Jerusalem: Keter, 2007).

Feinberg, A. 'Rays of Light and the Shadows of History'. *Modern Hebrew Literature* 7 (1991), 8–10.

Halbwachs, M. *On Collective Memory*. Chicago, IL and London: University of Chicago Press, 1992.

Hinchman, L.P., and S.K. Hinchman. 'Introduction', in L.P. Hinchman and S.K. Hinchman, *Memory, Identity, Community: The Idea of Narrative in the Human Sciences* (Albany: State University of New York Press, 1997), xiii–xxxii.

Jackont, A. ‫דורון, ליזי‬ ['Doron, Lizzie'], ‫לקסיקון הקשרים לסופרים ישראלים‬ [The Heksherim lexicon of Israeli authors] (Or Yehuda: Dvir, 2014), 309.

Judt, T. 'The Past is Another Country: Myth and Memory in Postwar Europe'. *Daedalus* 121(4) (1992), 83–118.

Leggewie, C. *Der Kampf um die europäische Erinnerung: ein Schlachtfeld wird besichtigt* [The fight for the European memory: Visiting a battlefield]. Munich: C.H. Beck, 2011.

Milner, I. ‫קרע עבר. ביוגרפיה, זהות וזיכרון בסיפורת הדור השני‬ [Past present: Biography, identity and memory in second generation literature]. Tel Aviv: Am Oved, 2003.

Neuburger, K. 'Does Literature Matter? On the Reception of Israeli Literature in Germany after 1989'. European Forum at the Hebrew University. Working Paper 136 (Jerusalem, 2014).

Olick, J.K. 'Collective Memory: The Two Cultures'. *Sociological Theory* 17(3) (1999), 333–48.

Snyder, T. *Bloodlands: Europe between Hitler and Stalin*. New York: Basic Books, 2010.

Steindler, G.M. 'A New Understanding'. *Modern Hebrew Literature* 7 (1991), 11–12.

Wei, Z., and A. Erll. 'Notes from the Periphery of Globalizing Memory: The Jewish Exile in Shanghai'. *Hagar* 12 (2014), 150–51.

Yerushalmi, Y.H. *Zakhor: Jewish History and Jewish Memory*. Seattle, WA and London: University of Washington Press, 1982.

Yudkin, L.I. 'Memorialization in New Fiction'. *World Literature Today* 72(3) (1998), 485–92.

CHAPTER 9

Who Lost Turkey?

The Consequences of Writing an Exclusionary European History

PAUL T. LEVIN

In 1959, Turkey and Greece applied for Associate Membership in the fore-runner of today's European Union – the EEC. Four years later, the 1963 Ankara and Athens agreements sealed this status for the two countries, but when Greece applied for full accession in 1975, domestic instability in Turkey and the fallout from the invasion of Cyprus prevented Turkey from following suit. This had to wait until 1987, when Turkish president Turgut Özal submitted the application for accession as a full member of the European Community, surprising many observers. After many twists and turns, Turkey was declared an official candidate for accession twelve years later (at the 1999 Helsinki Summit), and formal accession negotiations were initiated six years after that, in 2005. It had taken a long while for Turkey to get to this point, and since then, only fifteen of the thirty-five 'negotiating' chapters have been opened for treatment, with only one so far having been concluded. Several chapters are currently blocked by EU member states and the accession process today appears to be at a complete standstill, or even nearing a point of collapse, as the Turkish government rolls back much of the EU-inspired reforms on human rights and democratization it had enacted over the past decade and a half. In light of what must be interpreted as a loss of appetite for EU accession in the ruling party in Turkey, and a much-reduced support for that goal among the general public, we should perhaps expect a debate in Europe over 'who lost Turkey', akin to the similar debate in the United States about the 'loss' of China to the Maoists after the Second World War, much as Gordon and Taşpınar warned of back in 2008.[1]

There is by now a significant body of scholarship exploring the 'Othering' of Turkey that has occurred in and through the EU accession process, as well as the deep-rooted problems of Islamophobia and anti-Turkish prejudice in Europe that have influenced this process.[2] With the benefit of having ten years of accession negotiations to look back upon, this chapter considers the consequences of these practices in the context of Turkey–EU relations. Given the long history of the prejudices and stereotypes in question, as well as the manner in which they are 'historicized', particular attention will be paid to how representations of the past have interlinked with the present in consequential ways. Drawing on my own earlier research,[3] the first part of the chapter explores the history of Othering, key representations, and their place in the dominant historical narratives. Parts two and three focus on the legacy of this history of Othering: part two considers contemporary representations and popular attitudes in the EU to Turkish EU accession, whereas the third and final section of the chapter investigates the deterioration of Turkey–EU relations and tries to answer the question of what role if any the EU has played in triggering recent developments in Turkey.

The argument put forth below is that a full understanding of the trajectory of EU–Turkey relations requires consideration of the interaction between developments on the EU level and those within Turkey. Hence, I hope to contribute to a literature that moves beyond the top-down approach of some of the early Europeanization literature that primarily focused on what Vivien A. Schmidt called the Third Question: how 'the EU's supranational institutions themselves affected member states' institutions through the process of Europeanization'.[4] To understand the political transformation of Turkey since the opening of accession process in 2005, one must consider domestic sources of change.

However, I also try to show that it is insufficient to merely point to domestic Turkish factors such as the (hidden) intentions of the ruling Justice and Development Party (best-known under their Turkish acronym, the AKP) as the main explanation for the ultimate failure of the accession process to produce democratization in Turkey. As for the question of writing history, I argue that there is a significant Islamophobic and anti-Turkish legacy in Europe, and that it has had a detrimental impact on EU–Turkish relations, on attitudes towards the EU in Turkey, and on the enthusiasm for reforms in the country. I argue that the carrots and sticks of EU conditionality combined with civil-society pressures and domestic receptivity to it produced a partially virtuous cycle of significant reforms between 1999 and 2005. After 2005, the credibility of conditionality was undermined due to developments on the EU level, and the reform process in Turkey partially slowed down. Sometime between the years 2010 and 2013, internal and external developments combined to turn the virtuous cycle into a vicious one that entailed significant Turkish retrenchments from earlier reforms.

Part 1: The Historical Trajectories of Two Rival European Self-conceptions

In *Turkey and the European Union: Christian and Secular Images of Islam,*[5] I explored early Christian representations of Islam at some length. Building on primary sources and existing surveys of the field, I identified the two dominant clusters of roles in which Christian writers cast Muslims during the Middle Ages: *exclusionary* roles, in which Muslims were portrayed as fundamentally different, and *inclusionary* roles, where the antagonists were different but not essentially so. An underlying assumption in the theoretical framework of the book was that representations of a given collective Other in a familiar role (e.g. pagan, Antichrist, heretic) can be used to evoke a collective (imagined) Self by virtue of the contrast inherent in a familiar role-relationship, and the names exclusionary/inclusionary refer to the self-images evoked. Depicting Muslims as fundamentally alien helps to create and reproduce a self-identity that excludes Muslims from membership in the in-group, thus helping to maintain desired social distance.

Moreover, I used the concept of roles in a dual sense: not simply to invoke the dialectics of role-relationships and in order to rest on a body of existing empirical work on role/identity theory, but also to capture the fact that depictions of Muslims were often explicitly or implicitly narrative in format. Hence, in the depictions from this time, the Muslims were not merely presented as involved in familiar role-relationships with Christians (pagan, faithful, etc.), but also played important roles in driving a historical meta-narrative forward. In the Medieval texts I analysed, the dominant narrative was a Biblical meta-narrative.

I also argued that the stories in which these characters were cast tended either towards a 'tragic' mode of narration or 'emplotment', which was associated with defence and exclusion, or – as was more commonly associated with the use of inclusive imagery – with a 'comic' mode of storytelling. In contrast, the latter was typically associated with expansion, military offence, and a self-confident expansionary Christian self-image. This basic division into two narrative tendencies – one comic, the other tragic – is the beginning of two rivalling self-images that I will explore further below.

It is important to note that there was nothing inevitable or necessary about the 'Othering' narratives that emerged as the dominant accounts of encounters and relations between Christians and Muslims. Throughout the Middle Ages and the Renaissance, there occurred extensive cross-fertilization between what we might bluntly term Islamic and European or Christian civilizations – often facilitated by, for example, Jewish interlocutors – in places such as Andalusia and the Ottoman Balkans. To Richard Bulliet, the scale of interaction was such that he thinks we should reject the notions of separate civilizations and instead talk about a shared 'Islamo-Christian' civilization.[6] Moreover, while warfare was common between Muslim and Christian rulers, so was warfare among Christians – for example, between Protestant and Catholic armies –, and Muslim-Christian trade was as common as confrontation. Nevertheless, and partly as a reaction to such erosions of communal boundaries and as a means of trying to reassert them, a canon of anti-Turkish imagery and ways of writing a shared Christian, European history emerged, and it set the stage for chroniclers and historiographers down the road. Even at this early point in time, then, we can see a practice of crafting historical narratives along certain more or less standardized plot lines, in which Muslim Others were cast in roles where part of their narrative function was to stand in contrast to, and thereby help to define, a collective Christian identity.

Latin Christians appear to have inherited the Eastern Christian practice of defining the Christian collective self by contrasting it with an imagined Muslim other. In no small part thanks to the contributions of prominent Byzantine refugees like Cardinal Bessarion, who came from territories conquered by Ottoman armies and became active in the city states of today's Italy, the Renaissance saw the transfer of the medieval anti-Islamic canon from Saracens onto Christendom's new Other: the Ottoman Turks.[7] During the Renaissance, moreover, the terms 'Christendom' and 'Europe' were increasingly being used as synonyms, and the latter inherited much of the connotation of the former.

These two transfers reinforced one another: the Ottoman Turks became Europe's Other in the same way that "Saracens" had been Christendom's Other.[8] This was a significant step in what might be described as the European secularization of the religious anti-Muslim imagery from Eastern Christendom. This secularization process was in fact continued by many of the later thinkers of the reformation and the enlightenment, who are often simplistically portrayed as shedding the Medieval and Catholic heritage, such as Martin Luther and René Voltaire. In fact, rather than shedding it, these and other foundational thinkers continued to evoke versions of the Medieval canon of anti-Islamic and specifically anti-Turkish imagery as part of the process of delineating a distinct European family of nations, as Denys Hay, Anthony Pagden, Iver Neumann and many others have shown. In the remainder of this chapter, I focus less on contemporary practices of historiography and more on the consequences that such a kind of identity creation through writing exclusionary (and inclusionary) history, which I have described above, would come to have for Turkey's relationship to the European Union.

Part 2: A Vibrant Legacy – Attitudes and Perceptions of Turkey in the European Union Today

The European Parliament (EP) has long played an important role as a tough check on democratic reforms in EU applicant states, and Turkey is no exception in this regard. But the debates in the European Parliament on whether Turkey fulfils the Copenhagen political criteria are not only revealing when it comes to Turkey but also when it comes to how the Members of the EP (MEPs) view themselves, the EU, and Europe more broadly.[9] In fact, these debates could be viewed as a struggle over the identity of the EU itself – and rather transparently so. As one MEP noted in a 1996 debate on the political situation in Turkey: '[I]t is turning more and more into a debate about the way the European Union sees itself'.[10]

Indeed, two rival conceptions of Europe and the European Union have come to a head in the debate over the Turkish candidacy: one emphasizes progressive and more or less universal Enlightenment values as the core of the European project, while the other emphasizes the Christian heritage.[11] Put in the terms used in Part 1 above, one conception draws on the 'comic' historical meta-narrative and an inclusive/expansive European self-image metaphorically associated with looking outwards and forwards. The other is rooted in the 'tragic' historical meta-narrative in which an exclusionary Europe is on the defensive, under siege from culturally alien strangers within and on the outside. The latter historical meta-narrative – predominantly inwards- and backwards-looking – is most clearly visible in statements by far-right MEPs in the NI (Non-Attached) group when discussing the question of Turkish membership, in which they emphasize a shared Christian heritage as an argument against it. Paradoxically, these same MEPs are also some of the most vocal opponents of European integration and champions of retained national sovereignty. The exclusionary tragic European meta-narrative is thus strangely compatible both with a conservative conception of Europe, in which a shared culture warrants deepening integration as well as excluding a Turkish 'other', and a nationalist, xenophobic and highly Eurosceptic position that nevertheless also excludes Turkey on essentialist cultural grounds. The essentialist and defensive position is illustrated by statements such as:

Europe's cultural identity ... would without doubt be fundamentally under-mined by the presence of a Muslim Member State, and the mass immigration of millions of unemployed young Turks – which is a certainty – would result in a series of social and economic catastrophes.[12]

The statement is indicative of a recent development on the anti-immigrant extreme right in both Europe and the United States, namely the post-9/11 convergence of the exclusionary discourse around Islamophobia. Muslim immigrants are depicted as a simultaneous threat against distinct national cultures and values as well as against a shared Western, Christian heritage. Hence, the struggle between the exclusivist and the inclusive meta-narratives is fought both on the European and the national levels. In recent years, the exclusionary European self-image has gained significant ground across the continent.

Extreme right parties have made electoral gains in most EU member states by telling a story of a Europe again under siege by threatening foreign-ers, and most prominently by Muslims. It is a 'tragic' story, even apoca-lyptic in some versions, and it evokes the same kind of exclusionary and inward-looking identity as that which the early Eastern Christian predeces-sors employed, quite often invoking symbolically charged historical battles like the 1683 Siege of Vienna. Many mainstream European politicians have followed suit and adjusted their rhetoric. The assertion that Turkey is not European and therefore cannot become a member of the European Union, and that, by extension, being European meant being Christian, used to be heard primarily from politicians on the extreme right. In the past few years, similar claims have been made by some of the leading politicians in the EU, by former French president Nicholas Sarkozy, and in effect even by German chancellor Angela Merkel. Today, warnings of the 'Islamization of Europe' are commonplace, and not just put forth by the extreme right. The question to be explored here is what this has meant for Turkish–EU relations.

If we first consider some quantitative data on attitudes in the EU towards this quest and towards Turks in general, we find clear indications that the long historical legacy of anti-Islamic and anti-Turkish imagery in Europe is visible today. The Eurobarometer surveys conducted by the Commission of the European Union have long been collecting data on support for EU enlargement, including the level of support enjoyed by specific applicant countries and future or potential applicants. As a result, we have data that allows us to compare whether, as we would expect in light of the histori-cal legacy explored above, opposition to Turkey is stronger than to other countries, or whether it otherwise stands out.

Figure 9.1[13] shows that popular opposition in the EU towards an enlarge-ment that includes Turkey has consistently been stronger than opposition to other actual or potential applicants, and (with a brief exception in 2001–02)

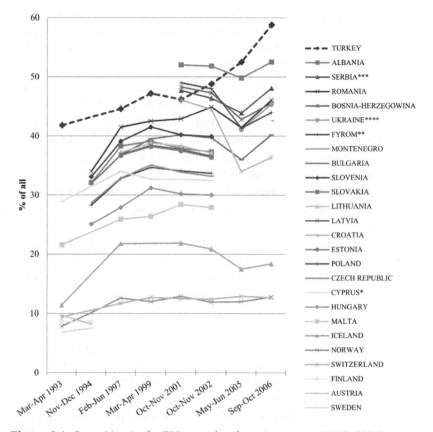

Figure 9.1 Opposition in the EU towards enlargement to . . . (1993–2006)

* CYPRUS: Nov–Dec 1994 data missing, Jan 1996 data used as proxy.
** FYROM: (Former Yugoslav Republic of Macedonia), 'Macedonia' in EB56.2 (2001)
and EB58.1 (2002). Data for 1999 missing, EB54.1 2000 used as proxy.
*** Serbia: 'Yugoslavia' in EB56.2 (2001), 'Serbia-Montenegro' in EB63.4 (2005). Data
missing for 1997, EB44.2 Jan–March 1996 used as proxy ('Serbia-Montenegro').
**** Ukraine: Data missing for 1997, EB44.2 Jan–March 1996 used as proxy.

it has grown stronger over the years. The exception concerns five of the
Balkan countries included for the first time in the 2001 Eurobarometer:
Croatia, Albania, Serbia, the Former Yugoslav Republic of Macedonia,
and Bosnia-Herzegovina. But opposition to enlargement to these countries
dropped quickly after 2001. In contrast, opposition to Turkish accession
grew again after a small (1 percentage point drop from the 1999 survey)
decline in 2001, so that in the 2005 survey Turkey regained the dubious
honour of topping this chart.

　　At the time of writing, opposition in the EU to Turkish EU accession is
strong across the political spectrum, and for good reasons. The increasingly

authoritarian turn of the AKP government, with truly massive purges after the failed coup of 15 July 2016, the harsh crackdown on dissenters during the 2013 Gezi protests and beyond, and the suppression of freedom of speech and such like have all combined to turn even the most supportive friends of Turkey in the EU into critics. Few today believe that EU accession is on the cards anytime in the foreseeable future. However, the Eurobarometer data that we are considering here goes back to the period before Turkey took an authoritarian turn.

Figure 9.1 gives us several good reasons to believe that the opposition to Turkish accession in the EU is conditioned at least in part by the long legacy of fear and animosity towards Islam and Muslims in Europe. First, opposition to Turkey has consistently been much stronger than opposition to other potential or actual applicant states. Second, the strong increase in opposition to Turkish EU accession between 2001 and 2005 was a marked exception to the general trend during the same years. Except for a minimal increase in the very low level of opposition to Switzerland (+0.4 percentage points), opposition towards enlargement to all other countries in the chart dropped rather dramatically between these years. In contrast, opposition to Turkey grew by 6.2 percentage points. Hence Turkey, as we would suspect, stands out with respect to the direction of change in the period 2001–05.

How should we explain this? Was there a dramatic surge in violence in Turkey or a series of troubling political developments in Turkey that shed doubt on the country's willingness to reform? The political and economic development as well as partial liberalization witnessed in Turkey's human rights regime during the early years of the accession talks hardly validates such an argument. In fact, the strong increase in opposition is particularly vexing in light of the fact that 2005 was the year when formal accession negotiations were opened with Turkey, which was only possible after its reforms to meet the Copenhagen Political Criteria had been deemed sufficient to allow for the start of negotiations. Indeed, as we shall see in Part 3 below, the diagram covers the period of the most ambitious EU reforms in Turkey. Between 2001 and 2004, the Turkish government passed nine constitutional reform packages inspired by the EU. Despite the (imperfect but undoubtedly significant) liberalizing and democratizing reforms that were conducted by successive Turkish governments in the first six years of the new millennium covered in this chart, popular opposition in the EU to Turkish accession grew. Hence, and regardless of the situation today where many oppose Turkish accession due to legitimate concerns over authoritarianism in the applicant country, popular scepticism in the EU towards Turkey during this period was clearly not only, or even primarily, driven by concerns over human rights abuse or the state of democratization in Turkey. In fact, there is additional direct evidence in support of this deduction, as 61 per cent of the respondents in the 2006 survey agreed with the statement that 'the cultural differences between Turkey and the European Union member states are too significant to allow it to join the European Union', whereas only 27 per cent disagreed. This is of course in line with what we would expect in light of the earlier discussion of the historical legacy, but it is also supported by recent research on perceptions of Turkey in the EU.

The current state of the art in research on perceptions of Turkey in the EU confirms rather unambiguously that Turkey has been suffering from a particularly bad image problem.[14] Much of this research has begun disaggregating attitudes towards Turkish EU accession, distinguishing between, for example, attitudes in different member states[15] or between elites and general publics.[16] There are clear and consistent differences between these groups/categories: opposition to the idea of Turkish EU accession is stronger in some member states than others, and the general public is more opposed than EU elites. As for what motivates this opposition, existing research supports our contention that it has much to do with European attitudes towards Islam, other cultures, and immigration/immigrants.[17] Canan-Sokullu's analysis of polling data from the German Marshall Fund's Transatlantic Trends Survey and European Elite Survey, for example, confirms the findings of existing literature that 'Turcoscepticism ... seems to be rooted in the perception of an Islamic fundamentalist threat'.[18]

However, these findings are by themselves clearly insufficient to explain the change in attitudes to Turkey's EU accession. We need to address what appears like a methodological-epistemological problem for our historically oriented approach: how can we explain a recent change in attitudes, such as the increase in opposition to Turkish EU accession, with reference to a historical legacy? It would seem impossible to explain change with reference to stasis. The answer is likely to be twofold. First, the prospect of Turkish EU accession provokes questions about the role of culture and religion in European identity, about Europe's borders, and about insiders versus outsiders.[19] In this context, each step that Turkey takes towards EU accession raises the discomfort among those in the EU who see the country and its people as culturally alien. Hence, rather than relieving concerns over the slow pace of reforms in Turkey, the reforms and relatively swift progress of the talks between 1999 and 2005 instead had the paradoxical effect of increasing opposition among the general public in the EU. This puzzling correlation is difficult to comprehend unless we accept that increased proximity to someone or something considered culturally alien often triggers discomfort.

Second, given the link between 'Turcoscepticism' and the perceived threat from Islam identified by Canan-Sokullu, it is unsurprising that the developments in Europe in the 2000s had nothing to do with Turkey's eligibility for EU accession but with something that fuelled latent European

Islamophobia and would spill over to Turkey–EU relations, as Ziya Öniş argued in 2008:

> Crucial developments in the internal politics of Europe over the past few years have undoubtedly made a deep, negative impact on Turkish membership prospects. One of the striking developments in Europe in recent years has been the development of right-wing populism based on the fears of immigration and loss of jobs fuelled by the rise of Islamophobia. There is no doubt that the events of 9/11 have left a deep imprint on the European landscape and have clearly helped to fuel anti-Muslim sentiments at the level of the general public. The clear swing of the pendulum toward right of center, Christian Democratic parties in recent years has also generated an unattractive environment for Turkish membership... [T]he 'Turkey question' is a reflection of deeper uncertainties and fears in European societies.[20]

This account is confirmed by my analysis of debates in the European Parliament between 1996 and 2010, which showed a significant rise in the use of exclusionary imagery and rhetoric after 2002.[21] The 2002 ascent to power in Turkey of a party with roots in political Islam – the AKP – arguably also worked against Turkey as far as popular perception in the EU was concerned, by making it easier for Turkey's detractors on the far right to evoke Islamophobic responses when talking about Turkey, despite the fact that the AKP during this period was busy conducting significant reforms in order to harmonize with EU law.

In short, while this is difficult to verify conclusively, we have seen that there is evidence to suggest that the continuation to the present day of a long tradition of employing anti-Turkish imagery to define a shared and distinct European identity – imagery in which Turkey is typically portrayed as backwards, dangerous and alien, both culturally and religiously – has had a lasting effect on popular perceptions of Turks and on attitudes towards the prospect of including Turkey in the European Union.

Part 3: A Problematic Legacy – Understanding the Failure of Conditionality in Turkey–EU Relations

The historical legacy described above and the continued practices of Othering Turkey by leading politicians in the EU have arguably had serious consequences for Turkey–EU relations, and have also had a negative impact on political developments in Turkey. Let us look at two troubling trends with respect to said relationship. First of all, support for EU membership in Turkey – once extremely strong across almost all demographics – has now declined significantly. Second, the high early pace of reforms aimed at harmonizing Turkish legislation and policy with the EU 'acquis communautaire' had slowed substantially by the year 2010, but a shift could be traced as far back as 2005. Today we see much more than just a slowed pace of reform, as evidenced both by the increasingly vocal and frequent accusations of growing authoritarianism in the sitting Turkish government by international organizations and NGOs inside Turkey, and by the deeply worrying spiral of intramural violence, the attempted military coup on 15 July 2016, and the massive purges that have followed in the wake of the coup and are taking place at the time of writing. In this chapter, however, I limit the discussion to the initial abatement of reforms, not the eventual reversal that we are now witnessing. It is of course difficult to determine with any high degree of certainty whether or which of these are effects of the practices of Othering that is our focus, or if they have other causes, but the final section of this chapter tries to disentangle ways in which these practices probably did contribute to the two above-mentioned outcomes in question.

Drop in Support for EU Accession in Turkey

Whereas very high numbers of Turks in almost all demographic and political categories used to favour membership in the European Union, more recent polls show a marked decline in support. In 2004, 71 per cent of Turkish respondents believed that Turkish EU membership was a good thing. By the 2010 Eurobarometer, this figure had dropped to 41 per cent.[22] There is now a body of literature examining Turkish attitudes towards the EU, EU accession, and Turkey's place in Europe, including a number of recent studies that investigate the rising Euroscepticism in Turkey and among the Turkish political elite.[23] Among these, Barış Gülmez argues that this change is at least in part a reaction to the 'EU's ambivalent and discriminatory approach in the application of its conditionality'.[24] This argument is supported by Akşit, Şenyuva and Gürleyen's finding that many Turkish legislators feel ignored by the EU, and have low levels of trust in EU institutions.[25]

It is exceedingly difficult – not least from a Turkish perspective – to distinguish between two distinct kinds of opposition to Turkey's membership bid. On the one hand, there is a contingent opposition on the basis that Turkey at the current time does not fulfil the Copenhagen criteria. The inclusive imagery described above fits in this category, and it is typically associated with comic meta-narratives. The tragic mode of employment and exclusionary imagery, on the other hand, are associated with a view that Turkey should not be allowed to join the EU because it is predominantly Muslim or (supposedly) culturally alien. While outright culturalist arguments are being heard more often these days, proponents of this latter school of thought have also tended to hide behind arguments about the state of Turkish democracy (i.e. the Copenhagen criteria), which explains why it has been so difficult for many Turks to distinguish between the two lines of reasoning. Turks have increasingly been saying, 'why should we listen to you lecturing us on human rights when you're really just using it to keep us out because we're Muslims?' It is quite clear that members and supporters of the sitting AKP government nowadays use this line of reasoning strategically, and quite cynically, to rebut criticism from the EU, but the reason it works is that it taps into widespread sentiments among the Turkish population. Unfortunately, this has had a negative impact on the EU's so-called normative power to propel reform in Turkey, which today is much diminished.

Slowed Pace of Reforms

The core of the normative power of the European Union is the power to affect democratic change in accession countries. This power stems from the logic of 'conditionality' mentioned by Gülmez, which is inherent in the accession process. In short, a candidate country is assumed to apply for accession because it desires membership in the EU, and by making membership conditional upon fulfilment of the so-called Copenhagen accession criteria, the EU can exert leverage and propel the candidate country to reform. While there has been backsliding in many of the countries in the Eastern and Central European enlargements after they gained accession, the logic of conditionality was clearly at work during those enlargement processes, and extensive reforms were adopted in the candidate countries.[26]

There are lively debates among Turkey experts about the phenomenon of 'Europeanization' in Turkey–EU relations: about the extent and significance of reforms enacted by the AKP after it came to power in 2002, about when more precisely the stream of reforms, such as they were, abated,[27] as well as about whether the party leadership were ever genuinely interested in securing full EU membership for Turkey.[28] Looking at the facts, however, it is indisputable that there were serious reforms between 1999 and 2005, and that significant forward movement continued in more isolated areas after 2005. Capital punishment was abandoned in two stages: in 2002 its use in peacetime was banned, and in 2004 a blanket ban was introduced.[29] The systematic and widespread practice of torture in detention facilities was eventually abolished (even though Amnesty International and other observers are voicing concerns that it may now have been reintroduced, following the 15 July 2016 coup attempt).[30] Legal changes regarding gender equality were introduced in 1998 and 2001, and a significantly revamped Criminal Code was enacted in 2004, which contained thirty amendments concerned the rights of women, and abolished most of the discriminatory provisions of the old law.[31] Restrictions on the public use of Kurdish were eased, a

Kurdish public radio and television station opened, and attempts – known by names such as the Oslo Process, the Kurdish Opening, the Democratic Initiative, and the Resolution/Peace Process – to resolve the long-standing conflict with the PKK were initiated. As mentioned above, nine constitutional reform packages, which were almost entirely guided by EU reform requirements, were adopted in the years between 2001 and 2004. At that point, the Commission of the European Union deemed Turkey's alignment with the Copenhagen political criteria for EU accession sufficient to warrant the opening of formal negotiations.

Sometime after 2005, however, the spurt of reform activity in Turkey slowed down. Alpan, for example, argues that the concept 'Europe' had constituted a 'hegemonic' reference point in the discourse between 1999 and 2005, but that it lost this position after 2005.[32] While reforms continued over the next decade,[33] they were arguably more selective and limited,[34] and implementation of some of these reforms left much to be desired. Informed in part by what might be described as the second-generation Europeanization literature on Turkey, which substituted the top-down orientation of the first generation of scholarship with a bottom-up focus on domestic politics in member states and applicant states,[35] I believe that this slowdown was partly a function of internal power-political developments and imperatives. However, it was also partly a function of the fact that conditionality was undermined by external developments: on the EU level and in EU member states. Or rather, the key to understanding the slowdown is to grasp how the internal and external interacted to create a partly virtuous cycle in the early years of the AKP, but that at some point the cycle turned vicious.

My focus in this chapter is on forces external to Turkey – on developments within the EU. Here, a number of factors contributed to gravely undermine the promise of membership upon which the logic of conditionality is premised, and several of them are best understood in light of the long history of Othering described above. First, the already mentioned fact that it was difficult for many Turks to discern between inclusionary and exclusionary positions on the Turkish accession process meant that the credibility of the promise of accession was undermined from the start. Turkish officials, journalists, and the broader population felt that they had good reason to question assertions by EU representatives that Turkey's accession would be assured if only Turkey would fulfil the Copenhagen criteria. Here centuries of writing a European history at the expense of Muslims and Turks mattered.

Second, these doubts were further fuelled by the addition of a statement in the official Negotiating Framework that the accession process was open-ended and need not result in full membership. EU candidates in Central and Eastern Europe (including Cyprus and Malta) had begun their negotiations with a clear roadmap to membership, and even a planned date of accession.

This set-up contributed to the 'rhetorical entrapment' of the EU, in the sense that an applicant state that enacted reforms and satisfied the Copenhagen criteria that had been set up as conditions for accession had a certain entitlement to demand full accession as a reward.[36] In the Turkish case, the novel caveat was flanked by public statements by a number of key EU leaders, either promoting alternatives to full membership, like Angela Merkel's famous 'privileged partnership', or promising outright to reject the Turkish application, as did France's Nicholas Sarkozy. His election in 2007 led to a more restrictive French line vis-à-vis the Turkish application than during the time of his predecessor, Jacques Chirac. The caveat and this rhetoric, which emphasized culture, religion and/or realpolitik over EU treaties and the Copenhagen criteria, was a sign that key players within the EU did not see themselves as fully entrapped by liberal democratic norms in the context of Turkey's application for full accession to the European Union.[37]

The promise of membership at the other end of the accession/reform process was also undermined by the inclusion of a still divided Cyprus as a full member of the EU in 2004. The Cypriot leadership had allegedly promised not to veto the Turkish accession if it became an EU member itself, and did refrain from blocking the decision to open negotiations with Turkey in 2005. Shortly after joining the EU, however, Cyprus mobilized opposition in the European Parliament to the easing of sanctions against the Turkish Republic of Cyprus. And when Turkey refused to extend the Customs Union between Turkey and the EU to Cyprus, the latter gathered a coalition of EU member states at the December 2006 EU Council behind a decision to partially freeze the accession negotiations with Turkey. According to the December decision, none of the thirty-five negotiating chapters could be closed, and eight negotiating chapters would be blocked from even being opened. In an interview with the author, a senior EU official with insight into the accession process commented on the effects of this decision: '[W]e noticed a significant drop in enthusiasm from the Turkish side after this'.

Whether to put the blame on Cyprus for blocking the negotiations, or on Turkey and the TRC for unnecessarily pushing the issue with the Customs Union (or, for that matter, on all parties involved for simply not doing enough to resolve the underlying issue of the divided and partially occupied island) is not the question here. However, it is clear that the Cyprus issue contributed to the 'drop in enthusiasm' for reform in Ankara that we had seen even prior to 2006. The December 2006 decision to block the opening of such chapters as 23 and 24 had troubling consequences for the Turkish reform process. Opening these two chapters would have enabled the EU to assist Turkey in conducting – and put pressure on it to implement – reforms in areas pertaining to the Judiciary and Fundamental

Rights (chapter 23) and Justice, Freedom and Security (24). As it now stands, these two chapters have still not been opened and hence the reform process in these policy fields never properly began.

It is difficult to weigh the exact balance: the significance of the unresolved Cyprus conflict compared to the more diffuse sentiment on behalf of many Turks that their country was not welcome in the EU for cultural or religious reasons (the result of centuries of Othering). What is less difficult to see is that these factors in one way or another combined to create a climate of growing mutual scepticism and suspicion in which Ankara eventually lost its appetite for reform and Brussels partially halted the negotiations. It could be objected that Ankara should have an incentive to enact democratizing reforms regardless of the prospects for EU accession. There is much to say in favour of this objection, but it underestimates the very real costs associated with the reform process for a variety of Turkish elites. Among other things, the reforms demanded the lifting of a number of long-lasting political taboos and the reconsideration of several fundamental cornerstones of Turkish politics and national security policy. Successfully concluding such endeavours would arguably be for the better for the country as a whole, but the unevenly distributed cost, the difficulty, and the potentially disruptive consequences of pursuing the reform effort should not be underestimated. The reforms brought transfers of wealth and power between different Turkish elites, and thus did have disruptive and unpredictable effects on Turkish society and politics.

As the 'second generation' research on Europeanization has emphasized, domestic political actors also have their own agendas, and EU reform demands interact in complicated ways with domestic political dynamics. With respect to Turkey, it is very tempting to evaluate the AKP of 2004 through the lens of today's party, which appears quite preoccupied with securing its grip on power in the country, and conclude that the current state of affairs is what they always desired. However, to do so would be to fall prey to hindsight bias ('I knew it would happen')[38] and teleological reasoning. Ziya Öniş describes three distinct periods in the evolution of AKP rule: the 'golden age' (2002–07); relative stagnation (2007–11); and real decline (from 2011 and on).[39] During the 'golden age' the AKP also attracted a large number of liberals and democrats with no prior connection to the Islamist movements in Turkey, but who supported the AKP for the reforms that they enacted and for their efforts to dismantle the authoritarian so-called 'deep state' (*derin devlet*) structures in the country. The party lost some of these allies during the period that followed, but most of them dropped off during the years of 'real decline', which included significant democratic backsliding.

The 'golden age' constituted a real window of opportunity for the European Union in which many leading representatives of the party showed a willingness to enact even some costly reforms. For a number of reasons, the EU failed to seize the opportunity to encourage continued reforms by extending a credible, conditional promise of full membership. The unresolved conflict over Cyprus was a key factor that disabled the EU in this regard, but so was the legacy of centuries of writing an exclusionary European history at the expense of Turks and Muslims. At some point between 2010 and 2013 perhaps, this failure of external pressure and weakened rhetorical entrapment had combined with internal political developments within Turkey to make selective democratization the more attractive option for the AKP leadership than the option of pursuing potentially costly reforms. Further political polarization and increasingly contentious power struggles in Turkey eventually meant that the AKP government turned from selective democratization towards heightened authoritarianism,[40] bringing us to where we are today.

Conclusion

We are now at a point where 'national conservative' parties on the far right have gained significant ground in many EU member states in recent years. The rise of these populist parties has shifted the discourse on topics such as immigration, the place of Islam in Europe, and ultimately also Turkey's bid for EU accession far to the right. Even though the increasing authoritarianism of the governing party in Turkey in many respects mirrors developments in some EU member states like Hungary and Poland, it has provided xenophobic and Islamophobic actors in the EU with an easy target. Accordingly, the 'threat' of Turkish EU accession figured prominently in the 'Brexit' referendum debate, where the Vote Leave campaign played on old prejudices and fears. According to one 'analysis' distributed by the campaign: 'Because of the EU's free movement laws, the government will not be able to exclude Turkish criminals from entering the UK'. Another campaign poster warned: 'Turkey (population 76 million) is joining the EU. Vote Leave, take back control'.[41] The 'tragic' metanarrative of a Christian Europe under siege, and the exclusionary identity constructs associated with it, have now gained even further strength.

In many ways, these developments have played right into the hands of conservative and anti-Western forces in Turkish politics and society, not the least within the ruling party. Increasingly, Turkish officials shrug off criticism by EU institutions of Turkish human rights abuses with the observation that the critique is mere prejudice or that the EU is in no position to lecture those it is asking to care for the refugees that EU member states failed to welcome. Following the failed coup on 15 July 2016, cabinet members and pro-government pundits lambasted the EU, and the West more broadly, for allegedly failing to come to the defence of the Turkish people or denounce the coup fast enough. A not-so-subtle line or argument has also emerged, holding the United States responsible for the failed coup. In Turkey, too, a 'tragic' and more or less paranoid meta-narrative of a country under attack by external forces that wants to divide and weaken it – along with a set of increasingly nationalistic and exclusionary identity constructs – has become nearly hegemonic after the coup.

What we see in Turkey–EU relations today are the centrifugal effects of a vicious circle of anti-Turkish sentiments in EU member states and anti-Western sentiments in Turkey feeding off each other. The historically anchored and increasingly exclusionary representations of the Other are mutually reinforcing. Turkish Muslim nationalists invoke the Conquest of Constantinople when European nationalists invoke the Siege of Vienna. In this chapter, I have not attempted to show that this turn for the worse in Turkey–EU relations is exclusively a function of the legacy of writing an exclusionary European history, but I hope to have shown that this legacy did play a significant role in this downward spiral. Coupled with the failure to resolve the long-standing conflict over Cyprus, the rightward turn in European politics (and thus the resurgence of the tragic and exclusionary metanarrative) effectively undermined the credible promise of full membership as the future reward for Turkey if it were to successfully conclude the reform process, and thus undermined the logic of conditionality in the accession process that is at the core of the EU's normative power to affect democratic change in applicant states like Turkey. This meant that the EU was unable to capitalize on the window of opportunity to prod the AKP to stick to the reform path that existed around 2004 and a few years thereafter.

There is widespread and justified scepticism of the Turkish ruling party's sincerity when it comes to the questions of EU membership and democratic reforms today, but this chapter has cautioned against viewing the AKP of, for example, 2004 through the lens of today's party. We should also be weary of viewing the AKP as a monolithic actor with unitary and set preferences since there were arguably a range of interests, incentives and agendas among the ruling AKP elite, which changed over time with the domestic political context and as the result of internal power struggles. This meant that the party was never by itself a reliable engine of democratic reforms in the long run (even though it arguably had been a reform engine in the early years). Precisely for that reason, the EU 'anchor' in the form of a forceful and credible promise of conditional membership was crucial. In the end, Turkey was never Europe's to 'lose', but the saga of Turkey–EU relations in the first decade and a half of the new millennium could well be told as a tragic story of missed opportunities.

Paul T. Levin is the founding director of the Stockholm University Institute for Turkish Studies (SUITS). Previously he served as programme director for Governance and Management Training, and taught international relations at the Department of Economic History, both at Stockholm University. He received his PhD from the School of International Relations at the University of Southern California. The author of *Turkey and the European Union: Christian and Secular Images of Islam*, and co-editor of *Migration from Turkey to Sweden: Integration, Belonging and Transnational Community*, Dr Levin is a frequent commentator on Turkish affairs in Swedish and international media.

Notes

1. P.H. Gordon and Ömer Taspinar, *Winning Turkey: How America, Europe, and Turkey can Revive a Fading Partnership* (Washington, DC: Brookings Institution Press, 2008).

2. P.T. Levin, *Turkey and the European Union: Christian and Secular Images of Islam*. First edition. (New York: Palgrave Macmillan, 2011). Iver B. Neumann and Jennifer M. Welsh, 'The Other in European Self-Definition: An Addendum to the Literature on International Society', *Review of International Studies* 17(4) (1991), 327. E. Canan-Sokullu, 'Turcoscepticism and Threat Perception: European Public and Elite Opinion on Turkey's Protracted EU Membership', *South European Society and Politics* (16)3 (2011), 483–97.

3. Levin, *Turkey and the European Union*.

4. V.A. Schmidt, 'The EU and its Member States: From Bottom Up to Top Down', in D. Phinnemore and A. Warleigh-Lack (eds), *Reflections on European Integration: 50 Years of the Treaty of Rome* (New York: Palgrave Macmillan/Springer, 2009), pp. 194–211. See also Alpan and Diez, 'The Devil is in the "Domestic"?', 1–10.

5. This section builds on Levin, *Turkey and the European Union*, and an unpublished paper titled 'Europe's Identity Crises and Their Consequences' presented at the 2012 annual conference of the European Consortium for Political Research, Tampere, Finland. Levin, *Turkey and the European Union*.

6. R.W. Bulliet, *The Case for Islamo-Christian Civilization* (New York: Columbia University Press, 2004).

7. N. Bisaha, *Creating East and West: Renaissance Humanists and the Ottoman Turks* (Philadelphia, PA: University of Pennsylvania Press, 2004); R. Schwoebel, *The Shadow of the Crescent: The Renaissance Image of the Turk (1453–1517)*, 2nd edition (New York: St. Martin's Press, 1969); Levin, *Turkey and the European Union*.

8. D. Hay, *Europe: The Emergence of an Idea* (Edinburgh: Edinburgh University Press, 1957).

9. C. Macmillan, *Discourse, Identity and the Question of Turkish Accession to the EU: Through the Looking Glass* (Farnham: Ashgate, 2013); Levin, *Turkey and the European Union*.

10. Levin, *Turkey and the European Union*.

11. C. Macmillan, *Discourse, Identity and the Question of Turkish Accession to the EU*; Levin, *Turkey and the European Union*.

12. German MEP Mölzer (NI), *Debates of the European Parliament: Turkey's Progress Towards Accession*, Monday 13 December 2004.

13. The Nov–Dec 1994 data for Cyprus is missing. A version of Figure 9.1 was previously published in Levin, *Turkey and the European Union*.

14. Canan-Sokullu, 'Turcoscepticism and Threat Perception', 483–97. J.C. Dixon, and A.S. Fullerton, 'For and Against European Union Expansion: Examining Mixed Opinion on Enlargement and Specific Countries' Entries', *International Journal of Comparative Sociology* 55(5) (2014), 357–78. Macmillan, *Discourse, Identity*; N. Tocci, *Talking Turkey in Europe: Towards a Differentiated Communication Strategy*. Talking Turkey II, IAI-TEPAV Project (Rome: Istituto affari internazionali, 2008).

15. S. Akşit, Ö. Şenyuva and I. Gürleyen, 'The Turkish Parliamentary Elite and the EU: Mapping Attitudes towards the European Union', *South European Society and Politics* 16(3) (2011), 395–407; Macmillan, *Discourse, Identity*; Tocci, *Talking Turkey in Europe*.

16. L.M. McLaren, 'Explaining Opposition to Turkish Membership of the EU', *European Union Politics* 8(2) (2007), 251–78; Canan-Sokullu, 'Turcoscepticism and Threat Perception', 483–97; Macmillan, *Discourse, Identity*.

17. H. Sjursen, 'Why Expand?: The Question of Legitimacy and Justification in the EU's Enlargement Policy', *JCMS: Journal of Common Market Studies* 40(3) (2002), 491–513; F. Cengiz and L. Hoffmann (eds), *Turkey and the European Union: Facing New Challenges and Opportunities* (London: Routledge, 2013); McLaren, 'Explaining Opposition'; C.H. De Vreese, H.G. Boomgaarden and H.A. Semetko, 'Hard and Soft Public Support for Turkish Membership in the EU', *European Union Politics* 9(4) (2008), 511–30.

18. Canan-Sokullu, 'Turcoscepticism and Threat Perception', 483–97.

19. Levin, *Turkey and the European Union*; Neumann and Welsh, 'The Other in European Self-Definition', 327; B. Rumelili, 'Constructing Identity and Relating to Difference: Understanding the EU's Mode of Differentiation', *Review of International Studies* 30(1) (2004), 27–47.

20. Z. Öniş, 'Turkey–EU Relations: Beyond the Current Stalemate', *Insight Turkey* 10(4) (2008), 45.

21. See esp. chapter 7 in Levin, *Turkey and the European Union*.

22. Macmillan, *Discourse, Identity*; A. Çarkoğlu and Ç. Kentmen, 'Diagnosing Trends and Determinants in Public Support for Turkey's EU Membership', *South European Society and Politics* 16(3) (2011), 365–79.

23. Akşit, Şenyuva and Gürleyen, 'The Turkish Parliamentary Elite', 395–407; S.B. Gülmez, 'Explaining the Rise of Euroscepticism in the Turkish Political Elite', in Cengiz and Hoffmann, *Turkey and the European Union*, 102; Çarkoğlu and Kentmen, 'Diagnosing Trends', 365–79; B. Saatçioglu and A. Elbasani, 'The AKP's Shifting Support for EU Accession: Secular Constraints, Organizational Capacities and Religious Ideas', in Cengiz and Hoffmann, *Turkey and the European Union*, 138.

24. Gülmez, 'Explaining the Rise of Euroscepticism', 102.

25. Akşit, Şenyuva and Gürleyen, 'The Turkish Parliamentary Elite'.

26. F. Schimmelfennig, 'The Community Trap: Liberal Norms, Rhetorical Action, and the Eastern Enlargement of the European Union', *International Organization* 55(1) (2001), 47–80.

27. For an interesting recent contribution to this debate, see Erik Meyersson's blog, where he uses the Varieties of Democracy data on liberal and other kinds/measures of democracy to argue that there never was much of an early reform period under the AKP. https://erikmeyersson.com/2016/10/04/the-reversal-of-what-little-liberal-democracy-there-ever-was-in-turkey/ Other quantitative indexes like Freedom House do capture a degree of liberalization in the early years of the AKP. In the remainder of Part 3, I substantiate the claim that there were indeed significant reforms enacted during the 'golden age' of the AKP.

28. For an overview of some of this literature, see the introduction to (as well as the various contributions in) the special issue by B. Alpan and T. Diez, 'The Devil is in the "Domestic"? European Integration Studies and the Limits of Europeanization in Turkey', *Journal of Balkan and Near Eastern Studies* 16(1) (2014), 1–10.

29. BBC News, 'Turkey Agrees Death Penalty Ban', 9 January 2004. Available from http://news.bbc.co.uk/2/hi/europe/3384667.stm (last accessed 13 October 2016).

30. Amnesty International, 'Turkey: Independent Monitors Must be Allowed to Access Detainees Amid Torture Allegations', 24 July 2016. Available from https://www.amnesty. org/en/latest/news/2016/07/turkey-independent-monitors-must-be-allowed-to-access-detainees-amid-torture-allegations/ (last accessed 13 October 2016).

31. B. Özdemir, 'The Role of the EU in Turkey's Legislative Reforms for Eliminating Violence against Women: A Bottom-Up Approach', *Journal of Balkan and Near Eastern Studies* 16(1) (2014), 119–36.

32. B. Alpan, '"Europe-as-Hegemony" and Discourses in Turkey after 1999: What has "Europeanization" Got to Do with It?', *Journal of Balkan and Near Eastern Studies* 16 (2014), 68–85.

33. See e.g. the discussion of the legal reforms that were part of the 2010 constitutional amendment, in E. Özbudun, 'Turkey's Judiciary and the Drift Toward Competitive Authoritarianism', *International Spectator* 50(2) (2015), 42.

34. See e.g. I. David, 'Strategic Democratisation? A Guide to Understanding AKP in Power', *Journal of Contemporary European Studies* (2016), 1–16.

35. Alpan and Diez, 'The Devil is in the "Domestic"?', 1–10.

36. Schimmelfennig, 'The Community Trap', 47–80. I am grateful to one of the anonymous reviewers and Caner Tekin for contributing to my thinking on the issue of rhetorical entrapment as it relates to the Turkish accession.

37. Beken Saatcioglu, 'The EU's "Rhetorical Entrapment" in Enlargement Reconsidered: Why Hasn't it Worked for Turkey?', *Insight Turkey* 14(3) (2012), 173.

38. For one of the original studies of the psychological phenomenon by which we reconstruct projections of the future, see B. Fischhoff and R. Beyth, 'I Knew It Would Happen', *Organizational Behavior and Human Performance* 13(1) (1975), 1–16.

39. Z. Öniş, 'Mopolising the Centre: The AKP and the Uncertain Path of Turkish Democracy', *The International Spectator* 50(2) (2015), 23.

40. See e.g. Özbudun, 'Turkey's Judiciary', 42.

41. D. Boffey and T. Helm, 'Vote Leave Embroiled in Race Row over Turkey Security Threat Claim', *Guardian*, 22 May 2016.

Bibliography

Akşit, S., Ö. Şenyuva and I. Gürleyen. 'The Turkish Parliamentary Elite and the EU: Mapping Attitudes towards the European Union'. *South European Society and Politics* 16(3) (2011), 395–407.

Alpan, B. '"Europe-as-Hegemony" and Discourses in Turkey after 1999: What has "Europeanization" Got to Do with It?'. *Journal of Balkan and Near Eastern Studies* 16(1) (2014), 68–85.

Alpan, B., and T. Diez. 'The Devil is in the "Domestic"? European Integration Studies and the Limits of Europeanization in Turkey'. *Journal of Balkan and Near Eastern Studies* 16(1) (2014), 1–10.

Bisaha, N. *Creating East and West: Renaissance Humanists and the Ottoman Turks*. Philadelphia, PA: University of Pennsylvania Press, 2004.

Boffey, D., and T. Helm. 'Vote Leave Embroiled in Race Row over Turkey Security Threat Claim'. *Guardian*, 22 May 2016.

Bulliet, R.W. *The Case for Islamo-Christian Civilization*. New York: Columbia University Press, 2004.

Canan-Sokullu, E. 'Turcoscepticism and Threat Perception: European Public and Elite Opinion on Turkey's Protracted EU Membership'. *South European Society and Politics* 16(3) (2011), 483–97.

Çarkoğlu, A., and Ç. Kentmen. 'Diagnosing Trends and Determinants in Public Support for Turkey's EU Membership'. *South European Society and Politics* 16(3) (2011), 365–79.

Cengiz, F., and L. Hoffmann. *Turkey and the European Union: Facing New Challenges and Opportunities*. London: Routledge, 2013.

David, I. 'Strategic Democratisation? A Guide to Understanding AKP in Power'. *Journal of Contemporary European Studies* 24(4) (2016), 1–16.

De Vreese, C.H., H.G. Boomgaarden and H.A. Semetko. 'Hard and Soft Public Support for Turkish Membership in the EU'. *European Union Politics* 9(4) (2008), 511–30.

Dixon, J.C., and A.S. Fullerton. 'For and Against European Union Expansion: Examining Mixed Opinion on Enlargement and Specific Countries' Entries'. *International Journal of Comparative Sociology* 55(5) (2014), 357–78.

Fischhoff, B., and R. Beyth. 'I Knew It Would Happen'. *Organizational Behavior and Human Performance* 13(1) (1975), 1–16.

Gordon, P.H., and O. Taspinar. *Winning Turkey: How America, Europe, and Turkey can Revive a Fading Partnership*. Washington, DC: Brookings Institution Press, 2008.

Gülmez, S.B. 'Explaining the Rise of Euroscepticism in the Turkish Political Elite', in F. Cengiz and L. Hoffmann (eds), *Turkey and the European Union: Facing New Challenges and Opportunities* (London: Routledge, 2013), 102–20.

Hay, D. *Europe: The Emergence of an Idea*. Edinburgh: Edinburgh University Press, 1957.

Levin, P.T. *Turkey and the European Union : Christian and Secular Images of Islam*. First edition. New York: Palgrave Macmillan, 2011.

Macmillan, C. *Discourse, Identity and the Question of Turkish Accession to the EU: Through the Looking Glass*. Farnham: Ashgate, 2013.

McLaren, L.M. 'Explaining Opposition to Turkish Membership of the EU'. *European Union Politics* 8(2) (2007), 251–78.

Neumann, I.B., and J.M. Welsh. 'The Other in European Self-Definition: An Addendum to the Literature on International Society'. *Review of International Studies* 17(4) (1991), 327–48.

Öniş, Z. 'Turkey–EU Relations: Beyond the Current Stalemate'. *Insight Turkey* 10(4) (2008), 53–40.

———. 'Mopolising the Centre: The AKP and the Uncertain Path of Turkish Democracy'. *The International Spectator* 50(2) (2015), 22–41.

Özbudun, E. 'Turkey's Judiciary and the Drift Toward Competitive Authoritarianism'. *The International Spectator* 50(2) (2015), 42–55.

Özdemir, B. 'The Role of the EU in Turkey's Legislative Reforms for Eliminating Violence against Women: A Bottom-Up Approach'. *Journal of Balkan and Near Eastern Studies* 16(1) (2014), 119–36.

Rumelili, B. 'Constructing Identity and Relating to Difference: Understanding the EU's Mode of Differentiation'. *Review of International Studies* 30(1) (2004), 27–47.

Saatcioglu, B.'The EU's "Rhetorical Entrapment" in Enlargement Reconsidered: Why Hasn't it Worked for Turkey?', *Insight Turkey* 14(3) (2012), 173.

Saatçioglu, B., and A. Elbasani. 'The AKP's Shifting Support for EU Accession: Secular Constraints, Organizational Capacities and Religious Ideas', in F. Cengiz and L. Hoffmann (eds), *Turkey and the European Union: Facing New Challenges and Opportunities* (London: Routledge, 2013), 138–55.

Schimmelfennig, F. 'The Community Trap: Liberal Norms, Rhetorical Action, and the Eastern Enlargement of the European Union'. *International Organization* 55(1) (2001), 47–80.

Schwoebel, R. *The Shadow of the Crescent: The Renaissance Image of the Turk (1453–1517)*. 2nd edition. New York: St. Martin's Press, 1969.

Schmidt, V.A. 'The EU and its Member States: From Bottom Up to Top Down', in D. Phinnemore and A. Warleigh-Lack (eds), *Reflections on European Integration: 50 Years of the Treaty of Rome.* (New York: Palgrave Macmillan/Springer, 2009), 194–211.

Sjursen, H. 'Why Expand?: The Question of Legitimacy and Justification in the EU's Enlargement Policy'. *JCMS: Journal of Common Market Studies* 40(3) (2002), 491–513.

Tocci, N. *Talking Turkey in Europe: Towards a Differentiated Communication Strategy.* Talking Turkey II, IAI-TEPAV Project. Rome: Istituto affari internazionali, 2008.

CHAPTER 10

Conceptualizations of Turkey's Past in the European Parliament

CANER TEKIN

The EU's enlargement policy and its discussions at European level reveal pan-European and national camps' opinions about candidate countries' compatibility with EU legislation, in particular with the accession criteria. From this standpoint, the EU's supranational institutions, notably the European Commission (EC) and the European Parliament (EP), are also expected to represent candidates' histories according to the same set of conditions. Among the EU's institutions responsible for enlargement, the European Parliament is one platform at which various understandings of European history exert influences on political debates over the candidates and their pasts. Turkey, a candidate for EU accession, and yet a country that had been perceived to be Europe's antithesis for many centuries, is a specific example. As recent works put forward, ever since Turkey was given a candidacy status in 1999, members of the European Parliament (MEPs) have drawn on their respective conceptions of history throughout their debates over Turkey's reform process towards accession.[1]

The present chapter elaborates on the debates by MEPs over Turkey's history in a number of cases. It also gives insights into the distances of political camps to the accession criteria when they discussed Turkey's past. To this end, it inspects the statements raised during the plenary sessions of the European Parliament, including those of the Committee on Foreign Affairs (AFET) during the 2000s, and highlights how European political camps employed the accession criteria in their arguments about Turkey's history. It opens with a short introduction to the connection between European identity and the accession criteria, and how European parties related these membership conditions to European identity, as their election programmes during the 2000s implied. Later, it highlights the textual data created in the European Parliament. The first source is the debates in the EP reserved for Turkey's progress towards accession, and the second involves the official Turkey reports tabled annually by the Committee on Foreign Affairs. The third sort of document is the proposals made by AFET members to amend Turkey reports (second type documents). Overall, MEPs' speeches as well as official documents, including their amendments, reflect the dichotomic influences exerted by national politics and European politics on debates over Turkey and its history.

In the beginning it is essential to clarify why blanket ideological terms are employed throughout the chapter. In general, traditional ideological lines at the European level and affiliations with pan-European parties restrict parliamentarians' arguments. Although left–right frictions diminished in time in European politics, European parties still represent their own political identities today. To give a very general example, the parties centred on the 'right' or 'centre-right' upheld a functioning free market and EU-led authority to control criminal and immigration issues, while the 'political left' rather remained the advocates of the social policies, equality, and fundamental liberties.[2] Similarly, the political parties represented in the European Parliament semi-officially designate themselves with references to their ideological lines in their political programmes. The members affiliated with the Party of European Socialists are called the 'Socialists' whereas the ones from the European Left and the European Green Party, including their parliamentary groups, are referred to as the Communists and the Greens respectively. ALDE's (Alliance of Liberals and Democrats for Europe) members champion liberal values, hence they are designated as 'the Liberals'. The European People's Party (EPP) is the political camp of the Christian Democrats, who still are part of the 'conservatives'. In fact, the conservative ideology has a broad array of divisions with ontological differences such the Christian Democracy and Euroscepticism. Here, the chapter stresses the Christian Democratic identity of EPP members almost everywhere, and mentions the rest, such as the members of the Independence/Democracy Group, as the conservatives. Next, the conservative parliamentarians of British origin are officially affiliated with the Conservative and Unionist Party, or the British Conservatives. Although they collaborated with the Christian Democrats in one parliamentary group for most of the 2000s, their views on core issues such as the EU's integration and enlargement structurally contrasted with their European partners, as they finally formed their own political party.

Taking into consideration their individual views on Turkey, this chapter respectively alludes to them as the British Conservatives. Other conservative MEPs, like the members of the European Alliance for Freedom (after 2010), or the independent ones such as Philip Claeys of Vlaams Belang, that of the Belgian/Flemish nationalist party, or William Dartmouth from the UK Independence Party, are referred to as the far-right or nationalist members in this chapter.

Conceptions of European Identity and the Accession Criteria

The European Commission tables its progress reports according to the Copenhagen Criteria, and the European Parliament (the Committee on Foreign Affairs) shapes country reports considering, inter alia, these earlier progress reports. Therefore, European political camps are presumed to primarily approach candidates' compatibility with EU legislation through the prism of the accession criteria. But the question remains how they perceive these conditions: the heart of European identity as fundamental, liberal-democratic principles, a product of the historical development underpinned by Christianity and thus only one component of Europeanness, or a legal ground on which European nation states cooperate so long as their interests match? Before seeing MEPs' statements about Turkey's past, it is important to take into account that European political camps do not agree on the accession criteria's scope.

Two main sources lay the foundations of the accession criteria. First, Article 49 of the Treaty on European Union (TEU) enshrines the territorial and political conditions of EU membership. It states: '[A]ny European State which respects the values referred to in Article 2 and is committed to promoting them may apply to become a member of the Union'.[3] The second source is the Copenhagen Criteria, a set of conditions stipulated by the Copenhagen European Council in 1993 to the EU's applicants, and specified as 'the stability of institutions guaranteeing democracy, the rule of law, human rights, respect for and protection of minorities, the existence of a functioning market economy, as well as the capacity to cope with the competitive pressure and market forces within the Union, and, the ability to take on obligations of membership including adherence to the aims of political, economic, and monetary Union'.[4] Given its border disputes between Greece and Cyprus, the Brussels European Council in 2004 introduced a new condition to Turkey entitled 'good neighbourly relations'.[5] This latest condition was given mention in the negotiating document adopted at the beginning of the membership negotiations with Turkey, on 3 October 2005.[6] Thus, Article 49 of the TEU and the Copenhagen Criteria together are expected to be the only standards of discussing Turkey in the European Parliament. All these conditions below shall be referred to as the accession criteria.

Democratic principles that Article 49 of the TEU and the Copenhagen Criteria involve are recently mentioned in EU legislation as 'European values'. Following the amendments made by the Treaty of Lisbon (2009), the Treaty on European Union enshrined democratic principles and responsibilities in Article 2: 'The Union is founded on the *values* of respect for human dignity, freedom, democracy, equality, the rule of law and respect for human rights, including the rights of persons belonging to minorities'.[7] The EU typically represents, and gives highest moral priority to, these secular, humanitarian and democratic characteristics.

Political camps of the European Parliament are also expected to acknowledge the accession criteria as the common values of the European Union. The parties of the political left mostly limited European values to the accession criteria while discussing Turkey's reform progress towards EU accession. The Socialists, the Greens, the Communists, and additionally the Liberals championed an organization principally defined by the Copenhagen principles.[8] In comparison with these parties, the Christian Democrats, the far-right members, and the other conservative members of the EP were more fragmented on the connection between European identity and the accession criteria.

The European People's Party is a particular example. Despite being the strongest representative of the Christian Democratic ideology in Europe, the European People's Party symbolized (and still does) the secular side of European politics. The EPP and its constituent national parties in Western Europe built on linkages between the political organization and social groups like trade unions, rather than the church.[9] That being said, in the party's conservative terminology, European values exceed the accession criteria. Since the EU's foundation, the Christian Democratic ideology has maintained that political integration is a prerequisite due to common cultural values of Europeans.[10] Put differently, to the European People's Party the European history shaped by Christian practices entails European integration. With regard to their reading of European history, then, the set of shared values the EPP suggested in the European Parliament during the 2000s was not limited to the Copenhagen Criteria.[11] Shortly before the membership negotiations began, the PES leader Martin Schulz denounced the EPP's construction of European values and its insistent opposition against Turkey: 'I can tell . . . that it does not want Turkey because Turkey is distant and Muslim, but that Croatia is acceptable on the grounds of being Catholic, conservative and close at hand'.[12] Next, the religious construction of Europe is certainly a common conception between the members associated with the radical right in Europe. As the chapter exemplifies below, these members stated bluntly in the EP that religion is one common ground of Europeans, and the adoption of European values by Turkey was only likely by leaving Islamic and 'Ottoman values' aside.[13]

A majority of the conservative MEPs from Britain contrasted with their European counterparts in conceptions of the accession criteria. The British Conservative Party, which collaborated with the EPP in the same group until 2009, confined European values to the Copenhagen Criteria and formed an opinion of the Turkish candidate only through the accession conditions that had already been set by the EU's founding treaties.[14] Other leading British national parties represented in the European Parliament, except the UK Independence Party, which stood against the EU entirely, also built their arguments about European enlargement primarily on the accession criteria – these were the Labour Party and Liberal Democrats, which were affiliates of the Party of European Socialists and ALDE respectively. Further, their election programmes for the European elections in the 2000s suggest that these parties, including the Conservatives, expressed their reliance on the Copenhagen Criteria throughout the enlargement process, including Turkey.[15] This is explained with the *sui generis* nature of British politics, and a public opinion notably sceptical of European integration. At least in the 2000s, the Eurosceptic British foreign policy followed a strategy of backing Turkey's accession, so that the membership of a culturally and historically 'different' country with a huge population would hinder the European Union's further integration.[16] In the European Parliament this was a familiar picture. Among the British MEPs only the far-right members (the UK Independence Party) excluded Turkey from Europe, while the other British parliamentarians embraced the country's accession process during the 2000s.

In brief, pan-European parties and some national parties represented in the EP did not agree on the relationship between the accession criteria and Europeanness. Therefore, how these camps use the accession criteria in parliamentary discussions about Turkey's past is a relevant question. Before anything else, it needs to admit that it is not possible to separate clearly the arguments about Turkey's history from those about Turkey's contemporary political and economic progress towards accession to the EU. In this case, MEPs approached Turkey's reform process as well as its history in the shadow of current developments. First, shortly after the accession talks commenced (2005), the European Commission declared in its report that Turkey had already slowed down its important legislative reforms.[17] In 2006 the European Parliament was also pointing out Turkey's downturn in fulfilling reforms.[18] The second development was Turkey's insistence on its Cyprus policy: the Council of the European Union blocked eight chapters of Turkey's existing negotiations in 2006 as a response to the candidate refusing to recognize Cyprus as one legitimate representative of the island. Despite these developments impacting on the image of Turkey, or the image of Turkish governments more precisely, reading the debates over the candidate's past through the usage of the accession criteria gives clues about what the deputies understand of European and Turkish histories.

Turkey's History as a Matter of Discussion in the European Parliament

Throughout the 2000s, parliamentarians discussed, alternately, not only Turkey's democratic performances towards EU accession but also its history. Overall, members of the European Parliament (MEPs) gave references to a number of historical cases from Turkey's past and linked them to the contemporary politics. Some of these much-debated cases were the Armenian Genocide of the Ottomans, Turkey's historical relationship with Cyprus, its Kemalist legacy, and its religious past going back to the Ottoman era.

First, parliamentarians discussed Turkey's relations with Armenia with references to the past. They largely presented the Armenian Genocide, the deportation and massacre of the Armenian subjects in the Ottoman realm, as a historic case concerning modern Turkey, and together called on the candidate to face its history. The European Parliament had first requested Turkey to recognize the act as genocide in 1987, and it revived the issue through its resolutions about the candidate in 2000, 2004 and 2005. The reports on Turkey and their amendments published during the 2000s suggest that the keywords 'past' and 'history' were employed primarily with the Armenian Genocide, and also linked to a contemporary aspect, the country's relations with its minorities.[19]

To give examples from parliamentary debates, in 2004 the Christian Democrats and other conservative parliamentarians (members of the Independence/Democracy Group), together with Liberals, were stating that recognizing the Armenian Genocide of the Ottomans was a natural precondition before Turkey's membership negotiations.[20] In return, a few in the EP were contending that the Ottomans' Armenian Genocide was not a precondition for Turkey's membership negotiations but something the candidate should immediately acknowledge.[21] In this case, parliamentarians welcomed Turkish intellectuals questioning Turkey's denial diplomacy, and equally criticized the prosecutions directed at these people and the act of discussing the genocide in public.[22] Later, Turkey managed to begin its accession talks without making any attempt in this case, and in this instance many MEPs maintained that the Armenian Genocide should be a condition for the candidate's accession. Still, although parliamentarians together acknowledged the case as 'genocide', and saw it as critical to Turkey's accession, they linked it to the Copenhagen Criteria differently. For instance, the European

Parliament's resolution published shortly before the opening of the membership negotiations with the candidate 'call(ed) on Turkey to recognise the Armenian genocide' and 'consider(ed) this recognition to be a prerequisite for accession to the European Union'.[23] In the following report tabled roughly one year after the beginning of the accession talks, the rapporteur intended to keep the mention of the genocide as a precondition, yet the entire statement would be amended following the intervention of Socialist and Liberal members: '[A]lthough recognition of the Armenian genocide as such is formally not one of the Copenhagen criteria, it is indispensable for a country on the road to membership to come to terms with and recognise its past'.[24] To these members the genocide should be recognized, inescapably, but not necessarily at the beginning of the negotiations, as it did not derive from the accession criteria.

Parliamentarians also linked Turkey's responsibility for the Armenian Genocide to the contemporary frozen relationships with its neighbour. The European Parliament's resolution on Turkey in 2004 had dealt with two issues in one context:

> [T]his process must be taken to its logical conclusion by re-opening the border between Turkey and Armenia . . . (the EP) calls on the Commission and the Council to demand that the Turkish authorities formally acknowledge the historic reality of the genocide perpetrated against the Armenians in 1915 and open the border between Turkey and Armenia at an early date, in accordance with the resolutions adopted by the European Parliament between 1987 and 2004.[25]

In its resolution, the European Parliament connected a historical case with current politics and discussed it under the 'good neighbourly relations', one of the accession conditions, which was individually stipulated to Turkey. Parliamentarians similarly remarked on history and contemporary politics together. In 2005, MEPs emphasized the current state of the freedom of thought in Turkey as something that hinders the liberal arguments about the Armenian Genocide. In parallel, they debated Turkey's recognition of the genocide together with the country's foreign policy of Armenia.[26] That is also why a possible rapprochement in current diplomatic relations between Turkey and Armenia partially affected genocide discussions in the EP. The European Commission and European Parliament commended Turkey in taking steps towards an agreement with Armenia in 2008.[27] Debates on the Armenian Genocide abated, relatively speaking; the EP did not mention the term 'genocide' in its later reports, at least until its resolution (2015) on the centenary of the tragedy, and parliamentarians directed their attention towards the possibility of reconciliation between two neighbours.

The second issue that stemmed from Turkey's past and caused contemporary consequences was the candidate's strained relations with Cyprus.

Here, Turkey's historical image emerged on the whole as 'an occupier'. The EU's attitude towards the existence of Turkish military on the island since 1974 is known to be negative when aligned with the principle of good neighbourly relations. In 2000, the European Parliament denounced Turkish armed forces in Northern Cyprus, referred to them as 'occupation forces', and called for their immediate withdrawal.[28] Following the negotiations' beginning, the European Parliament repeated its warnings against Turkey's military involvement in Cyprus, although it refrained from using the term 'occupation'. The early negotiation years also featured Cypriot and Greek members' joint participations in plenary discussions on this subject. To give examples, conservative members of Cypriot origin made use of the terms 'occupation' and 'colonization' in their proposals,[29] and communist, liberal, and conservative members from Greek and Cypriot origins also agreed together on the immediate withdrawal of Turkish forces and on the steps to take to recognize Cyprus.[30] Similarly, Greek and Cypriot members representing different ideological spectrums called on Turkey to end its veto against the membership of Cyprus in international organizations (i.e. NATO).[31]

Another dimension of this issue needs to be mentioned: Turkey's long-expected recognition of Cyprus, which is stipulated by the EU to be a precondition of the candidate's accession. In the early 2000s a plan was developed for the unification of the island, which was initiated by the United Nations and supported by the EU, Turkey and Greece, and it was famously called the 'Annan Plan'. The Greek Cypriots rejected the plan in a referendum, and joined the EU in 2004 as the sole representatives of the island. Consequently, Turkey would not recognize an EU member, and this caused a highly serious problem under the principle of the good neighbourly relations, as the European Commission's progress report in 2005 proclaimed.[32] Following the EU's enlargement in 2004, Turkey was expected to extend the implementation of the Association Agreement and Additional Protocol, which it once signed with the EU's founding members. Updating the documents to the total number of EU members would eventually mean the full recognition of Cyprus by Turkey. In return, the candidate declared that it would involve Cyprus in the protocol as soon as the EU ended the isolation of the Turkish Cypriot community. As a stalemate occurred, Turkey's restrictions against the country continued mostly in security and transportation, at the expense of receiving a series of reactions by the European Union. In 2006, the Council of the European Union blocked eight chapters of Turkey's membership negotiations and announced that they would remain suspended 'until Turkey fulfils its commitments under the additional protocol to the EU–Turkey association agreement, which extended the EU–Turkey customs union to the ten member states, including Cyprus'.[33] The European Parliament also declared in the same year that the candidate's denial to fully recognize Cyprus was to set a serious barrier in the accession process.[34] In return, the Socialists, Greens, Liberals and the British Conservatives asked the EU to take a more constructive initiative for the solution. In plenary sessions during 2006 and 2007, they separately called on the EU and Cyprus to end the isolation of the Turkish community on the island, as Turkish Cypriots had accepted the Annan unification plan in referendum.[35] Conservative members instead continued to condemn Turkey for its Cyprus policy, and largely lacked a proposal against the Turkish community's isolation in the north. Philip Claeys, an MEP representing the nationalist Belgian/Flemish Party, Vlaams Belang, was a particular example: he asserted right at the beginning of the negotiations that the lack of progress in Turkey's recognition of Cyprus must put an immediate stop to the accession talks.[36] He also disagreed with the EU's prospective support for the Northern Cypriot authority, including financial incentives, and contended that financial assistance to the Turkish Cypriot community would infringe international law.[37] In the end, Turkey's image as the occupier on the island remained undisputed, and the contemporary frozen relationship with Cyprus hindered any change in this conception.

The secular modernization movement called 'Kemalism' since the early republic, named after its founder Mustafa Kemal Ataturk, was another subject of discussion and was mainly approached in political and religious terms derived from the EU's accession criteria. Parliamentarians representing different ideologies questioned the Kemalist ideology's compatibility with minority rights in Europe.[38] They tended to link Article 301 of the Turkish Constitution to the nationalist origins of the Kemalist legacy in Turkey,[39] and thus that the recent authoritarianism witnessed in Turkey dated from the Kemalist past.[40] Charles Tannock, from the European Conservatives and Reformist Group (Eurosceptics), exemplified this view in his statement that Kemalist traditions in Turkish politics should evolve to a more pluralistic political environment as it was now largely motivating the nationalist opposition to Turkey's reformist policies in minority rights.[41] In contrast, some conservative and nationalist members credited the modernist lines of Kemalism with being essential for the candidate's reform process and contended that Ataturk's legacy was to be saved for the sake of the secular and democratic Turkey.[42] There were members considering Kemalism to be the source of Turkish enlightenment against political Islam, such as Gerard Batten from European Freedom and Democracy, who stated: '[T]he reforms of Kemal Ataturk in the 1920s were to be applauded, as they sought to leave behind the antiquities of the Ottoman Empire and the worst of the Dark Age Islamic practices, and to take Turkey forward into the twentieth century'.[43] To Batten, Ataturk stood against and repelled the radical Islam in the country. The militant Islam would have a greater chance to thrive against Kemalist legal traditions if Turkey joins the European Union because EU laws would take precedence over the secular Turkish laws and help the radical Islam to flourish.[44] In another instance, Kemalism was presented in opposition to the Ottoman past. Mogens Camre, the parliamentary vice chair of Eurosceptic and nationalist Union for Europe of the Nations, commented at the beginning of the membership negotiations: '[I]f Turkey really wanted to live by Kemal Ataturk's famous words "there is only one civilization", we would not be standing here year after year stating that Turkey is most certainly not willing to comply with the EU's demands concerning the adoption of European values and give up Ottoman values'.[45]

The Kemalist legacy was additionally connected to the military influence over Turkish politics. Consensus remained between European political camps in the case of civil–military relations in the country. Shortly after the beginning of the membership negotiations, the dominant view was that the 'Kemalist' Turkish army sought to infiltrate the civil politics on certain occasions, and it contributed to the illiberal democracy, the deepening of the minority problems in Turkey, and the lack of a resolution in the conflict with Cyprus.[46] In its 2006 report, the European Parliament called on the civil politicians and judiciary in Turkey to act against a number of military officers accused of illegal actions in Kurdish-populated districts.[47] In another instance, the Socialist and Liberal members denounced the memorandum that the Turkish military released to manipulate the presidential election in 2007. Despite these views, the historical image of the Turkish army as the saviour of the secular regime was also expressed. As some conservative members argued, the military in Turkey had the crucial role of protecting the secular regime against political Islam, and this role should be maintained throughout the country's accession process.[48]

The final subject was Turkey's religious past. Arguments about the current implementation of the freedom of belief and the rights of religious minorities in Turkey drew on the country's religious history at times. Conservative members of the European Parliament showed striking examples. In these examples they associated the 'Islamic devotion' in Turkey with authoritarianism, and asserted that Turkey's history did not prove the country European.[49] Zbigniew Zalewski from the European People's Party stated in the European Parliament: 'Their religious tradition is directing them along their own specific course, which differs from that of us Europeans. In addition, the unwritten social codes do not suggest that the Turkish people are gravitating towards a European identity'.[50] Non-attached Andreas Mölzer, representing solely the Freedom Party of Austria, similarly asserted: 'Europe's cultural identity, which has evolved through history, would without doubt be fundamentally undermined by the presence of a

Muslim Member State'.[51] To these members it was particularly the Islamic tradition that was diverging Turkey from European values.[52] Marine Le Pen, France's National Front representative in the EP, who would later assume the party's leadership, expressed in September 2005, shortly before the beginning of the membership negotiations: 'In a period marked by Islamic terrorism . . . and at a time when our republican laws and our principle of secularism are coming into conflict with the development of a radical kind of Islam on our soil, how can Europe take the responsibility of forcing upon Europeans a country with an Islamic government?'[53]

In these arguments, Islam was being held responsible for Turkey's illiberal politics. The 'Turkish Islam', as named by Philip Claeys and William Dartmouth, was the main reason for the violence against Christian minorities.[54] It also preceded the discrimination of women in Turkey.[55] Mogens Camre put in words in 2006: 'The government of Turkey has demonstrated again and again that it does not recognize European values, whilst at the same time demanding that we should respect unacceptable Turkish and Islamic values'.[56] Aside from righteously questioning the freedom of religion in Turkey, in all these statements what remains is religious conceptualizations of the country and its history as a different, anti-civil and anti-European existence. For a suggestive example, non-attached Jim Allister, representing conservative Traditional Unionist Voice from Britain, stated in a parliamentary session in 2004:

> Turkey itself has a shameful history of expansionism. Witness its brutal invasion and occupation of Northern Cyprus. Witness its genocide of the Armenian people. Witness also, despite the massive inducements of pre-accession aid from Brussels, its intolerant suppression of religious freedom, in particular with regard to Christians.[57]

In parallel with the statements above, the conservative parliamentarians condemned Turkey's membership in the Organization of the Islamic Conference, whose declaration made use of the word 'Sharia'. Turkey's involvement in the organization was arguably incompatible with 'the separation between church and state in Turkey'.[58] As one example, Charles Tannock from the European Conservatives and the Reformists Group asserted: 'One concern . . . is Turkey's membership of the Organisation of the Islamic Conference (OIC), where such common Western values as we all share in the European Union are not evident because the OIC cites Sharia law as a basis for human rights in the Islamic world'.[59] Yet, it needs to be remembered here that the Organisation of the Islamic Conference is a legitimate establishment represented in the United Nations. Also, through its official Arabic language, the declaration of OIC inherently involves the term 'Sharia', which merely connotes the minimalist conception of Islamic ethics.[60]

In other respects, Turkey's Islamic past was mainly accompanied by its Ottoman history. In contrast to the above conservative and far-right members seeing 'Ottoman values' as antithetical to 'European values', there were members who tended to see Islam and the country's Islamic past as a source of multiculturalism. Regarding positive references to the Ottoman past, the European Green Party came into prominence. Cem Ozdemir, the party's former co-president, had stated in 2004 that Turkey's EU membership would ensure that many religious communities flourish together 'as they once did during the history of the Ottoman Empire'.[61] Similarly, in their proposal to amend the EP's report in 2006, the Greens internalized Turkey's cultural background by calling on the candidate to heed the cultural and historic legacy inherited from the Ottomans. The amendment, as approved by the other deputies in return, involved that the European Parliament 'respects the sensitivities that exist in a country where the large majority are Sunni Muslims, but reminds Turkey of the important cultural and historic heritage handed down to it for safekeeping by the multicultural, multi-ethnic and multireligious Ottoman Empire'.[62] The Greens pointed out the Ottoman heritage, famously credited with the 'Millets', the Ottoman administration system based on autonomous religious groups. The Ottoman history was thus constructed as compatible with the freedoms expected from the contemporary Turkey: the 'multicultural, multi-ethnic and multireligious Ottoman Empire' had once bestowed various kinds of social rights on its subjects, and so should the Turkish regime today. The social rights given in the Ottoman past were to inspire the Turkish government to advance religious freedoms. The overall argument, therefore, brought multiculturalism to the fore.

Conclusion

This chapter builds on the argument that there are conceptual relationships between the understandings of the EU's accession criteria and the debates over Turkey's past and its compatibility with European history. Accordingly, what pan-European political camps understand of the accession criteria can be grouped into two categories: the accession criteria being the heart of European identity as fundamental, liberal-democratic principles, and the accession criteria as a product of the historical development underpinned by Christianity, and thus only one component of Europeanness. To draw the main conclusion, the members of the European Parliament, who regarded the accession criteria as identical to Europeanness, principally discussed Turkey's history with political terms, and even in certain instances they implied the intersections between European and Turkish histories. On the other hand, many conservative deputies who drew on a Christian history of Europe debated the candidate's past alternately. In addition to the accession criteria, this latter group stipulated other, mostly religious and geographical, conditions to Turkey, and tended to describe the candidate's history as completely opposed to European history.

In other respects, there was often consensus among delegates on certain instances of the candidate's history. Turkey's recognition of the Armenian Genocide was generally discerned to be a precondition before the candidate's membership. The parliament's reports and MEPs' statements involving the Armenian Genocide indicated the shared, strong position against Turkey's official denial. This precondition was mostly discussed together with the contemporary relations with Armenia or intellectual freedoms in Turkey, and connected to the EU's accession criteria. Turkey's responsibility for the conflict in Cyprus was another issue debated with references to the past and the present day. The Council of the European Union denounced Turkey for persistently rejecting the recognition of Cyprus, and took measures against the candidate, in particular suspending some chapters of the membership negotiations. The responsibilities of the EU and Cyprus for the conflict and the isolation of the Turkish community on the island rather remained subjects of disagreement, and national interests often structured discussions. In this sense, the image of Turkey as the 'occupier' of Cyprus was expressed in the European Parliament at times. Finally, parliamentarians commonly ascribed the Turkish army's impact on civil politics to Kemalism, the ideology that founded the Turkish Republic. MEPs either questioned it as a doctrine, over which a more pluralistic understanding of governance should prevail, or they saw it as a necessary, ideological source of the secular regime. In this latter group siding with Kemalism, the ones preoccupied with Turkey's Islamization advocated the existing military influence on civil politics, and equated Kemalist ideology with the means of de-Islamizing national politics.

During the 2000s, political camps represented in the European Parliament were highly fragmented over the Islamization in Turkey. Parliamentarians mentioned the Islamic aspect of Turkish history alternately, and debated whether it conformed to their constructions of European history. In religious terms, conservative parliamentarians who conceptualized European history in parallel with the Christian line of development tended to estrange Turkey's history. Among them, the apologists of a Christian Europe and especially far-right members asserted that Turkey's history was not compatible with the European past. These arguments were also accompanied by views on the rise of political Islam in Turkey. These members were inclined to use Turkey's Islamic past and their concerns about the current state of Islamism in Turkey within one argument.

Finally, we need to underline the import of national politics exerting certain influences over the debates about Turkey's history at the European level. As a striking example, the conservative parliamentarians affiliated with the British Conservative Party contrasted with their European counterparts marginalizing Turkey's history, as the British Conservatives debated the candidate's past, as well as its present candidature, in rather political terms. British foreign policy and public opinion, perhaps the most pro-Turkish of their time (during the 2000s), led to the British Conservatives expressing positive messages about Turkey's EU membership and its history. Second, MEPs from Cyprus and Greece showed an almost uniform attitude towards contemporary and historical aspects of Turkey, which were linked to long-term political disputes over the Mediterranean region. These examples underpin the argument that European political elites principally approached European and Turkish histories with contemporary interests and beliefs structured by national contexts.

Caner Tekin is a member of the Centre for Mediterranean Studies at the Ruhr University Bochum, where he has recently received his doctoral degree. He worked previously at the Georg-Eckert Institute for International Textbook Research in Brunswick, Germany as a postdoctoral fellow. He is also a review editor working for H-Nationalism, the online scholarly forum on nationalism studies. His research interests revolve around the linkages between nationalisms, representations of the past, and migration.

Notes

1. P. Levin, *Turkey and the European Union: Christian and Secular Images of Islam* (New York: Palgrave Macmillan, 2011), 181–204; S. Aydin-Duzgit, *Constructions of European Identity: Debates and Discourses on Turkey and the EU* (London: Palgrave, 2012).

2. S. Hix, *The Political System of the European Union* (New York: Palgrave Macmillan, 2005), 167–68.

3. Ibid., 43.

4. Council of the European Union, Presidency Conclusions, Copenhagen European Council, 21–22 June, 1993, SN 180/1/93.

5. Brussels European Council, Presidency Conclusions, Brussels, 16/17 December 2004.

6. Negotiating Framework, 3 October 2005.

7. Consolidated Versions of the Treaty on European Union, *Official Journal of the European Union* 55 (2012), C326, 17.

8. Party of European Socialists, Manifesto for Elections, June 2009. Amendments 17 and 18 for recital c. Amendments 1–162 for the Draft Motion for a Resolution PE402.879v01-00, PE404.587v01-00, 07.04.2008, 9/142; Amendments 6 and 7 for recital a, amendment 28 for paragraph 1 and amendment 39 for paragraph 5, Amendments 1 –243 for the Draft Motion for a Resolution PE430.695v02-00, PE431.004v02-00, 04.01.2010, 5–6, 15, 19–20/127;

Amendment 11 for paragraph 8, Amendments for the Draft Motion for Resolution on the 2012 Progress Report of Turkey, PE.504.377v01-00, 12.02.2013, 7/118; European Liberal, Democrat and Reform Party, European Liberals' Top 15 for EP Election, Manifesto for the European Election 2009, Adopted at the Stockholm Congress, 31 October 2008; ELDR Manifesto, 2004 European Parliamentary Election, Approved in Amsterdam, 14 November 2003; The European Green Party, Manifesto for the 2004 European Election, Fourth European Greens Congress, Rome, 20–22 February 2004; European Left, United for a Left Alternative in Europe, European Left Election Manifesto 2004.

    9. S.N. Kalyvas, *The Rise of Christian Democracy in Europe* (Ithaca, NY: Cornell University Press, 1996), 1–2; T. Jansen and S. Van Hecke, *At Europe's Service: The Origins and Evolution of the European People's Party* (Heidelberg: Springer, 2011), 180–81.

    10. Jansen and Van Hecke, *At Europe's Service*, 20–22.

    11. Amendment 13 for recital c, Amendments 1–188 for the Draft Motion for Resolution PE414.936v01-00, PE416.543v01-00, 07.01.2009, 8/103.

    12. Martin Schulz's address, Debate on Opening of Negotiations with Turkey, Additional Protocol to the EEC–Turkey Association Agreement, European Parliament, 28 September 2005.

    13. Lydia Schenardi's address, Debate on Women in Turkey, European Parliament, Strasbourg, 12 February 2007; Mogens Camre's address, Debate on Turkey's 2007 Progress Report, European Parliament, Strasbourg, 21 May 2008.

    14. British Conservative Party, 'Vote for Change: European Election Manifesto', Manifesto for European Election 2009.

    15. Labour Party, 'Britain Forward not Back', The Labour Party Manifesto 2005; Liberal Democrats, 'The Real Alternative', Election Manifesto 2005; Liberal Democrats, 'Stronger Together, Poorer Apart', The Liberal Democrat Manifesto for the 2009 Election to the European Parliament. Also see, 'It's Time for Action', Conservative Election Manifesto, 2005.

    16. A.V. Menéndez-Alarcón, *The Cultural Realm of European Integration: Social Representations in France, Spain, and the United Kingdom* (Westport, CT: Praeger, 2004), 127.

    17. Commission of European Communities, Progress Report of Turkey, SEC(2005)1426, 9 November 2005, 137.

    18. European Parliament, European Parliament Critical of Slowdown in Turkey's Reform Process, Press Service 20060922IPR10896, 27 September 2006.

    19. Paragraph 56, European Parliament Resolution on Turkey's Progress towards Accession P6_TA(2006)0381, paragraph 34; European Parliament Resolution of 12 March 2009 on Turkey's Progress Report 2008, P6_TA(2009)0134, paragraph 44; European Parliament Resolution of 21 May 2008 on Turkey's 2007 Progress Report, P6_TA(2008)0224; Amendment 99, paragraph 20a, amendment 13 for recital c, Amendments 1–188 for the Draft Motion for Resolution, PE416.543v01-00, 7 January 2009, 54/103; Amendment 104 for paragraph 19a, amendment 185 for paragraph 32; Amendments 1–243 for the Draft Motion for a Resolution, PE431.004v02-00, 1 January 2010, 55, 98/127.

    20. Addresses by Bernard Lexideux, Paul-Marie Coûteaux, Nils Lundgren, Ioannis Kassoulides, Thomas Savi and Christine de Veyrac, Debate on Turkey's Progress towards Accession, European Parliament, Strasbourg, 13 December 2004.

    21. Veronique de Keyser, Debate on Turkey's Progress towards Accession (2004).

    22. See the commentaries in: Debate on Opening of Negotiations with Turkey – Additional Protocol to the EEC–Turkey Association Agreement, European Parliament, Strasbourg, 28 September 2005. Warner Langen and Louis Michael's addresses, Debate on Turkey's Progress towards Accession, European Parliament, 26 September 2006, Strasbourg. Also see amendment 372 for paragraph 31, Amendments 1–461 for the Draft Motion for a Resolution on the 2011 Progress Report on Turkey PE473.875v02-00, PE478.719v01-00, 1 February 2012, 64/274.

23. European Parliament Resolution on the Opening of Negotiations with Turkey, (PA_TA(2005)0350), 28 September 2005..

24. Paragraph 56, European Parliament Resolution on Turkey's Progress towards Accession, P6_TA(2006)0381, 27 September 2006. For its draft version, see paragraph 49, Report on Turkey's Progress towards Accession (2006/2118(INI)), 13 September 2006.

25. European Parliament Resolution on the 2004 Regular Report and the Recommendation of the European Commission on Turkey's Progress towards Accession P6_TA(2004)0096, 15 December 2004.

26. Addresses by Francis Wurtz, Ioannis Kasoulides, György Schöpflin, Richard Seeber, Marie-Arlette Carlotti and Martine Roure, Opening of Negotiations with Turkey – Additional Protocol to the EEC–Turkey Association Agreement, European Parliament, Strasbourg, 28 September 2005.

27. Olli Rehn's speech, Debate on Enlargement Strategy 2009 Concerning the Countries of the Western Balkans, Iceland and Turkey, European Parliament, Strasbourg, 25 November 2009.

28. European Parliament, Report on the 1999 Regular Report from the Commission on Turkey's Progress towards Accession, A5-0297/2000, 19 October 2000.

29. Amendments 206 and 207 for paragraph 19, amendment 217 for paragraph 19a, Amendments 1–236 for the Draft Motion for a Resolution PE392.298v02-00, PE393.947v02-00, 25.09.2007, 69–70, 73/79.

30. Amendment 262 for recital Ca, amendments 179 and 186 for paragraph 30, Amendments 1–343 for Draft Report on Turkey's Progress towards Accession 2006, PE 376.373v02-00, 04.07.2006, 62–64, 88/115. Amendments 208, 213 and 214 for paragraph 19 and amendment 222 for paragraph 20, Amendments 1–236 for the Draft Motion for a Resolution PE392.298v02-00, PE393.947v02-00, 25.09.2007, 70–72, 75/79.

31. Amendment 173 for paragraph 29a, amendment 195 for paragraph 30a and amendments 201, 202 and 203 for paragraph 31a, Amendments for Draft Report on Turkey's Progress towards Accession 2006, PE 376.373v02-00, 04.07.2006, 60, 67–68, 70/115.

32. European Commission, Turkey 2005 Progress Report, Brussels, SEC (2005)1426, 09.11.2005, 137.

33. European Parliament, Report on Turkey's Progress towards Accession 2006/ 2118(INI), 13.09.2006, 15/22.

34. Ibid.

35. Amendment 22 for recital d, and amendments 181 and 184 for paragraph 30, Amendments 1–236 for the Draft Motion for a Resolution, PE393.947v02-00, 25.09.2007, 7, 61-62/79. Amendment 187 for paragraph 30, Amendments for Draft Report on Turkey's Progress towards Accession 2006, PE 376.373v02-00, 04.07.2006, 65/115. Amendment 216 for paragraph 19, Amendments 1–236 for the Draft Motion for a Resolution PE392.298v02-00, PE393.947v02-00, 25.09.2007, 73/79. Amendment 331 for recital U, Amendments for Draft Report on Turkey's Progress towards Accession 2006, PE 376.373v02-00, 04.07.2006, 111/115.

36. Amendment 200 for paragraph 31, Amendments for Draft Report on Turkey's Progress towards Accession 2006, PE 376.373v02-00, 04.07.2006, 69/115.

37. Amendment 177, paragraph 30, Amendments for Draft Report on Turkey's Progress towards Accession 2006, PE 376.373v02-00, 04.07.2006, 61/115, and amendment 220 for paragraph 19, Amendments 1–236 for the Draft Motion for a Resolution PE392.298v02-00, PE393.947v02-00, 25.09.2007, 74/79. Amendment 221 for paragraph 20, Amendments 1–236 for the Draft Motion for a Resolution, PE393.947v02-00, 25.09.2007, 74/79.

38. Bernd Posselt's address, Debate on Turkey's Progress towards Accession (2006).

39. Alexander Lambsdorff and Charles Tannock's addresses, Debate on EU–Turkey Relations, European Parliament, 24 October 2007.

40. Marios Matsakis's address, Debate on Democratic Process in Turkey (2009). Elmar Brok, Debate on Situation in Turkey (2013).

41. See Charles Tannock's address, Debate on Democratization in Turkey (2010); and Bastian Belder's address, Debate on Democratic Process in Turkey (2009).

42. Geoffrey Von Orden and Christiana Muscardini's addresses, Debate on Situation in Turkey (2013).

43. Gerard Batten's address, Debate on Democratization in Turkey, Strasbourg, 20 January 2010.

44. Gerard Batten's address, Debate on EU–Turkey Relations, 2007.

45. Mogens Camre's address, Parliamentary Debate on Turkey's 2007 Progress Report, European Parliament, 21 May 2008, Strasbourg.

46. For example, see amendment 156 for paragraph 28a, Amendments 1–343 for Draft Report on Turkey's Progress towards Accession PE 376.373v02-00, 4 July 2006, 54/115 and Werner Langen and Marios Matsakis's addresses, Turkey's 2007 Progress Report, Strasbourg, 21 May 2008.

47. European Parliament, European Parliament Resolution on Turkey's Progress towards Accession (2006), Article 20.

48. For example, see Gerard Batten's address, Debate on EU–Turkey Relations (2007); Geoffrey Von Orden and Christiana Muscardini's addresses, Debate on Situation in Turkey (2013).

49. Veronique Mathieu and Mchi Ebner's addresses, Debate on Progress towards Accession by Turkey, European Parliament, Strasbourg, 1 April 2004.

50. Zbigniew Zalevski's address, Debate on Turkey's 2007 Progress Report, European Parliament, Strasbourg, 21 May 2008.

51. Andreas Mölzer's address, Debate on Turkey's Progress towards Accession, European Parliament, Strasbourg, 13 December 2004.

52. Daniel Hannan's address, Debate on Women in Turkey, European Parliament, 12 February 2007; and Peter Van Dalen's address, Debate on Enlargement Strategy 2009 Concerning the Countries of the Western Balkans, Iceland and Turkey, European Parliament, Strasbourg, 25 November 2009.

53. Marine Le Pen's address, Debate on Opening of Negotiations with Turkey, European Parliament, Strasbourg, 28 September 2005.

54. Philip Claeys and William Dartmouth's addresses, Debate on Enlargement Strategy 2009 Concerning the Countries of the Western Balkans, Iceland and Turkey, European Parliament, Strasbourg, 25 November 2009.

55. Amendment 77 for paragraph 16a, Amendments for Draft Report on Turkey's Progress towards Accession 2006, PE 376.373v02-00, 04.07.2006, 27/115. Amendment 160 for paragraph 15, Amendments 1–236 for the Draft Motion for a Resolution, PE393.947v02-00, 25.09.2007, 54/79.

56. Mogens N.J. Camre's address, Debate on Turkey's Progress towards Accession, European Parliament, Strasbourg, 26 September 2006.

57. Jim Allister's address, Debate on Turkey's Progress towards Accession, European Parliament, Strasbourg, 13 December 2004.

58. Amendment 378 for Paragraph 26a, Amendments for the Draft Motion for Resolution on the 2012 Progress Report of Turkey II, PE.504.402v01-00, 12.02.2013, 103/126. Amendment 84 for paragraph 18a, Amendments for Draft Report on Turkey's Progress towards Accession 2006, PE 376.373v02-00, 04.07.2006, 29/115.

59. Charles Tannock's address, Debate on Democratization in Turkey, European Parliament, Strasbourg, 20 January 2010.

60. See Cairo Declaration on Human Rights in Islam, 5.08.1990, UN GAOR, World Conference on Human Rights, 4th Session, Agenda Item 5, UN Doc. A/CONF.157/PC/62/Add.18 (1993) [English translation].

61. Cem Ozdemir's address, Debate on Turkey's Progress towards Accession, European Parliament, Strasbourg, 13 December 2004.

62. Amendment 76 paragraph 16a, Amendments for Draft Report on Turkey's Progress towards Accession 2006, PE 376.373v02-00, 04.07.2006, 26/115. Paragraph 56, European Parliament Resolution (2006).

Bibliography

Archival Sources

British Conservative Party. 'It's Time for Action'. Conservative Election Manifesto, 2005.

————. 'Vote for Change: European Election Manifesto'. Manifesto for European Election, 2009.

Brussels European Council. Presidency Conclusions, Brussels, 16/17 December 2004.

Cairo Declaration on Human Rights in Islam, 5 August 1990, U.N. GAOR, World Conference on Human Rights, 4th Session, Agenda Item 5, U.N. Doc. A/CONF.157/PC/62/Add.18 (1993) [English translation].

Commission of European Communities. Progress Report of Turkey, SEC(2005)1426, 9 November 2005.

Consolidated Versions of the Treaty on European Union. *Official Journal of the European Union* 55 (2012), C326.

Council of the European Union. Presidency Conclusions, Copenhagen European Council, 21–22 June 1993, SN 180/1/93.

European Commission. Turkey 2005 Progress Report, Brussels, SEC (2005)1426, 9 November 2005.

European Green Party. 'Manifesto for the 2004 European Election'. Fourth European Greens Congress, Rome, 20–22 February 2004.

European Left. 'United for a Left Alternative in Europe'. European Left Election Manifesto, 2004.

European Liberal, Democrat and Reform Party. 'European Liberals' Top 15 for EP Election'. Manifesto for the European Election 2009, adopted at the Stockholm Congress, 31 October 2008.

————. 'Manifesto, 2004 European Parliamentary Election'. Approved in Amsterdam, 14 November 2003.

European Parliament. Amendments 1–162 for the Draft Motion for a Resolution 2007/2269(INI), PE402.879v01-00, 7 April 2008.

————. Amendments 1–243 for the Draft Motion for a Resolution AM\801213EN.doc, PE431.004v02-00, 4 January 2010.

————. Amendments for the Draft Motion for Resolution on the 2012 Progress Report of Turkey, PE.504.377v01-00, 12 February 2013.

————. Amendments 1–188 for the Draft Motion for Resolution (PE414.936v01-00), PE416.543v01-00, 7 January 2009.

————. Debate on Opening of Negotiations with Turkey, Additional Protocol to the EEC–Turkey Association Agreement, 28 September 2005.

————. Debate on Women in Turkey, Strasbourg, 12 February 2007.

————. Debate on Turkey's 2007 Progress Report, Strasbourg, 21 May 2008.

————. European Parliament Critical of Slowdown in Turkey's Reform Process, Press Service 20060922IPR10896, 27 September 2006.

————. Resolution on Turkey's Progress towards Accession, P6_TA(2006)0381, 27 September 2006.

————. Resolution of 12 March 2009 on Turkey's Progress Report 2008, P6_TA(2009)0134.

————. Resolution of 21 May 2008 on Turkey's 2007 Progress Report, P6_TA(2008)0224.

————. Debate on Turkey's Progress towards Accession, Strasbourg, 13 December 2004.

————. Debate on Opening of Negotiations with Turkey – Additional Protocol to the EEC–Turkey Association Agreement, Strasbourg, 28 September 2005.

————. Debate on Turkey's Progress towards Accession, Strasbourg, 26 September 2006.

————. Amendments 1–461 for the Draft Motion for a Resolution on the 2011 Progress Report on Turkey (PE473.875v02-00), PE478.719v01-00, 1 February 2012.

————. Resolution on the 2004 Regular Report and the Recommendation of the European Commission on Turkey's Progress towards Accession P6_TA(2004)0096, 15 December 2004.

————. Debate on Enlargement Strategy 2009 Concerning the Countries of the Western Balkans, Iceland and Turkey, Strasbourg, 25 November 2009.

————. Report on the 1999 Regular Report from the Commission on Turkey's Progress towards Accession, A5-0297/2000, 19 October 2000.

————. Amendments 1–236 for the Draft Motion for a Resolution (PE392.298v02-00), PE393.947v02-00, 25 September 2007.

————. Amendments 1–343 for Draft Report on Turkey's Progress towards Accession 2006, PE 376.373v02-00, 4 July 2006.

————. Report on Turkey's Progress towards Accession 2006/2118(INI), A6-0269/2006, 13 September 2006.

————. Debate on EU–Turkey Relations, Strasbourg, 24 October 2007.

————. Debate on Progress towards Accession by Turkey, Strasbourg, 1 April 2004.

————. Debate on Turkey's 2007 Progress Report, Strasbourg, 21 May 2008.

————. Debate on Opening of Negotiations with Turkey, Strasbourg, 28 September 2005.

————. Amendments for the Draft Motion for Resolution on the 2012 Progress Report of Turkey II, PE.504.402v01-00, 12 February 2013.

————. Debate on Democratization in Turkey, Strasbourg, 20 January 2010.

Labour Party. 'Britain Forward not Back'. Labour Party Manifesto, 2005.

Liberal Democrats. 'The Real Alternative'. Election Manifesto, 2005.

————. 'Stronger Together, Poorer Apart'. The Liberal Democrat Manifesto for the 2009 Election to the European Parliament.

Negotiating Framework between the European Union and Turkey, 3 October 2005.

Party of European Socialists. Manifesto for Elections, June 2009.

Secondary Sources

Aydin-Duzgit, S. *Constructions of European Identity: Debates and Discourses on Turkey and the EU.* London: Palgrave, 2012.

Hix, S. *The Political System of the European Union.* New York: Palgrave Macmillan, 2005.

Jansen, T., and S. Van Hecke. *At Europe's Service: The Origins and Evolution of the European People's Party.* Heidelberg: Springer, 2011.

Kalyvas, S.N. *The Rise of Christian Democracy in Europe.* Ithaca, NY: Cornell University Press, 1996.

Levin, P. *Turkey and the European Union: Christian and Secular Images of Islam.* New York: Palgrave Macmillan, 2011.

Menéndez-Alarcón, A.V. *The Cultural Realm of European Integration: Social Representations in France, Spain, and the United Kingdom.* Westport, CT: Praeger, 2004.

Conclusion

European and National Ways of Politicizing European History

STEFAN BERGER AND CANER TEKIN

With regard to its objective of collective identity construction, one of the primary strategies of the European Union has been to initiate an effective way of representing its integration history as a success story of overcoming previous trauma and violence. The House of European History in Brussels is arguably the latest and most ambitious of the European Union's projects to base notions of a common Europe on history. Yet historical narratives within the European Union remain highly contested. Despite the EU's transnational designs, national politics today continues in a number of cases to put forth their own, sometimes mutually exclusive, conceptualizations of European history. The aim of the present volume, therefore, has been to explore both the motivations behind establishing a shared European historical narrative and the diverse national resistances to this process of developing a European historical consciousness. The previous sections have discussed European and national approaches to the representation of the European past – in particular, the twentieth-century European past. They have focused attention, respectively, onto European Union and national history politics – with the latter often contesting the dominance of the former.

Such history politics has been discussed prominently on the previous pages vis-à-vis European museums, in particular the House of European History. Like national history museums, first conceptualized in the nineteenth century, European history museums still tend to come up with single

Notes for this section begin on page 199.

unitary narratives aimed at producing cosmopolitan memories based on stories of suffering and victimhood. A past characterized by violence and trauma becomes justification for the political project of the European Union. Such European history narratives can accommodate and arguably even thrive upon the many contradictory and eclectic images of European identity. An outward profession of multi-perceptivity and pluralism still produced a powerful singular legitimatory narrative of uniting Europe politically.

Such narrativizations of Europe have not only been visible in museums, but they are also present in professional historical writing on Europe, as has been discussed in the previous pages. The European Commission has long promoted a uniform way of writing the history of European integration. It began this undertaking in the 1970s, in parallel with its cultural policy, as a complementary strategy to its economic rationale. At a time when the European Economic Community faced its first serious economic crisis, it discovered that an economic rationale on its own was not sufficient for justifying European integration. Building a cultural and historical foundation now became a key target of the European Union. Among a whole range of initiatives, the European Commission also initiated two partnerships with professional historians. In 1977, it initiated a research programme on the history of European integration at the European University Institute, which only existed for less than four years. With this failure the commission endorsed a transnational academic forum entitled the Liaison Committee of Historians between 1982 and 1999. This committee proved critical this time, as it gave rise to new collaboration channels and generated a transnational vocabulary in the historiography of European integration. There was, however, still no agreement among historians of European integration on how this history would best be written. On the one hand there were those, like Walter Lipgens, the founding chair of the programme of the history of European integration at the European University Institute, who argued that the European Union was key to maintaining and developing European culture, and that therefore scholars had a responsibility for contributing to European unity. On the other hand, there were those like René Girault, the first chairman of the Liaison Committee, who retained a strong distance from any project of narrating European integration in a uniform and unilinear way. Instead, he insisted that European history did not teleologically lead to the unification of Europe. Today the history of European integration still moves somewhere between these two poles of legitimating the European Union project and emphasizing the diversity of past futures in relation to this project.

If the histories of European integration and representations of European history in European history museums grapple with national histories and national representations, national institutions representing national cultures to non-national audiences in Europe deal with Europe selectively, and only where it fits into national storylines. As this volume demonstrates in relation to the European Union National Institutes for Culture, Europe's nation states rarely engage European histories in a common narrative framework. Instead, the EU's member states prioritize their national contexts, and only promote any national linkages with a supposedly common European framework if they will benefit from making such linkages. A similar logic of national prerogatives can be observed in the field of history textbooks for schools and school curricula. Whilst there are advances in the Europeanization of national history textbooks, they still betray strong national biases in almost every case. The much-advertised joint history textbooks, in particular the Franco-German and the Polish–German initiatives, were successful, but where pasts are more alive and contested, similar initiatives have failed. Overall, most school children identify Europe through the lens of the nation state. Transnational history textbooks exist, but they are not (yet?) in use much anywhere in Europe.

If national perspectives on European history are still dominant in contemporary Europe, these national perspectives reveal not only incompatibilities between nation states but also within them. In England, for example, two versions of Euroscepticism draw on different historical characteristics of English national identity. Both represent England as the birthplace of representative democracy and the centre of world trade, but the 'soft' version of Euroscepticism suggests that English history is compatible with Europe in certain areas whereas the 'hard' version rejects the Europeanness of England altogether. The discussions surrounding Brexit in the run-up to the historic decision to leave the European Union were rich in historical references.[1] Nostalgia for empire was mixed with traditions of xenophobia and with institutionalized memories of Britain's long parliamentary and constitutional history, and it was used as an exceptionalist argument of not belonging to continental Europe. Of course, there were a range of other factors at play, some of them arguably more important than history: the strength of anti-politics, the feeling that a vote for Brexit would be a protest vote against a political class who did not represent the large sections of the population who were afraid of further economic decline. Nevertheless, history was an important weapon against Europe, whereas the 'Remain' camp did not try to rally history to its cause, instead relying almost exclusively on a negative campaign of 'we would be worse off outside the EU'. Arguably, no other historical memory was as powerfully instrumentalized by the Brexiteers as the memory of the Second World War, when Britain, thus the historical myth, for a brief period stood alone fighting a National Socialist Germany that had conquered almost the whole continent. Seventy years on, Winston Churchill's war rhetoric still powerfully underpinned the claims that Britain should be wary of the Continent.

Apart from England, there are many examples in this volume of how diverse representatives speaking on behalf of nations instrumentalize the past for present nation-centred political concerns. Thus, the post-Yugoslav states made widespread use of history to legitimate their new-found independence in the 1990s. Interestingly, the way in which they narratively constructed their past in the wake of independence was remarkably similar, even if the respective politics differed quite substantially. Outside of Serbia we find a thorough delegitimation of antifascism, which was now portrayed as an imperialist ideology of Serbia to subjugate the diverse nationalities of Yugoslavia. Anticommunism came to the fore, and united with often very traditional forms of legitimating a collective national identity. In Serbia, partly as a response to the national challenges from other post-Yugoslav republics, socialism was tied even more strongly to Serbian nationalism and pan-Slav feelings that included a positive evaluation of the historical ties to Russia.

National viewpoints also dominate the way in which European nation states memorialize past crimes in their histories. In East European countries, the condemnation of crimes committed under Communism are widely depicted as 'foreign' crimes, committed by an occupying power – namely, the Soviet Union. They become part of the national collective remembrance as national suffering from a foreign ideology, where its representatives become henchmen of an alien force in national history. In contemporary Western Europe, anticommunist reflexes, a shadow of Cold War ideology, are also strong but they take second place in the memorial landscape in relation to the Holocaust. Only in Germany (and perhaps increasingly also in Austria) has the Holocaust become a central anchor of national identity, whereas elsewhere in Western Europe it has become an important lens through which to view aspects of national history. With the extension of the European Union eastwards after the fall of Communism, the new members states of the EU also had to accept Holocaust memory as central to their own history politics and memorial landscapes. In return, the EU included the memory of Stalinist crimes in the repertoire of the EU's memory diplomacy. Since 2009, largely due to pressure from East-Central European countries, the EU observes a European Day of Remembrance for the Victims of Totalitarian Regimes.[2] The date 23 August was declared as this annual day of remembrance, as it was on this day in 1939 that the Ribbentrop-Molotov pact was signed. In Eastern Europe it was widely seen as a day to remember the Communist gulag and the Communist crimes. It is undoubtedly far more popular in East-Central than in Western Europe. Nevertheless, this quid pro quo arrangement in official European collective memory discourses can also be observed in the direct juxtaposition of Stalin and Hitler in one of the central halls of the House of European History. Still, the memory of

Communist crimes carries arguably less resonance in transnational European (and global) memory than the United Nations' International Holocaust Remembrance Day on 27 January, marking the liberation of the annihilation camp of Auschwitz by Soviet forces.[3]

Holocaust remembrance, both at national and European levels, is also a widely contested affair as has been discussed in the previous pages in relation to literary challenges to the authenticity of Holocaust memory within national and European Holocaust discourses. Both the national mediation of Holocaust memories and the processes of their global exchange live in constant tensions with each other. The cultural and social memories of the Holocaust are reproduced through highly localized forms of memory adaptations that are by no means universal, even if they aspire towards universalism. Hence it is vitally important to find a pluralistic way of representing the European history of the Holocaust that keeps the highly local aspects of this history alive. Refraining from abstract categorizations about the Holocaust and instead learning from the victims' perspectives without generalizing them is one of the key challenges of contemporary memorialization of the Holocaust.[4]

In this book there is also much sustained discussion about the place of Turkish history within the representations of European history. Contemporary debates over Turkey's EU candidature are firmly connected to the candidate's 'controversial' past, essentially on two grounds: the history of Ottoman/Turkish modernization that took shape in relation to European modernization, and the Ottoman history allegedly ridden with religious conflicts with a Christian Europe. When Turkey was given the green light to begin accession talks in 2005, Jack Straw, the foreign minister of Britain, was congratulating EU members for their decision that the EU was 'founded on values, not on history', and also not on religion.[5] Still, the following years witnessed the power of history and religion over values in many core European nation states. Turkey was not just measured against particular values but also against history. Turkey-sceptic politicians across the European Union put up strong opposition to the candidate on historical and religious grounds. They were successful in torpedoing the accession talks leading to the EU declaring those talks 'open-ended' in 2005, and refraining from giving any clear membership perspective for Turkey, despite it having been previously granted to other candidates. Such cold-shouldering of Turkey contributed in turn to Turkey's turn away from Europe. Admittedly, there were many factors underpinning the opposition to Turkey, such as the candidate's geographical location and its huge population. However, Turkey's negative historical image in the eyes of sceptical European political camps also played a key role in explaining the failure of the accession talks in the 2000s. The confrontation of Europe with Turkey thus shows, above all, the continuing powerful hold of religion over the European memorial landscape. It proved to be more powerful than the much-proclaimed European values that were upheld by centre-left political forces in the European parliament and that had formed the basis for the official 'accession criteria', but with little consequences in practice. Turkey, with its Ottoman shadow, remains one of the key 'others' in the European imaginary, which is why it is unlikely to enter the European Union any time soon, regardless of how democratic, liberal and Western it might be. The power of religiously motivated memorial landscapes is stacked against it.

Overall, the contributions to this volume all shed light on the manifold tensions that exist between the history and memory politics of the EU on the one side, and of the individual European nation states on the other. They thus highlight the long-standing and ongoing discrepancy between European and national conceptions of European history. In the light of this, one can only remain sceptical about the prospective success of framing a common understanding of European history in Europe today, especially if that framing is connected with top-down Brussels-based attempts to homogenize the highly diverse landscapes of historical culture in Europe today.

At the same time, however, many of the contributors to this volume also stress that national narratives in Europe do relate to references of Europeanness in manifold and often contradictory ways. Hence there is a tension between the widespread rejection of uniform representations of Europe emanating from within EU institutions, and the attempts to relate national narratives to Europeanness that are ongoing within a variety of different European nation states. The differences and similarities between those attempts to align the national and the European need to be explored at greater depth. What kinds of Europeanness are championed in different parts of Europe today? How integrated and at the same time contested are those narrative constructions of Europe? How do they relate to the construction of long-established national historical narratives? The answer to these questions will give some indication of the prospective success or failure of the European project in the twenty-first century.

Stefan Berger is professor of history at the Ruhr University Bochum, where he is the director of the Institute of Social Movements and the chairman of the History of the Ruhr Foundation. He was appointed honorary professor at Cardiff University in 2017. He has published numerous books and articles on historiography and comparative labour history, and his most recent book publications include *Industrial Heritage and Regional Identities* (edited with Christian Wicke and Jana Golombek, 2018), *The Transnational Activist: Transformations and Comparisons from the Anglo-World since the Nineteenth*

Century (edited with Sean Scalmer, 2018), and *Popularizing National Pasts: 1800 to the Present* (edited with Chris Lorenz, 2017).

Caner Tekin is a member of the Centre for Mediterranean Studies at the Ruhr University Bochum, where he has recently received his doctoral degree. He worked previously at the Georg-Eckert Institute for International Textbook Research in Brunswick, Germany as a postdoctoral fellow. He is also a review editor working for H-Nationalism, the online scholarly forum on nationalism studies. His research interests revolve around the linkages between nationalisms, representations of the past, and migration.

Notes

1. O. Gust, 'The Brexit Syllabus: British History for Brexiteers', *History Workshop Journal*, 5 September. 2016, http://www.historyworkshop.org.uk/the-brexit-syllabus-british-history-for-brexiteers/ [last accessed 11 February 2017]; J. Lanchester, 'Brexit Blues', *London Review of Books* 38(15) (2016).

2. European Parliament, 'Declaration of the European Parliament on the Proclamation of 23 August as European Day of Remembrance for Victims of Stalinism and Nazism', 23 September 2008, Brussels, P6_TA(2008)0439.

3. 'About the Holocaust and the United Nations Outreach Programme', The United Nations Outreach Programme, http://www.un.org/en/holocaustremembrance/ [last accessed 11 February 2017].

4. W. Kansteiner, *In Pursuit of German Memory: History, Politics and Television after Auschwitz* (Athens, OH: Ohio University Press, 2006); S. MacDonald, *Memorylands: Heritage and Identity in Europe Today* (Abingdon and New York: Routledge, 2013), 205; A. Bull and H.L. Hansen, 'On Agonistic Memory', *Memory Studies* 9(4) (2016), 390–404.

5. 'EU Opens Historic Talks with Turkey', *Philippine Daily*, 5 October 2005, 12.

Bibliography

Archival Sources

Lanchester, J. 'Brexit Blues'. *London Review of Books* 38(15) (2016), 3–6.

'About the Holocaust and the United Nations Outreach Programme'. The United Nations Outreach Programme, http://www.un.org/en/holocaustremembrance/ [last accessed 11 February 2017].

European Parliament, 'Declaration of the European Parliament on the Proclamation of 23 August as European Day of Remembrance for Victims of Stalinism and Nazism', 23 September 2008, Brussels, P6_TA(2008)0439.

'EU Opens Historic Talks with Turkey'. *Philippine Daily*, 5 October 2005.

Secondary Sources

Bull A., and Hansen, H. L. 'On Agonistic Memory'. *Memory Studies* 9(4) (2016), 390–404.

Gust, O. 'The Brexit Syllabus: British History for Brexiteers'. *History Workshop Journal*, 5 September 2016, http://www.historyworkshop.org.uk/the-brexit-syllabus-british-history-for-brexiteers/ [last accessed 11 February 2017].

Kansteiner, W. *In Pursuit of German Memory: History, Politics and Television after Auschwitz.* Athens, OH: Ohio University Press, 2006.

MacDonald, S. *Memorylands: Heritage and Identity in Europe Today.* Abingdon and New York: Routledge, 2013.

Index

MAKING SENSE OF HISTORY
Studies in Historical Cultures
General Editor: Stefan Berger
Founding Editor: Jörn Rüsen

Bridging the gap between historical theory and the study of historical memory, this series crosses the boundaries between both academic disciplines and cultural, social, political and historical contexts. In an age of rapid globalization, which tends to manifest itself on an economic and political level, locating the cultural practices involved in generating its underlying historical sense is an increasingly urgent task.